THE LOVE OF NATURE
AMONG THE ROMANS

THE
LOVE OF NATURE
AMONG THE ROMANS

DURING THE LATER DECADES OF THE REPUBLIC
AND THE FIRST CENTURY OF THE EMPIRE

BY

Sir ARCHIBALD GEIKIE, K.C.B.

D.C.L., Ll.D., D.Sc., Ph.D., F.R.S.

LONDON

JOHN MURRAY, ALBEMARLE STREET, W.

1912

PREFACE

THE publication of this volume by an author who has spent a long life in the active prosecution of Science may need a few words of explanation. Let me at once disclaim any pretension to classical scholarship. I can only say that, in the midst of wholly different pursuits, I have never lost the taste for those classical studies which were a joy to me in youth, but which since then have been taken up only fitfully and at long intervals, as a restful refreshment. Two years ago, induced by the representations of my lamented friend the late Samuel Henry Butcher, I accepted the Presidency of the Classical Association, and had, as the main duty of my year of office, to deliver an Address in January 1911. I chose a subject which seemed in some measure to combine the classical interests of the members with my own deep love of Nature. I had often found much enjoyment in tracing among the authors of antiquity the mental attitude shown by them

towards the varied aspects of the world around
them, and in thus learning how far their writings
expressed feelings that resembled or differed from
those which the same objects awaken in our
own day. Accordingly I selected two or three
parts of the wide realm of Nature, and discussed
the literary and artistic treatment of them at
Rome during the last decades of the Republic
and the first century of the Empire.

I had originally no intention of proceeding
further in a field whereon I had perhaps somewhat rashly trespassed. But the fascination of
the subject tempted me to continue the congenial occupation which the preparation of the
Address to the Classical Association had provided. Expanding the treatment of those sections
that were dealt with in that Address, I extended
my survey over the rest of the broad domains
of Nature, but still keeping on the whole within the chronological limits of Latin literature
originally chosen, that is, from the period of
Lucretius to that of Statius.

The outcome of these studies is contained in
the present volume which, though it is only a
sketch of so wide a subject, I have after some
hesitation decided to publish. The classical scholar
who may look over its pages will probably find
in them nothing with which he is not already
familiar, though it may not have occurred to him

to collect and compare the scattered passages in Latin authors which reveal how far and in what ways these writers were influenced by the features of the external world. To the ordinary reader, however, it may, I hope, be of some interest to see the familiar aspects of Nature as they appeared to Roman eyes and appealed to Roman hearts nineteen hundred years ago.

The subject of the feeling for Nature among the Romans has been briefly touched on by many authors. It has been treated somewhat more fully by several French and German writers, particularly by Secretan, De Laprade, Friedländer, Motz, and Woermann. But in no language, including our own, have I found it discussed with the fullness and detail which it appears to me to deserve.

It was at first my intention to give in the original language, as well as in translation, all my quotations from Latin authors, but such a duplex citation was found to involve an increase in the size of the book beyond the limits that seemed to me desirable. In regard to translation it would have been easy to select from some of the many published versions of the authors quoted, but one chief attraction of my self-imposed task was the pleasure of attempting once again to turn the Latin into metrical English with as close adherence to the original text as the different structure of

the two languages and the exigencies of rhythm
would permit. Entirely satisfactory translation is
probably impossible, but the attempt to attain it
will continue to employ and delight men as long
as literature is cultivated.

SHEPHERDS' DOWN, HASLEMERE,
      4th June 1912.

CONTENTS

THE LOVE OF NATURE
AMONG THE ROMANS

CHAPTER I

THE SATURNIAN LAND AND ITS PEOPLE

FROM all the evidence now available the early
founders of the City and State of Rome appear to
have been a race of farmers and shepherds. Their
fields and pastures spread over the plain of the
Campagna to the skirts of the primeval forest,
which then clothed a great part of Italy. That
forest harboured bears, wolves, wild boars, and other
creatures, against whose depredations constant guard
had to be maintained. It was needful, also, from
time to time to take up arms for the purpose of
repelling incursions of rival tribes of men. The
life of the Latin settlers must thus have been
laborious and vigilant. Their outlook on the
world around them could not fail to be in many
respects different from that of their descendants
towards the end of the Republic. Some dim perception of what this outlook probably was may be
gathered from the traces of early customs and
beliefs, some of which survived from primitive

1   A

times down to the end of paganism in Italy. The religion of the first builders of Rome seems to have been a kind of nature-worship or animism. The active processes of Nature were looked on by them as manifestations of the presence and working of invisible and impersonal spirits, with which their imagination filled the world. Some of these spirits were conceived to be beneficent and willing to attach themselves to mankind. Thus each family had its central hearth guarded by the fire-spirit, while a company of other similar beings (Penates, Lares, and many more) watched over the material well-being of the household. Outside the homestead a concourse of equally invisible and impersonal beings, each with its special though limited functions, included some who were both malevolent and capricious, and whose good-will had to be solicited by appropriate oblations. The dark forest that stretched far away up into the hills, formidable enough from its dangerous wild beasts, would gain an added terror from the conviction that it was the chosen abode of unseen beings who could be potent for evil. Down through all the subsequent centuries, amid the changes of belief which the Roman people underwent, traces of this primitive agrestic faith, especially in its domestic parts, were never wholly lost.[1]

When in course of time, after the community had come into contact with the Greek colonies

---

[1] This subject has recently been ably discussed by Mr Warde Fowler in his "Religious Experience of the Roman People," 1911.

farther south, a national cult was formulated at Rome, a number of important deities were recognised by name, and provision was made for their due worship on certain festivals throughout the year. The pious Roman, who had now learnt, probably from Hellenic influences, that these gods and goddesses could assume bodily form and appear visibly to men, was continually reminded of their presence as he moved about. If he was caught in a thunderstorm, he knew that Jupiter was angrily launching his bolts to punish or terrify some offending mortal. If he stood by the shores of the sea, he might perchance catch sight of Neptune borne across the deep in his golden shell, or " hear old Triton blow his wreathèd horn." If he sat by a clear spring, in the cool shade of trees, he felt himself to be at the haunt of some fair naiad, to whom the place was sacred. If he wandered by the banks of a river, he believed that under its waters dwelt the god whose special care it was to watch over that stream, alike in drought and flood. If he sought the solitude of some woodland, he might pause to listen for the strains of the pan-pipe of old Silvanus, but he would usually fear to venture too far alone into the sombre forest lest, if he encountered no wild beasts, he might nevertheless be set upon by a company of frolicsome fauns.

The farmer or peasant who, while devoutly attending to the requirements of his domestic *numina*, also diligently observed the other religious duties which the State had prescribed, was thus furnished with opportunities, if he desired to use them, of rising above the sordid cares of his daily avocations and recognising the supervision and beneficent assistance of higher powers. And it would seem that a simple piety of this kind was prevalent in the community during its early history. There was little, however, in the religion to awaken sympathies and affections with regard to the surrounding world. The husbandman would, of course, appreciate the light and warmth of the sun, in which he could bask when the chills of winter had fled ; the coolness of leafy shade, where he could rest and sleep ; the freshness of rippling streams, where he could drink or bathe ; the fragrance of flowers ; the advent of spring, with its blossoms of promise, followed by the coming of autumn, with its bountiful harvests. But above and beyond his regard for what was useful or agreeable to him in his daily life, it might perhaps be seldom possible for him to rise. Nevertheless a life spent in rural pursuits placed him in the midst of influences which, where he was susceptible to them, were more fitted to foster his better qualities than were the conditions to be found in the growing city.

According to ancient tradition, the early in- habitants of Latium lived under a mythical king, Saturnus, from whom their country was called the Saturnian Land. They were reputed to have been pious followers of the primitive faith, simple and moral in their lives, hardy, industrious, and thrifty.

Their praises and those of their descendants through many generations down to the time of the Empire were sung by successive generations of writers, both in verse and prose, their virtues being held up as a contrast to the accumulating vices of later times. But in the course of centuries the manners and habits of the entire population underwent a gradual deterioration. The national religion which, carefully framed to guide the people in their relations to the gods, had come down from the days of the kings and was still maintained by the State, began to lose its hold. With the increasing laxity of belief and practice, growing into indifference and open disbelief, there came also a falling off from the traditional simple and upright life, with its steady industry and contentment. The country districts, as might be expected, were affected by these changes more slowly than the urban community. Even down to the time of the Empire the inhabitants of remote, and especially of upland, districts seemed by contrast with the townsmen to have still retained the piety and simplicity of their ancestors.[1]

This national demoralisation seems to have set in with quickened pace after the close of the Punic Wars and the establishment of direct political relations between Rome and Greece. The process of Hellenisation, which had probably begun long before, through the influence of the colonies of Magna Græcia, now advanced more rapidly.

[1] This subject is more fully noticed in the following chapter.

Greek mythology, Greek literature, Greek philosophy, and even Greek license, exercised a powerful influence on the Romans. Although the rites and ceremonies of the State religion continued to be maintained by public authority, and a law existed prohibiting the introduction of foreign divinities, the comparative simplicity of the old pantheon was overlain and lost amidst the rich exuberance of the Greek myths. When the somewhat austere gods of Latium were identified with the anthropomorphic deities of Hellas, they were credited with the history and deeds of these deities. Thus a moral code utterly alien to the habits of the early population appeared to come with divine sanction. There was introduced, likewise, the Greek conception of the underworld, with all its repulsive details. The Romans seem to have previously held no very clear opinions as to the future state after death ; but the Greek presentation of this subject obtained wide acceptance, especially among the less educated classes. Eventually foreign cults became fashionable, and the mystic rites of Isis and Mithras attracted many worshippers to whom the national religion had ceased to appeal.

So long as men continued to believe that the world was filled with an innumerable company of impersonal spirits or of divinities that could assume the human form, and that these beings had the command of all the forces of nature, which they wielded as they pleased and could direct for the benefit, or capriciously and even vindictively to the

injury, of mankind, the feeling which we understand
by the love of Nature, instinctive as it is in the soul
of man, could hardly be fostered into growth.   But
there was one influence from Greece, which, though
it could directly reach only a limited section of the
population, was of a benign and ultimately of a
far-reaching kind.   Greek philosophy had been
received with acclaim by the more cultivated
society of Rome.   The two great philosophical
schools had each its partisans in the capital—the
Stoics with their monotheism or pantheism, and the
Epicureans with their professed atheism.   Much as
these disputants differed from each other in their
respective creeds, they were tolerably unanimous
in their disbelief of the national mythology, though
many of them judged it expedient for the general
good of the community that the State religion
should be maintained.   They seemed at times to
vie with each other in the vehemence of their
contempt for the childish and grotesque fables
about the gods which had been invented in Greece
and had been so widely accepted in Italy, but
which they declared, with a confidence certainly
premature, that no stripling or old woman could
now be found to believe.   How far the teachings
of philosophy may have accelerated the rejection of
the established religion among the educated portion
of the community can only be guessed.   The
influence of these teachings on the general body
of the people must for a long time have been
slight, by a slow process of diffusion, for the

pagan beliefs of Rome continued to flourish for
several centuries after the introduction of Greek
philosophy.

But there was one conclusion of transcendent
importance to which the leaders in both of the two
chief schools of thought had come.   Casting aside
the multiplicity of gods and goddesses and their
supposed functions in the economy of the world,
the philosophers recognised the essential unity of
nature, the orderly reign of law, and the harmonious co-operation of all the sources of energy
that maintain the system of the universe.   Cicero,
who did so much to make these subjects familiar
and interesting to his countrymen in his own lucid
and sonorous prose, when he contemplated the
marvellous order manifest throughout the world,
recognised "such an admirable continuity and
succession of things that each part seems to be
connected with the others and all to be bound
and linked together." He inferred that "there
must be some most excellent and pre-eminent
Nature that originally made and now moves,
directs, and governs those stupendous works,—
the universe with all its parts, heaven, earth, sea,
sun, moon, and stars."[1]   And he affirmed that
"the beauty of the world and the order of all
celestial things compel us to confess that there is
an excellent and eternal Nature which deserves to
be worshipped and admired by all mankind."[2]

[1] *De Nat. Deor.* I. xxxvi. 100.   [2] *De Div.* II. lxxii. 148.

On the other hand, Lucretius, the great Latin exponent of the Epicurean philosophy, was not less emphatic in his insistence on the unity, beauty, and majesty of Nature. The followers of Epicurus were accused of atheism because they denied that the gods took any concern in human affairs or even in the government of the universe. Lucretius maintained that the gods must dwell apart in some remote abode, far from this earth, and certainly take no interest in mankind nor any share in the direction of the world. He fearlessly asserted that Nature, free and uncontrolled by any deities, is seen to do all things of her own accord. Appealing to the holy gods themselves, he asked who among them could rule the immense universe, or control the immeasurable deep or cause the heavens to roll on in their course and warm with their fires the fruitful earth.[1] But though he discarded the national gods and goddesses, he recognised that the world is regulated by fixed law (*certa ratio*), that by "the conditions of Nature (*foedera naturai*) it stands decreed what each part can do and cannot do," and that the "law whereby all things are made is that by which they must abide, for they are impotent to rescind the binding statutes (*leges*) of time."[2] Though he believed in an atomic theory of the origin of the universe, and discoursed on the clash of atoms out of which the cosmos has emerged, it is clear that he

---

[1] *De Rer. Nat.* II. 1090, *seq.*
[2] *Id.* I. 586 ; II. 710 ; V. 56.

felt the presence of some creative, directing, and governing power which he called " Nature, the parent of things, that brings everything to the utmost limit of its growth." [1]   Certainly no writer of antiquity ever formed a nobler conception than did Lucretius of the nicely adjusted economy of Nature, and no one was ever more keenly and even rapturously alive to its infinite charm.

It was thus a notable advance in man's conception of the universe, and a memorable service to the fostering of the love of Nature, to discard the multitudinous divinities of paganism, with all their wayward doings and incalculable caprice, and to proclaim the unity and harmonious co-operation of all the forms of energy in the world under the sway of immutable law.   Even cultivated minds wherein the old gods had not been entirely dethroned, and wherein long use and wont and the traditions and associations of the past were still powerful, could not but feel the influence of the wider views proclaimed by philosophy, which came like a gleam of light from heaven.   In the midst of the prevailing indifference and disbelief there must have been many Romans who, though they could not accept all the legends of the received mythology, clung to the national religion, discarding the grosser features that had overlain it, but keeping a simpler and older faith.   Men like Virgil, for example, conservative in their instincts,

---

[1] *De Rer. Nat.* II. 1116. Further reference to Lucretius will be found in chapter iii.

reverent of the past, and full of natural piety, combined with a keen pleasure in the beauty and interest of the outer world, which philosophy taught them all the more to appreciate, probably indulged in this eclecticism. They made the most of those parts of the mythology which they could accept, and explained away or quietly ignored the rest. The poetic beauty of many of the myths of Greece appealed to such natures. The recorded traditions of the interposition of their own Italian gods on behalf of Rome in her struggles for the supremacy of Italy and of the world likewise warmed their patriotism and strengthened such hold as the State religion still had upon their acceptance. Thus their religion, their philosophy, and their love of nature were blended into a union which, illogical as it might be, was often poetical, and probably afforded satisfaction to those who adopted it.

The Romans are often spoken of as essentially a practical, or even a prosaic, people. It is admitted that in law, in administration, in military affairs, in engineering, in architecture, and in other spheres of political and industrial activity, they were unrivalled by any race in ancient times. But it is contended that in literature, in philosophy, in art, and in science, they owed their knowledge and inspiration to the Greeks. There is a common belief that even when they gave expression to their own genuine and spontaneous sentiments, they consciously or unconsciously

imitated or actually reiterated what they had imbibed from the Hellenic world.

That the intellectual debt of Rome to Greece was gigantic has never been disputed, and was freely admitted by the Romans themselves. The greatest of their philosophers candidly confessed that whatever he had been able to accomplish in literature and philosophy he owed to his study of Greek authors.[1] The poets were not less frank in their confessions of indebtedness. Virgil admitted that he began his poetic career by imitating the Sicilian muse of Theocritus, as he afterwards drank inspiration from the *Iliad* and the *Odyssey*. Horace makes the fullest acknowledgment when he affirms that Greece, though vanquished, overcame her conqueror by teaching rude Latium the arts of life, and he repeatedly boasts of his share in introducing Greek lyric measures into Latin poetry. It was the proudest title that Propertius claimed—to be called the Roman Callimachus. In art the debt of Rome to Greece was so overwhelmingly vast that the very existence of a native artistic vein has been almost lost sight of amidst the paramount influence of Greek sculpture.

Nevertheless, when the fullest acknowledgment

---

[1] Cicero, *Epist. Quint. Frat.* I. i. 9. Elsewhere he urges his fellow-countrymen to seize the literary glory from the languishing hands of Greece and transfer it to Rome (*Tusc. Disp.* II. ii.). Varro was likewise indefatigable in his efforts to bring all departments of Greek culture within the range of Latin studies. *See* on this subject Gaston Boissier's "Varron," p. 376.

is made of the influence of Greek thought and
literary form upon the Roman mind in regard to
the feeling for Nature, it must be obvious that
such a masterful race as the Romans could not
rest contented in a merely imitative mood. Undoubtedly they drew inspiration from the Greeks,
and so far as concerned the form into which their
literary effusions were thrown and their painting
and sculpture were conceived, they continued to
follow Greek models. But as the Roman poets
felt the growth of their own powers of conception and expression, they found a fresh source
of inspiration in their native surroundings and
adequate modes of expression in their own language,
which grew more and more tractable and musical
in their hands. There may be difficulty in always
discriminating what was borrowed from what was
truly the product of Italian soil. Yet there cannot
be any doubt that a genuine national Roman spirit
was eventually developed alike in literature and
in art.

It is, indeed, inconceivable that an intellectual
people could dwell in such a land as Italy without
being directly and powerfully impressed by the
various natural features around them, and without
finding for these impressions and feelings literary
forms suited at once to the subject and to the
genius of their own language. Probably no part
of Europe is more eminently fitted to awaken
national enthusiasm, to quicken the growth of a
patriotic spirit, and at the same time to stimulate

the love of Nature. Italy includes a conspicuous portion of the loftiest mountain-chain on the Continent; it is traversed by ample rivers; it comprises numerous lakes, some embosomed among the northern mountains, others farther south, nestling within the craters of extinct volcanoes. From the cool, mossy springs among its hills rippling brooks descend into the plains. The geographical form and position of the country have given it a remarkably mild climate (*indulgentia caeli*), but with a wide enough range to ensure a pleasing diversity of vegetation. The soil in the cultivable areas is usually deep and fertile, yielding all kinds of crops, as well as the choicest flowers and fruits. On either side of the peninsula a coast-line of long extent and endless variety is washed by two wide gulfs of the Mediterranean Sea, which on their placid surface reflect the deep blue of the Italian sky.

Some of the physical features of the country have undoubtedly had a potent influence upon the history and development of its inhabitants. Among these features, of special significance has been that of the broken and rugged chain of the Apennines, which runs down the whole length of the peninsula. In early times it served to separate various tribes from each other. To the dwellers on the plains along either flank of this great back-bone, the wider landscape has always been bounded by a mountainous distance on the one side, and by the far gleam of the open sea on the other. The western lowlands are diversified by many isolated eminences, on whose summits citadels were built long ages ago, and by many groups of hills, up whose steep slopes, from time immemorial, little towns have climbed (*scandentes de vallibus arces*), which still remain inhabited, and form so characteristic and delightful an element in Italian scenery. From the northern frontier, with its snowy, pine-covered Alps, the traveller passes southward across the rich corn-lands, rice-fields, and mulberry plantations of the Lombardy plains to the flanks of the Apennines, with their woods and meadows, their vineyards and olive-groves, which accompany him league after league, until he finds himself among the palms, orange- and lemon-trees, myrtles, laurels, and the other characteristic plants of the southern provinces.

In one important respect the sea - shores of Italy wear an aspect different from that which is familiar in the countries of Western Europe. The Mediterranean being a nearly tideless sea, there is comparatively little variation in the level of its surface. Hence the frequent wide tidal flats, exposed between high- and low-water in so many bays and estuaries on the coasts of the Atlantic, are here absent. Day after day the water keeps nearly within the same limit along the shore, and the storms which disturb it, though sometimes severe, are less so than those of the ocean outside.

Another characteristic which marks off Italy from the rest of Europe is furnished by the volcanic energy of which the country has been the theatre since long before the advent of the earliest human population. The eruptions of Mount Etna were a source of wonder and awe throughout the basin of the Mediterranean ere the dawn of history. Made known to the Hellenic world by the Greek colonists and traders, they afforded a theme for Greek poets before any Latin singer had arisen to record their terrors. It was not only in Sicily, however, that such manifestations of subterranean commotion took place. The islands of Lipari and Volcano occasionally broke out in eruption. Stromboli, which is still constantly active, appears to have been in this state as far back as history extends. Ischia, too, has again and again been the scene of destructive outbreaks. Nor is it difficult to believe that some of the numerous now extinct craters that stud the region from Campania to Tuscany may have continued their eruptions after the aboriginal settlers appeared among them, for even now hot springs and emissions of sulphurous and other mephitic vapours show that the subterranean fires are smouldering not far beneath the surface. Furthermore, Italy from the remotest time has been subject to earthquakes, not infrequently of a disastrous type. These various manifestations of mysterious underground energy could not but deeply impress the imagination of primitive races, engendering superstition and colouring the popular conceptions of an under-world.

A land so varied in its scenery, so benign in its climate, so fertile in its soil, so exuberant in its vegitation, so prolific, therefore, in its ministration to the well-being of man, has been feelingly claimed by one of its modern poets to have been dowered with "the gift of beauty."[1] Two thousand years ago the same natural charms existed, and it would have been strange had the Romans proved insensible to them. There can be little doubt, indeed, that an appreciation of these charms was one of the grounds of that national sentiment of patriotism for which the Romans were distinguished among the peoples of antiquity. The more they saw and learnt of other countries, the stronger grew their conviction that none of these was so pleasant a land to dwell in as Italy, for nowhere had Nature so bountifully poured out her riches for the service of man. This pride in their fatherland is well brought out in the picturesque scene with which Varro prefaces his treatise on agriculture. He describes how, when he entered the temple of the goddess Tellus, he found there a group of his friends waiting for the return of the sacristan, and looking at a painting of Italy which appropriately decorated the opposite wall. One of the company

---

[1] Filicaja, in the sonnet so charmingly translated by Byron in his *Childe Harold* (iv. xlii) :—

> "Italia! oh Italia! thou who hast
> The fatal gift of beauty."

B

jocosely remarked that as, according to the old proverb, "the Roman conquers by sitting down," they should meanwhile seat themselves on the benches. The map (or perhaps allegorical figure) of their country led to a conversation on the various merits of Italy, which in their opinion might be regarded as a vast orchard that yielded in abundance everything useful to man. What spelt, they asked, could be compared to that of Campania, what corn to that of Apulia, what wine to that of Falernum, what olive-oil to that of Venafrum ?[1]

The same patriotic fervour breathes through the poetry of ancient Rome. It finds its fullest expression in the writings of Virgil. The contemplation of the manifold glories of Italy awakened in that sweet singer a vivid emotion, and became a main inspiration of his muse. Now and again, as in the often-quoted passage in the second *Georgic*, his feelings on this subject found vent in a burst of enthusiasm, which grew more overmastering as the varied elements of Italy's loveliness and strength passed in succession before his poetic vision—her eternal spring, her rich fields of corn, her vines and olives, her abundant flocks and herds, her many lakes— the huge Larius and sea-like Benacus — her winding shores, washed by two seas, her numerous havens, her wealth in veins of brass and silver and in the gold of her rivers, her noble cities, her

[1] *De Re Rust.* I. ii. 6.

many towns perched on rugged heights, with rivers gliding beneath their antique walls.[1] Such passages may be cited not only in proof of the poet's intense loyalty to the land of his birth, but as evidence of his vivid appreciation of the beauties of Nature. The richness of the Italian landscape filled him with joy, while at the same time it brought to his remembrance the deeds of the illustrious men of the past by whom the country had been fused into one nation and had been made the mistress of the world :—

> "Salve, magna parens frugum, Saturnia tellus,
> Magna virum !"

This commingling of the most devoted patriotism with a deep and pure affection for rural scenes gives to the poetry of Virgil an undying charm.

In a less lofty strain, a similar natural pride was expressed by Virgil's contemporary, Propertius, who declared that all the wonders of the world must yield to the Roman land which Nature had gifted with all that she had anywhere placed on earth. In his eyes it was a country more apt for arms than prone to crime, of whose history Fame had no reason to be ashamed ; for its people, while potent with the sword, were no less powerful from their devotion to duty ; they well knew how to temper victory with clemency.[2] Horace caught up the same enthusiasm for his country's greatness and glory. To him it seemed

---

[1] *Geor.* II. 136-176.
[2] *Eleg.* IV. xxii. 17.

that, besides Rome's success in foreign wars, her internal condition under the sway of Augustus was eminently auspicious, for "golden Plenty, from her full horn, pours forth her fruits upon Italy.[1]

In the following chapters I propose to consider the evidence which may be gleaned that a genuine feeling for Nature existed among the Romans, and to enquire in what forms this feeling found utterance in literature and art during the later decades of the Republic and the first century of the Empire, or from the time of Lucretius to that of Statius. This period, embracing what has been called the golden age of Latin literature, was marked by a series of political changes which had a profound influence on the intellectual progress of the country. The civil dissensions that led to the downfall of the Republic restricted and almost closed the openings into public life which had for centuries attracted the ambition of the governing class.[2] The establishment of the Empire still further narrowed these avenues.

---

[1] *Epist.* I. xii. 28. The national sentiment of patriotism is well expressed by Cicero : "Cari sunt parentes, cari liberi, propinqui, familiares ; sed omnes omnium caritates patria una complexa est, pro qua quis bonus dubitet mortem oppetere, si ei sit profuturus?" (*De Off.* I. xvii.). Another striking illustration of the same feeling is given by Catullus when he represents Attis, overwhelmed with remorse at his condition and self-chosen exile, and uttering as his first exclamation :

"Patria, o mei creatrix, Patria, o mea genetrix !" (lxiii. 50).

[2] Lucan gives a graphic picture of the ruin caused by the civil wars. Even in the more quiescent intervals,

"temporis angusti mansit concordia discors" (*Phars.* I. 24 *seq.*, 99).

When the whole power and patronage of the commonwealth were centred in one man, who might be jealous and vindictive, the sense of political freedom was so weakened that men sought their liberty in other fields of activity. Some, like the historians and poets, turned to literature, and produced works, alike in prose and verse, which are the immortal glory of Rome. Others, like Cicero, found their consolation in philosophy, and introduced the doctrines of the Greek schools into the literature of their own country, at the same time bringing Latin prose to its highest perfection.[1] Others, again, like Lucretius at the beginning of the period and the elder Pliny and Seneca towards its close, gave themselves to the scientific contemplation or attentive observation of the world around them, and made contributions to the foundation of natural and physical science.

It could hardly be that men should not turn to the fields, the woods, the hills, the rivers, and the sea-shore for the solace of peace and joy which the fresh face of Nature is ever so ready

[1] The numbing effect of the political condition of the country towards the end of the Republic is by no writer more vividly portrayed than by Cicero. Thus he writes : " As I have been shut out from political affairs and forensic business by impious arms and by force, I live continuously in retirement ; not from want of business, nor from a desire for rest. The senate being extinguished and the law-courts abolished, what is there left which I could worthily do either in the Curia or the Forum?" (De Off. II. i. and III. i.). He therefore betook himself to philosophy, and with amazing energy and fecundity poured forth a succession of treatises, which are among the masterpieces of Latin literature.

to afford.   How far they found consolation from this source can only be imperfectly gathered from the records which have survived from their times. But an examination of these records brings abundant proof that to some of the greatest minds of that period the love of Nature was an inspiring influence which, breathing through their souls and finding expression in their writings, must have found its way into the hearts of many of their fellow-countrymen, as, across the centuries, it still does into ours.

CHAPTER II

COUNTRY AND TOWN

THE founders of Rome, being an agricultural people, and thus living in continual contact with the open face of nature, led healthy lives, and were noted for their industry, sobriety, and thrift. The work of the farm being the common occupation of the community, there was no loss of dignity in sharing in the manual labour of the fields. The owner of a little farm, such as each single family possessed, with the help of his wife and his sons, worked the soil and reaped the harvest. And in long subsequent times, when larger properties had been acquired, it continued to be the practice for the proprietors of such estates to share in the usual operations of farming. Though these patricians would have shrunk from engaging in any kind of handicraft or trade,[1] they might be seen guiding the plough, or joining in some of the other menial work of their land. Tradition recorded that the founder of the city was himself not only a horseman, skilled in managing the bridle, but also expert with the plough.[2] It

[1] Cicero, *De Off.* I. xlii.
[2] Propertius, V. x. 19.

23

was the prevalent belief down to the end of the
Republic that in the olden time the land was
more diligently cultivated than in later years,
that the senator pastured his own sheep and
worked his paternal farm, that the consul went
straight from the plough to the fasces or to
dispense justice to the people, and that in those
days it was thought no disgrace to have hard
hands.[1] The story of Cincinnatus ploughing his
four jugera of land and stripped for the work,
when the delegates came to announce to him
his election to the dictatorship, was typical of
the simple life of the early Republic.   When,
centuries later, in the first days of the Empire,
Horace's neighbours used to smile as they saw
him moving sods and stones on his Sabine fields,
it was, doubtless, the awkwardness of his untrained
efforts rather than the occupation itself that
amused them.[2]

The Roman country-gentleman in the best
times of the Republic was well placed for appre-
ciating the pleasure and interest of rural pursuits.
Sharing in these with his free labourers and slaves,
he had an intimate practical acquaintance with
their details, and with all the trials and risks and
disappointments of a farmer's life.   Besides these
duties in the country, which of themselves must
in many cases have been enough fully to engross
his time and thoughts, he had other imperative

---

[1] Ovid, *Fasti*, III. 779-782, and I. 204-207.
[2] Horace, *Epist*. I. xiv. 39.

calls upon his attention. The more important families in the rural districts were likewise those of most consequence in the city. As members of the senate, they took part alike in the municipal government of Rome and in the political and military administration of the Republic. The patricians filled the succession of civic offices, and in due course were entrusted with the command of armies and with the administration of the various provinces which, one after another, were embraced within the sway of the Republic and the Empire. Yet, though the interest and attractions of city life grew increasingly strong, many of these men retained their love of the country, and spent as much of their time on their estates as could be spared from their senatorial and other duties. They were a living link between the rural community that remained on the land, and the inhabitants of the growing city who found residence and employment within its walls. They included many admirable specimens of their class—keen, public-spirited farmers, delighting in rural life, good sportsmen, sometimes accomplished in literature, and yet keeping in close touch with the politics of the Capital, joining in the debates of the Curia, ready to take their turn in the tenure of the magistracies, to march an army and quell an insurrection on the farthest frontiers of the dominions, or to spend years in settling and governing some remote and half-civilised province.

There was another influence by which some
of the landed proprietors might be brought into
touch with the wildest parts of the southern half
of the peninsula, far away from their own paternal
estates. As a result of the confiscations which
followed the wars waged by Rome in Italy, vast
tracts of the best grazing-grounds in the country
became the property of the Republic.[1] Cattle-
breeding on an extensive scale was thereby
developed, which became a lucrative employment
for men who had capital to invest in it. Varro
gives some interesting information regarding this
industry. He divides the raising of stock into two
kinds: one of a humbler type—the *pastio villatica*,
in which comparatively small flocks and herds were
tended on the lands around the country villa, and
in the care of which even boys and girls might
be employed; the other of a much more important character (*nota et nobilis*, Varro calls it)—the
pastio agrestis, which lay, at least in summer,
among the distant uplands of the Apennines,
including the wildest and most inaccessible ground,
where large herds of oxen, horses, mules, and asses
were pastured, and where numerous companies of
able-bodied men—slaves and freemen, were engaged.
In the transport of these herds from their higher
summer quarters to lower ground for wintering,
it was no light task to guide the animals along

---

[1] *See* a paper on *Pascua*, in Pelham's posthumous " Essays," 1911,
p. 300. Ovid alludes to a practice of illegal grazing of the public
pastures (*Fasti*, V. 283).

the narrow, rough, and often steep drove-tracks (*calles*). The men were themselves a wild set, ready for insurrection, and often engaged in it. They went armed against robbers, as well as against wolves and wild beasts of the chase, and were attended by packs of fierce dogs.[1] Although each proprietor was represented by a skilled and trusted overseer (*magister pecoris*), we may well suppose that, where he was young and adventuresome, he himself from time to time visited his far-lying dependencies, and thus made acquaintance with the sterner aspects of his native country, which otherwise he would have had little chance of ever seeing.

Records of the lives of some of these accomplished and patriotic country-gentlemen have come down the stream of time, and glimpses into their private life have been left by a few of them in their writings. One of the most notable of their number, Cato, the Censor (B.C. 234-149), filled a distinguished place in the history of Rome, and was also a voluminous author, though only fragments of his writings have survived. Among these the most important is his treatise on agriculture, written in a quaint, abrupt, and sententious style, indicative of a strong, authoritative, and conservative nature, which loved the country and rural life. He contrasts the pursuit of agriculture with that of the merchant. The latter he admits to be a strenuous and assiduous

---

[1] Varro, *Re Rust.* II. ix., x. ; III. i., ii.

calling, yet full of danger and risk. But he holds that from the ranks of the farmers the bravest men and the most vigorous soldiers are produced.[1] Cato's treatise is full of practical directions for all the various operations of husbandry, couched in terse language, which indicates not only intimate familiarity with the subject, but an evident delight in its pursuit. He was, moreover, a pious observer of the national religion. Thus, when a grove is to be thinned after the Roman manner, he enjoins that the operation must be begun by the sacrificial offering of a pig, and he even gives the words of the prayer which is to be addressed to the god or goddess of the place. His directions for the proper lustration of a farm state in still more detail the formula to be used in addressing Mars and the other deities concerned.[2]

Cicero, who was born little more than forty years after the death of Cato, and who must have known some of Cato's younger friends, has left a pleasant picture of the old patriot in his surroundings, discoursing of old age. In Cicero's essay he is represented as remarking :—

" I can name some Roman country-gentlemen in the Sabine district, neighbours and friends of mine, in whose absence hardly any of the more important farm-work is done, such as sowing and

[1] *De Re Rust.* I. *ad init.*
[2] *Op. cit.* cap. cxxxiv. cxli. Ovid gives a good description of the lustration of a pagus or hamlet by its coloni or small free tenants (*Fasti,* I. 657-704).

reaping or storing the crops. These same gentlemen also give themselves much trouble about matters which, as they are well aware, do not particularly concern themselves."

Cato himself is described as taking the keenest delight in the pleasures of farming. These, he remarks, " are not hindered by old age, and seem to come nearest to the life of a wise man." Cicero makes him conclude his panegyric on agricultural occupations with these words :—

" Nor is country-life delightful on account only of corn-fields and meadows, vineyards and plantations, but also of gardens and orchards, the pasturing of cattle, the swarming of bees, and the variety of every kind of flowers."[1]

Cato's love of Nature is characteristically Roman and practical. The beauty that more particularly appeals to him is that of Nature subdued by the hand of man, brought into his service, and ministering to his welfare.

To a later generation belongs the illustrious M. Terentius Varro (B.C. 116-27), who was born before the Jugurthine War, saw the fall of the Republic, survived the establishment of the Empire and the reign of Augustus, and did not pass away until he had nearly reached the age of ninety, and Tiberius had been thirteen years on the throne. He was the most learned and the most prolific writer of his time. Accomplished in almost every field of intellectual enquiry, he was likewise a

[1] Cicero, *Cato Major*, vii. xv.

strenuous country-gentleman and farmer. Un-
fortunately nearly all his writings have perished.
His little treatise on agriculture, already cited, is
the only one which has survived entire. In this
work, composed when its author was eighty years of
age, he puts his discourse into the form of dialogue,
and introduces a group of his agricultural friends
and neighbours, who give their views on the details
of farm management. The occasional flashes of
humour in the conversations throw a pleasant
light on the social intercourse of the day. With
regard to the problem of the country *versus* the
town, Varro remarks that

" two distinct kinds of human life have been handed
down to our time—that of the country and that of
the town. There can hardly be any doubt but that
these are distinct from each other, not only in place,
but also in time, and have separate origins. The
country life is much the more ancient, for men
were cultivating the land before they had any
towns." [1]

In another passage he states that

" the great men who have preceded us had good
cause to prefer the country people to the town-
bred population. They thought that as in the
country those who live at villas are more idle
than those who work on the fields, so those who
are settled in the town are lazier than those who
are engaged in the country. Accordingly, they so
divided the year that only each ninth day was
employed in town business, while the intervening

[1] *De Re Rust.* III. i.

seven [1] days were devoted to country-pursuits. So long as they kept to this arrangement they obtained the greatest yield from their fields, and they were themselves much stronger in health, having no need for the urban gymnasia of the Greeks." [2]

This brave old conservative stood stoutly on the ancient ways in all the affairs of life. In religion he continued to reverence the old national divinities that his forefathers had worshipped, calling them by their original Latin names, and not by the Greek appellations that were supplanting these. We may be sure that after every sojourn in Rome, he was delighted to get back to his country home, where his first care would no doubt be to look diligently into every detail of the farm work, and make sure that in his absence it had all been carried out satisfactorily without deviation from ancestral custom.

More than a century later than the time of Varro flourished Pliny the Younger (A.D. 61-113?) —the most excellent example of a Roman country-gentleman whose record has been preserved with some measure of fullness. Trained for the bar, he acquired a considerable practice there, and attained some distinction as an orator. He had a strong bent towards literature, and among his friends and correspondents was the historian Tacitus. Although most of his writings have perished, his letters remain as one of the most delightful books

[1] That is, counting each ninth day inclusively as the end of one interval and the start of another.

[2] *De Re Rust.* II. i.

in Latin literature. While they have not the unconstrained ease and grace and the deep interest of those of Cicero, they are, nevertheless, full of charm. His correspondence with the Emperor Trajan possesses some historical importance. But the main value of the letters is to be found in their revelations of the life of cultivated society at Rome and in the country. They show their author to have been wealthy and full of generous impulses in the employment of his riches, kind-hearted and considerate in his relations to his dependents, a keen observer, and gifted with no common power of describing what he saw. He had filled the usual civic offices, had served in Syria as military tribune, and for nearly two years was Propraetor of the province of Pontica in the north-east of Asia Minor. He was thus a thorough man of affairs, a conspicuous member of the best society of his day, the associate, and in some cases the friendly helper, of literary men. But with all these various interests to fill his thoughts and his time, he retained his love of the country and country life. His gardening operations, which will be referred to in a later chapter, prove how keenly devoted he was to the improvement of his estates, and how delighted to escape from Rome to the quiet and rest of his various homes in the country.

Among the sketches of character scattered through Pliny's correspondence none are more charming than those of some of his neighbours who, like himself, lived on their estates and enjoyed there the pleasures of rural retirement. At his native Como, for instance, he had near him the illustrious Verginius Rufus, who had been his guardian, and during many years had been endeared to him by endless acts of kindly friendship. Rufus, after an active and distinguished public life, in the course of which he had again and again been pressed in vain by his victorious soldiers to accept the succession to the Empire, had retired to his northern villa, which he called the "little nest of his old age." The description of the intimacy between these two friends, written by Pliny immediately after the death of his senior, is a touching tribute to the goodness of heart of a Roman patriot under the early Emperors.[1]

With another northern friend and neighbour, Caninius Rufus, Pliny shared the love of a country life and devotion to literary studies. The tastes and interests which they had in common may be judged from one of Pliny's letters which contains the following string of questions :—

"What is going on at Como, that darling place in your eyes and mine? What about that delightful suburban retreat of yours, that portico with its perpetual spring, that shadiest of plane-tree groves, that sparkling canal between its green banks, with the neighbouring convenient lake? What about your soft but solid promenade, your bath filled and surrounded with the fullest sunshine, your dining-rooms for public and home parties, your sleeping rooms for day and those for night?"[2]

[1] Pliny, *Epist.* II. i. ; VI. x.   [2] *Id.* 1. iii.

c

Pliny thinks that having all these comforts and advantages his friend must be happy and blest, and should therefore be able to dedicate himself to studious pursuits, and, in pressing such pursuits upon him, he adds a remark which significantly reflects his own ambition:

"Every other possession will pass away from you to one owner after another, but a literary work once accomplished will never cease to belong to yourself."

The same correspondence contains a pleasant narrative of how Pliny discovered among his neighbours another retired official with literary tastes not unlike his own. He describes a visit which he paid to Terentius Junior, who, after an honourable career in the public service, had resigned the office of Procurator of Narbonensian Gaul, and had settled quietly on his own property.

"I accepted his invitation," Pliny writes, "and, regarding him as a worthy father of a family and a most diligent farmer, I began to speak of such matters as I thought he would be interested in. But he with the most cultivated talk led the conversation into literary topics. With what purity he spoke alike in Latin and in Greek! He is such an adept in both tongues that he seems especially to excel in that which he is speaking at the moment. How much he has read, and how much he remembers! You would think that he lives in Athens and not in a remote country house."

Pliny draws from this experience the moral—

" Oh, what a number of learned men are concealed by their own modesty or love of retirement, and whose existence is thus unknown to fame." He concludes his letter with the remark :—

"As in the camp, so also in our literary field, you will find many men who, in spite of their country training, are well equipped and armed and possess the most ardent disposition." [1]

In the early days of the Republic, when Rome was comparatively small and its inhabitants were still for the most part engaged in cultivating the surrounding land, probably little or no difference in habits and tastes existed between those who dwelt within the walls and those whose daily work and domicile lay outside them. But with the growth of the city and the consequent increase in the requirements and amusements of urban life, there gradually grew up that diversity of manners and morals between the town-bred and the country - bred parts of the population to which allusion has already been made. The rural inhabitants, who included proprietors, coloni or small free tenants, and slaves, long retained, especially in the upland districts, much of the simple life, the morality, industry, and frugality of the olden time when, as Ennius wrote,

" Moribus antiquis stat res Romana virisque."

But in the city the growing luxury and

---

[1] *Epist.* VII. xxv. Interesting accounts of Pliny's own life at his country homes will be found in his Letters, *e.g.*, I. ix. ; II. xvii. ; IV. vi. *See* also IV. xxiii. To some of these, further reference will be made in later chapters.

extravagance of the upper classes, the idleness
and thriftlessness of the lower orders, the influx
of aliens attracted from the various countries under
the rule of the Republic, together with all the
evils arising from a constantly increasing servile
population, led to a serious relaxation of the
pristine virtues of the Latin race. Before the
end of the Republic this deterioration was plainly
perceived by observant men, and some efforts
were made to stem its progress. Varro, who held
that " divine Nature had given the fields, while
human art had built the cities," [1] thought it wise
policy to bring the people back to the land. He
maintained that the peasantry " had led a pious
and useful life and were the only representatives
left of the virtuous race that lived in the reign
of King Saturnus." [2]

---

[1] *De Re Rust.* III. i. 4. It has often been pointed out that his
words were almost exactly repeated by Cowper in the now somewhat
hackneyed line in *The Task* (I. 749).

"God made the country and man made the town."

The same idea, however, had appeared in an earlier English poet :—

"God the first garden made, and the first city Cain."
—Cowley's *Of the Garden.*

[2] *De Re Rust.* III. i. 5. The higher moral worth of the Sabine
and Apulian peasantry in their remote farms was praised by the poets
in many passages which might be cited from their writings. As samples
reference may be made to Virgil, *Geor.* II. 532 ; Horace, *Carm.* III. vi. 37 ;
Epod. II. 41 ; Propertius, IV. xiii. 25 ; Juvenal, VI. 1-12, 287, XIV. 179 ;
Statius, *Silv.* V. i. 122. The younger Pliny relates that among the
tenantry around his Tuscan home there were grandfathers and great-
grandfathers whose speech was so remote from the ordinary language
of his day that any one who listened to it might fancy himself to have
been born in an older century (*Epist.* V. vi. 6). He specially
mentions Brixia as a district where the antique " verecundia, frugalitas,
atque etiam rusticitas" were still in large measure preserved (*Epist.*
I. xiv. 4). The physical strength of the country-folk, stoutly affirmed

The attractions of Rome, however, were growing apace as the wealth of the State increased. Long before the end of the Republic the gratuitous distribution of corn and the large sums expended on gladiatorial shows and animal hunts in the circus or forum, drew an augmenting tide of rural immigrants from the country districts. Besides the slaves, strangers from many different lands found their way in increasing numbers to the capital in search of employment in the various industries and professions which grew up to meet the demands of advancing luxury and refinement. To the educated citizen who could take part in public life and enjoy the advantages and pleasures to be found at the heart of a great empire, there was obviously no place like Rome. Well might Cicero, when far off governing Cilicia, write to an unsteady friend at home—

"The City, the City, my dear Rufus—stick to that and live in its full light! Residence elsewhere, as I made up my mind in early life, is mere eclipse and obscurity to those whose energy is capable of shining at Rome."[1]

by Cato and Varro to be so superior to that of the town population, would seem to have still more differentiated the rural from the urban community a century or more after their time. Seneca remarked that the most athletic soldiers came from rugged regions, those from the city being much less robust. "Men who are transferred from the plough to arms shrink from no manual labour, but in the first march the perfumed cit gives way" (*Epist.* li. 10).

[1] *Epist. Fam.* II. xii. Mr Shuckburgh's translation. No one ever felt more sincerely or expressed more pathetically his passionate love of Rome than Ovid did in his exile :—

"O quater, O quotiens non est numerare, beatum
Non interdicta cui licet Urbe frui."—*Trist.* III. xii. 25.

Horace gave the same advice to his restless friend Bullatius: "While you may, and while fortune wears a smiling face, abide in Rome, and indite from there your praises of Samos, Chios and Rhodes."[1] The general opinion on this matter was tersely summed up in a couple of lines by Martial—

> "Rome, goddess of all lands and peoples,
> No equal hath, nor second."[2]

On the other hand, life in Rome was not without some serious drawbacks. The streets were narrow, and many of them tortuous, and the great increase of population led to a continual augmentation of their crowds and their noise. From morning to night they resounded with a ceaseless tumult of traffic—the various loud and discordant cries of itinerant vendors and beggars, the din from every kind of workshop, the rumbling of wheeled vehicles on the hard and rough stone pavements, the multitudinous shouts of teamsters and drivers, and the other countless varieties of hubbub incident to the everyday life of a large city.[3] Even the nights were broken by characteristic disturbances, such as the mill-grinding of the bakers, the hammering of the braziers, the lumbering of carts and waggons, and not infrequently by the alarm of

[1] *Epist.* I. xi. 20.
[2] *Epig.* XII. viii. 1.
[3] Martial, XII. lvii. Tibullus alludes to the tumult when a column is being dragged to the mansion of a rich man by a thousand pairs of strong oxen! (*Eleg.* II. iii. 43. *See* also Juvenal, III. 236).

a house on fire.[1]   Then the air was often redolent
of unpleasant odours coming from the numerous
cookshops and other sources.   In spite of the
excellent system of drains under the streets, the
general sanitary arrangements were probably somewhat primitive.   The wealthier portion of the
community could no doubt find, in their urban
gardens and roomy mansions, an escape from many
of these discomforts.   Even when the city was
crowded with sight-seers gathered together for
the great games in the circus, it would be possible
for one of that more fortunate class to find quiet
for study,[2] or a sequestered retreat where rest
and sleep could be enjoyed unbroken by sounds
from the outside.[3]

But in the most favourable conditions, the life
of the capital, for those who threw themselves fully
into it, could hardly be other than exhausting.
They might be able to screen themselves from
the *strepitus nocturnos atque diurnos* ; but the
whirl of society went on all the while, together
with the multitudinous cares and anxieties, and the
absorbing strife of the political and professional
arena.   A man wholly immersed *fluctibus in
mediis et tempestatibus urbis* must have been
glad to repair to the fresh air and restful quiet of
the country where he could enjoy "the indolent
but pleasant condition of doing nothing and being

---

[1] Martial, XII. lvii. ; Juvenal, III. 197.
[2] Pliny, *Epist.* IX. vi.
[3] Martial, *Epig.* XII. lvii. 21.

nothing."[1] Hence when the sultry season approached, Rome began to grow so intolerable that escape from it was sought by all who could afford the expense of removal. Tibullus thought that a man must be made of iron who could then remain in Rome.[2] As the Dog-days drew near, the throng of society in the city used rapidly to thin, and the numerous country retreats received their summer visitors. Some of the citizens made for Praeneste, others for the cool grove of Diana at Lake Nemi or the forests of Mount Algidus, or shady Tusculum, or the pleasant freshness of the Anio among the woods of Tibur.[3] A large proportion of the migrants went to the seaside, which all the way from the mouth of the Tiber southward to the far side of the Bay of Naples was dotted with little towns and an almost continuous chain of villas.[4] To receive this annual crowd of visitors there seems to have been no adequate provision of what we should now call "hotel accommodation" in the various places to which they flocked. Polybius, indeed, has put on record that food was cheap and abundant in Italy, and that at the inns travellers did not bargain for particular articles but simply

[1] Pliny, *Epist*. VIII. ix.

[2] *Eleg*. II. iii. 2. Martial affirms that Rome would soon bleach a man's complexion, even though travel might have tanned him as black as an Ethiop (*Epig*. X. xii. 11).

[3] Statius, *Silvae* IV. iv.

[4] The Bay of Naples itself was an especially favourite resort. In Strabo's time, and doubtless much earlier, the whole coast of the "Crater" from Misenum to Minerva's Point (Punta della Campanella) was adorned with towns, villas and their grounds, placed so close together that the whole looked like one continuous city (*Geog*. V. iv. 8).

asked what was the charge per head for board, the innkeepers being usually content to supply their guests with every necessary at a charge rarely exceeding an as a day each.[1] If, however, we are to take Horace's account of his journey to Brundisium as an unexaggerated narrative, the inn accommodation on that frequented route was not always satisfactory:[2] only when he and his fellow-travellers were fortunate enough to find quarters in some country villa did they secure comfort. It was obviously impossible to make a stay in these country inns, and it therefore became necessary, especially for those who had no estates in the country, but who chose to reside for part of the year at a distance from Rome, to buy or build houses of their own. Even comparatively poor men made every effort to acquire at least a modest cottage and garden, at a sufficient distance from the capital to be in the full quiet and freshness of the country. Thus Martial, who, though a popular poet, was not a rich man, was proud of the little farm which he had secured at Nomentum, some fourteen miles from Rome, and to which he betook himself at intervals when the capital became too much for his endurance.[3] Another literary man, Suetonius, the historian, enlisted the kind offices of Pliny the Younger in his endeavour to buy a small

---

[1] *Hist.* II. 15.   [2] *Sat.* I. v.
[3] *See* especially *Epig.* VI. xliii. ; X. xlviii. ; XII. lvii.

farm (*agellus*) not far from Rome and accessible by good roads.[1]

Those who enjoyed larger incomes were usually not content with a single retreat in the country.[2] Thus, Cicero, who in his own days would hardly have been pointed to as specially wealthy, possessed some seven houses along the shores of Latium and Campania, besides his larger properties at Arpinum and Tusculum.[3] Even tradesmen who had retired with a competence were possessors of country-houses, like the successful barber mentioned by Juvenal, whose numerous villas the poet could hardly count.[4]

[1] Pliny, *Epist.* I. xxiv. In some districts, as in a part of Latium alluded to by Juvenal (*Sat.* III. 223), an excellent house could be bought for the price paid for one year's rent of a dark lodging in Rome.

[2] Nor sometimes with a single house in Rome. Martial was exasperated with a man who had three houses in the city, and for whom he never knew where to look. The poet consoled himself with the reflection that he who lives everywhere lives nowhere (*Epig.* VII. lxxiii.).

[3] It appears from his Letters that he had a house of his own at each of the following places, Antium, Astura, Formiæ, Sinuessa, Cumae, Puteoli, and Pompeii. He uses the diminutive *prædiola* in speaking of these retreats, and they were probably for the most part modest enough, but he describes them as "belle aedificata et satis amoena" (*Ad Att.* XVI. iii. 4). Even when referring to his larger inland establishments, he is fond of diminutives ; the Tusculan villa has an *atriolum*, a *porticula*, etc., one of his places in Campania he refers to as a "minuscula villa" (*Ad Att.* XIV. xiii. 5). Sometimes when the distance between two country villas was considerable, the proprietor, in order not to trespass on the hospitality of friends who had houses in the neighbourhood, would buy a *deversorium*, or mere house of call, on the high road, wherein he could break his journey and rest for the night. Cicero thought of acquiring such a local halting-place at Tarracina (*Ad Fam.* VII. xxiii. 3).

[4] *Sat.* X. 225, and also I. 94. The custom of multiplying country abodes in Italy has descended to our own day. "When Prince Marcantonio Borghese died in 1886, the family estate comprised fifteen or twenty

The owner of a number of properties in different parts of the country could vary his residence according to the season of the year, one place being more suitable for winter, another for summer. Thus Pliny the Younger had a seaside villa near Laurentum, about seventeen miles from Rome, which, after a day's business in the capital, he could easily reach in the evening. It was so planned as to be available at any season, some of the rooms being warm in winter and cool in summer.[1] He had also cool summer retreats at Tusculum, Tibur, and Praeneste, and more than one house on the Lake of Como. But his favourite summer abode lay in Tuscany, far up the vale of the Tiber.[2] When considering the question of purchasing an addition to his landed property, Pliny admitted that it is perhaps best to distribute our possessions, and that "change of place and climate affords a great deal of pleasure, especially when the peregrination lies between one's own different estates."[3] On the other hand, Seneca strongly condemned this practice of shifting residences. He thought that to be jumping from one place to another was not consistent with stability of mind, for in his opinion to ensure such stability it was necessary to keep the body from

villas of which three were at Frascati and three between Anzio and Nettuno" (Lanciani, "Wanderings in the Roman Campagna " (1909), p. 43).

[1] Horace alludes to the luxury of large porticoes facing the cool north (*Carm.* II. xv. 15).

[2] Further particulars about Pliny's villas will be found in chap. vi.

[3] *Epist.* III. xix.

running about.[1]   This was not the opinion of
Cicero, who used to make the tour of his seaside
houses in Campania, spending a few days in each
and dating his delightful letters from them.

During most of the time of the Republic
country-houses were planned on a far more modest
scale than was afterwards reached towards the
close of that time and in the days of the Empire.
Of one of these simpler retreats a good account
has been left by Seneca. It was the home to
which the great Scipio Africanus retired in exile
from the ingratitude of his country. It stood
on the coast at Liternum, a little to the north
of Cumae. The humble aspect of the dwelling,
and especially the small size and darkness of its
bathroom to which the hero who had conquered
Carthage repaired when wearied with the rustic
labours of his farm, made a deep impression
on the philosopher, who, in describing it to his
correspondent, asked what Roman would now
put up with such accommodation. The contrast
between its antique simplicity and the prevailing
luxury of his own day afforded him a more than
usually telling illustration for one of his characteristic diatribes against the extravagance of the age.[2]

How far things had advanced from the days

---

[1] *Epist.* lxix. 1.   This was a favourite theme of Seneca's animadver-
sions.   In another letter he calls the habit a sign of an unbalanced
mind—"aegri animi ista jactatio est" (ii. 1).   Again he counsels
Lucilius against thinking that change of place will lighten sorrow and
care—"animum debes mutare, non caelum" (xxvii.), an expression
which Horace had already used (p. 47).

[2] *Id.* lxxxvi.

of Scipio to those of Trajan may be gathered
from the accounts of his villas left by Pliny the
Younger, which probably afford a good idea of
the general arrangement of the country-houses
of the better class.[1] Great care was taken in
the planning of a villa to place the various rooms
in appropriate position with reference to the sun.
The winter dining-room faced southwards, while
that for summer was shielded from the heat. Nor
was less regard shown with reference to the outlook from the house. The windows were arranged
so as to command the best views, a prospect
of the sea being especially desired. If the house
lay inland it might afford glimpses of the open
country and distant hills, with the garden as a
foreground. Cicero tells how his architect provided him with narrow windows through which
to look into the pleasure-ground, while Atticus
would have had them wide so as to take
in more of the surrounding landscape.[2] The
philosopher, while careful of the views outside,
was not less eager to ornament the interior of
his Tusculan retreat with works of art, for the
acquisition of which he used to give commissions
to some of his correspondents. He had a taste
for pictures and decorated the walls of that villa
with them.[3] There was obviously no limit to
the amount of money that might be expended in

---

[1] Described in chapter vi.

[2] *Epist. Ad Att.* II. iii. 2. Horace remarks :
"Laudaturque domus longos quae prospicit agros."—*Epist.* I. x. 23.

[3] *Ad Fam.* VII. xxiii.

the adornment of these country-houses, especially when it included the use of Greek and other far-fetched marbles and precious ornamental stones.[1]

By the time of the early Empire the taste for houses and gardens in the country had risen to such a height that Horace, in a vein of exaggeration, could exclaim that soon there would be no room for the plough, so numerously were these palatial mansions scattered over the land. The poet, in the typical spirit of the antique Roman, lamented that so much space should be given to the merely ornamental instead of to the useful. Thus he regretted that the plane-tree, grown merely for its shade, should supplant the elm which had been so long employed to support the vine, and that the olive should be replaced by beds of violets, myrtles, and all kinds of fragrant flowers. Such, he said, was not the way of the olden time when men of the type of Romulus and the unshaven Cato led the people.[2] Looking

[1] Juvenal, *Sat.* XIV. 86.

[2] *Carm.* II. xv. Seneca in one of his outbursts against what he considered to be the luxury of his time, asks—"When will there be a lake which the gable-ends of your villas will not overhang, or a river whose banks will not be fringed with your buildings? Wherever springs of warm water shall gush forth, there new and luxurious hotels will be erected, wherever a coast-line shall curve into a bay, you forthwith will throw down your foundations, and not content with the ground unless you have made it up artificially, you will push back the sea. Though your roofs may shine everywhere, in one place perched on an eminence and commanding a wide view of land and sea, in another place, built on the plains but carried up to the height of a hill, though you shall have piled up many and vast erections, yet consider that you are yourself single and a very small individual. Of what use, then, are your many bedrooms? You can only lie in one, and that is not yours when you are not there yourself" (*Epist.* lxxxix. 21).

at the matter from our modern point of view, we may be inclined to regard the increase in the cultivation of the ornamental as not so much an indication of growing luxury, as a distinct advance in taste, and a further stage in the development of the love of Nature.

It became the vogue to quit Rome during at least the sultry season of the year, and the demands of fashion appear to have been not less imperious in those days than they are now. Of the multitude that fled from the city the proportion may have been small of those who had a genuine love of the country and of a simple life there in the enjoyment of Nature. As many urban dissipations as could be transported were no doubt carried to these various summer resorts, and probably many of the sojourners were glad enough when the passing of the summer heats allowed them to resume their gay life in the city.[1] Horace described what was no doubt a common disposition among his fellow-countrymen when he wrote:—

"Our cares are removed by reason and prudence, not by an abode commanding a wide sea-view; we change our sky not our minds by running across the sea. We are engaged in a strenuous idleness."[2]

---

[1] Martial gives an interesting contrast of the counter-attractions of town and country (*Epig.* X. li.). Sulpicia's question—" Dulcius Urbe quid est?"—was no doubt asked by many a visitor wearied with the dullness of country life (Tibullus, IV. viii. 3).

[2] *Epist.* I. xi. 26; or, as Goldsmith expressed the idea,

"Thus idly busy rolls their world away."

One of the first and most obvious forms of
relief enjoyed by city-men at their country
quarters was freedom from the etiquette and
routine which custom exacted at Rome. A
sign of this relaxation was doffing the toga which,
as a symbol of what the rules of society required,
may be compared to the usage of the modern
frock-coat. "Let our wrinkled skin drink in
the warmth of the vernal sun, and avoid the
toga," was Juvenal's recommendation,[1] and one
of the causes which led Pliny to prefer his
Tuscan to his other villas was that, being so far
inland from Rome, it involved "nulla necessitas
togæ."[2] Juvenal remarks that, if the truth were
told, throughout a great part of Italy the toga
was never put on except upon the dead.[3]

Another relief which must have been inex-
pressibly welcome to busy political and professional
men, and indeed to everybody of any consequence
in Rome, was escape from the crowd of importunate
clients and hungry applicants for favour and
assistance who dogged their footsteps in the
city.[4] When men with rural tastes could go
far enough from Rome to find once more at their

---

[1] Sat. XI. 203.

[2] Epist. V. vi. 45. Martial uses the expression "tunicata quies,"
where the toga was discarded and the tunic became the outer garment
in the restful life of the country (X. li.).

[3] Sat. III. 171.

[4] It was necessary to go to a good distance from Rome to escape the
crowd of callers. Even at Formiæ Cicero was inundated with them, and
exclaimed to Atticus that if he could not be alone he would rather have
the company of mere country-folk than that of superfine fellows from
Rome (Ad Att. II. xv.).

country-homes quiet and fresh air, we can imagine
with what renewed interest they would survey
the latest improvements in their own villas and
gardens and in those of their neighbours, and
how the familiar features of rustic life—the farms
and fields, the voices of birds, the hum of insect
life, the shady woods, the herds in pasture, the
peasants at their wonted tasks, and above all
the life and stir of the farms on festive days when
the whole countryside was alive and gay with
flowers for the lustration or other appointed
ceremonial—would bring a sense of peace and
rest to men jaded by the turmoil of the capital.[1]

[1] The joy of these country festivals may be gathered from the
animated descriptions of them that have come down to us: Virgil,
Geor. I. 338-350 ; Tibullus, II. i. 1-30 ; Ovid, *Fasti* I. 663-704, II.
639-684.

D

CHAPTER III

To many of those who from time to time could get far away from the crowd and out of hearing of the "magnae vaga murmura Romae," the peacefulness and freshness of the country, the beauty of field and woodland, of flower and tree, the lights and shadows on the distant hills, the changing aspects of the sky, the wide expanse of open sea, and the plunge of the waves along the shore must have brought health and pleasure to mind as well as to body. How keenly the benefit of this contact with Nature was felt by contemplative and impressionable spirits may be gathered from many passages in Latin literature. To such a man as Cicero, for example, wearied with professional practice, worried with political anxiety, or bowed down with domestic sorrow, it must have been of the utmost service in resting and restoring his mental powers. He tells that it was his habit to keep up his spirits by seeking rivers and solitude, and when at rare intervals he could escape for a few days from his duties

50

in Rome, he was glad to retreat to his native
home at Arpinum, among the picturesque defiles
of the Fibrenus and Liris, where the extreme
beauty of the scenery, the loneliness and the
health-giving air of the place re-invigorated him.[1]
In the remarkable scene with which he opens the
second book of his work, *De Legibus*, he introduces Atticus as his guest at that place, and
represents him as delighted with the landscape
at the gorges of the two streams and the island
at their junction. Cicero's other country-houses,
more especially those at Tusculum, Antium and
Astura, likewise afforded him the mental rest and
refreshment of which he often stood in much
need. In a later generation, the younger Pliny,
in describing his Laurentine villa, breaks out into
an apostrophe to its charms—"O Sea, O Shore,
true and retired place for study! how much have
you taught me! how many thoughts have you
inspired!"[2]

The feelings of pleasure awakened by country
sights and sounds find full and joyous utterance
among the Latin poets. Most of these writers
delighted in depicting rural scenes. Even when
they lived in Rome, it was not in the city, but
in the memory of what they had seen and heard
among the woods and meadows, by the brooks
and rivers, or by the shores of the sea, that
some of the greatest among them found their

---

[1] *Epist. Ad Att.* XIII. xvi.; *ad Quint. Frat.* III. i.; *De Leg.* II. i. 1.
[2] *Epist.* I. ix.

chief inspiration.   It is interesting to trace how
these rural influences impressed the colossal
genius of Lucretius (B.C. 97-53).   Among all
the poets of ancient or modern time, he stands
out as the one who may, perhaps, most fittingly,
and in the widest sense, be called the poet of
Nature.   As a philosopher and man of science,
he devoted his life to the contemplation and
investigation of the universe.   His intense and
insatiable desire was to seek out and to interpret
to mankind the hidden causes and interconnec-
tions of the changes that are unceasingly in
progress in earth, sea, and sky.   Following the
teaching of his masters Epicurus and Empedocles,
he had gathered much knowledge, which he
believed would benefit his fellow-men, and he
threw his whole soul into the task of expound-
ing this knowledge and showing what he believed
to be its practical utility in dealing with the
most serious problems of human life.

There is a strangely modern tone in his
discussion of an atomic theory of the universe
and in his enunciation of the proofs of an orderly
system of evolution alike in the inorganic and the
organic kingdoms.   His explanations of natural
phenomena and his philosophy of the world do
not come within the scope of my present enquiry.
But we must recognise that no writer has ever
had a more vivid perception of the beauty and
harmony, the regulated movement and order of
the universe.   Decay and renewal, in never-ending

sequence, were seen by him to be the invariable process, everything being directed and governed by immovable law. As he contemplated this marvellous system with what he called "a kind of divine pleasure and awe,"[1] his poetic imagination embodied his conception of it in language often rugged, but sometimes impressively noble and solemn. Yet he seems at times to feel that at least the Latin tongue was inadequate to convey to others an idea of what with his mental vision he had seen and learnt, or to impart the thrill of delight with which his survey of the inner workings of nature had filled his own soul.[2]

The feeling which Lucretius had for Nature thus differed, as we have seen, from that of his fellow-countrymen. Discarding with contempt the national religion, he relegated its gods to a remote region of perpetual calm and unbroken inactivity. In their place there floated through his meditations a conviction of the transcendant unity of Nature, and a dim consciousness of some universal creative and regulating power. In his view we are all of celestial origin, children of the same father, who sends down the life-giving moisture that enables our mother earth to produce not only the human race, but all other living

---

[1] " Quaedam divina voluptas atque horror "—*Rer. Nat.* III. 28.

[2] *See* especially I. 133, 832, III. 260. The faculty which Ovid attributes to Pythagoras was amply possessed by Lucretius :

" Quae natura negabat
Visibus humanis, oculis ea pectoris hausit."—*Metam.* XV. 64.

things.[1] In the majestic opening of his poem[2] where he avails himself of the time - honoured usage of invoking divine help in his poetic undertaking, he selects, not the Muses, but "Alma Venus" as his inspiring deity. Yet, although he invests her with some of the familiar and sensuous attributes by which she was known in the popular mythology, it is clear from the whole tenor of the poem that he had in his mind a great life-giving Spirit in Nature. He continually refers to " Natura gubernans" " Natura creatrix," " Natura daedala rerum."[3] To this universal pervading spirit he appeals as his pilot and helper. He knows how dark is the way before him, but a great hope has entered his heart that he will be sustained in his enterprise of visiting the distant haunts of the Muses, which had never yet been trodden by the foot of man. In his

[1] *Rer. Nat.* II. 991, 992.

[2] It is interesting, as evidence of the popularity of Lucretius, to find that the first words of this fine opening occur several times among the graffiti on the walls of the houses in Pompeii (Mau, " Pompeii," 2nd ed., p. 509).

[3] He alludes also to a " vis abdita quaedam" that tramples on man, regardless of his greatness and glory (V. 1233). The spiritual meaning of this invocation is finely expressed in Tennyson's poem on Lucretius, who is represented as appealing to the goddess—

> " Ay, but I meant not thee ; I meant not her
> Whom all the pines of Ida shook to see
> Glide from that quiet heaven of hers, and tempt
> The Trojan.   Rather, O ye Gods,
> Poetlike did I take
> That popular name of thine to shadow forth
> The all-generating powers and genial heat
> Of Nature, when she strikes thro' the thick blood
> Of cattle, and light is large, and lambs are glad
> Nosing the mother's udder, and the bird
> Makes his heart voice amid the blaze of flowers."

invocation, thoughts and images seem to crowd upon each other as they hurry through the poet's mind, swept onward by the rapid flow of his imagination. The stately music of his language, however, is lost in translation.

" Mother of the Aeneadae, delight of men and of gods; fostering Venus, who, under the gliding stars of heaven, fillest with life the sea that bears the ships, and the lands that yield the crops; since through thee every living creature is conceived and beholds the light of the sun: at thy coming the winds and the clouds of heaven flee away; for thee the daedal earth unfolds her sweet flowers; for thee the level fields of ocean smile, and the calmed sky beams with widespread light. For so soon as the face of spring is laid bare, and the fruitful breath of the west wind, once more let loose, blows freshly, first the birds of the air, O goddess, herald thee and thine advent, their hearts stirred by thy power. Then the cattle frisk wildly over the glad pastures and swim the rapid streams; captivated by thy charm, each eagerly follows thee whithersoever thou leadest. And thus over seas and mountains and rushing rivers and the leafy homes of birds and the verdant plains, inspiring fond love into the hearts of all, thou makest them, each after its kind, eager to renew their race." [1]

As he contemplates his self-imposed mission the poet breaks forth in exultant anticipation of his ultimate success—

" glad am I to approach these untasted Pierian springs, there to drink a deep draught: glad

[1] *De Nat. Deor.* I. 1-20.

am I to cull new flowers, and to gather for my
head a noble crown from where the Muses have
never yet wreathed the brow of any mortal."[1]

And yet this sublime poet, soaring amid the
heights of his atomic philosophy, had the tenderest
and most human of hearts, full of sympathy for
sorrow and suffering, whether in man or beast.
Amid all his speculation he retained his love of
the simple beauty of the lowliest flower, and his
interest in the welfare of every living creature.
His great poem abounds with passages which
show how closely he noted the changes of the
sky and the varied aspect of the earth in the
succession of the seasons, and, at the same time,
with what kindly feeling he watched the toil of
the husbandman. The tender sympathy and
profound melancholy, with which he regarded
the sadness and the frailty of human life, found
vent in the following passage :—

" Now no more shall thy glad home welcome
thee, nor thy dear wife, nor will thy sweet children
run to meet thee and get thy first kisses, touching
thy heart with a quiet thrill of pleasure ; nor hence-
forth wilt thou, flourishing in thy affairs, be a
strong tower to thine own dear ones. 'Pitiable
art thou,' they say, 'and pitiably has one direful
day carried off from thee all the many prizes of
life !'"[2]

How genuine and all-embracing was the love

[1] *Rer. Nat.* I. 927.   [2] III. 891-896.

which Lucretius had for the country is well illustrated in this further quotation.

"At last the rains cease which our father the sky has showered upon the lap of our mother the earth. Luxuriant crops spring up, and the branches grow green upon the trees, which are soon heavy with fruit. From these sources our own race and the race of beasts are nourished; thence, too, we see happy towns alive with children, and the leafy woods ringing on every side with the voices of young birds; thence, also, the fat cattle rest their wearied bodies amid the glad pastures, while the milky stream flows from their distended udders, and a new brood, made light-hearted with the pure milk, sports wantonly with feeble limbs upon the tender grass." [1]

By none of the Latin poets were the rural landscapes of Italy sketched so often and with such loving devotion as by Virgil (B.C. 70-19). Born on the fertile plains of the Po, yet within sight of the towering Alps on the one side and the heights of the Apennines on the other, he was fortunate in the smiling landscapes of meadow, woodland, and river amidst which his youth was passed. They inspired his earliest verse, and in after years when he had risen to fame and had long quitted his paternal home, these same scenes continued to fill his imagination and to give a special charm to all his poetry.[2] Thus, what he called, in a

---

[1] *Rer. Nat.* I. 250-261.

[2] If the last eight lines of the fourth *Georgic* can be understood to mean, what they seem literally to imply, that the whole poem was written at Naples, Virgil's memory for the details of the scenery and rural life amidst which he spent his youth must have been extra-

striking phrase, the "divini gloria ruris," which
had irradiated his boyhood, remained with him as
a bright and animating influence to the end of
his life.

For an adequate estimation of Virgil's attitude
towards Nature it is more necessary, than in the
case of many other poets, to take note of the
circumstances of his life. He was born on 15th
October, B.C. 70, near Mantua, where his father
lived as a small farmer, cultivating his own land.
His native province was so largely inhabited by a
Celtic population as to have been known long before
his time as Gallia Cisalpina. The suggestion has
been made that Virgil himself may have come of
a Celtic stock, and that to this source he owed his
exuberant delight in Nature, his meditative disposition and the vein of tender melancholy that runs
through his poems. His health seems never to
have been robust, and he consequently led a quiet
and abstemious life. His father gave him the best
education then procurable, first at Cremona and
subsequently at Milan. On his 16th birthday,
which is said to have been the same day that
Lucretius died, Virgil assumed the *toga virilis*,
and soon thereafter (B.C. 53) went to Rome to
complete his studies. How long he remained in
the capital is uncertain, for there is a gap of some
ten years about which little or nothing is known
in regard to his movements.

ordinarily retentive. His descriptions and allusions are given not only
in that poem but also in the *Æneid*, with as much force and accuracy as
if he were still living among the landscapes of the north.

In the year B.C. 49, through the action of Julius Cæsar, the inhabitants of the Transpadane province received the "civitas," and the poet thereby became a Roman citizen. No one to whom this privilege was conceded could surpass Virgil in his whole-hearted devotion to Rome and his pride in her history and achievements. At this time he may have been residing at his paternal farm by the Mincius, continuing his studies and not improbably composing verses. At the date of the momentous battle of Philippi he would seem to have been at his old home, busy with his *Eclogues*. Some of his poems had by this time attracted the attention of the higher Roman officials of the province, especially of the governor, Asinius Pollio, in honour of whom the fourth *Eclogue* was written. His studious and meditative life, however, was rudely broken up by the confiscations made by the triumvirate to provide land for discharged soldiers. The poet, dispossessed of his farm, was recommended by his friends Pollio, Varus, and Gallus to go to Rome and lay his case before Octavianus. His land was eventually restored to him, but on his return to re-occupy it, the violence of the soldier who had obtained the place compelled him to flee for his life, and he seems to have taken no further steps to be reinstated. He then left his native district, and there is no record of his ever having revisited it, though the remembrance of its beauties remained as a vivid and inspiring impression to the end of his life. Through the

kindness of patrons and friends, especially of
Octavianus, he was amply compensated for the loss
of his paternal property.[1] He appears now to have
lived at Rome for a short time, and published there
his *Eclogues* in B.C. 37. These poems at once
made him famous, and gained him the personal
friendship of Octavianus and Maecenas. He had
a house on the Esquiline Hill, near the gardens of
Maecenas. But Virgil was by nature a recluse
who found his greatest happiness in the enjoyment
of a quiet meditative life in the restful country.
The attractions of the city and the fervid appreciation of his fellow-citizens could not long detain
him in Rome. He acquired a house at Naples and
also a villa near Nola, between the western flanks
of the Apennines and the eastern slopes of
Vesuvius, and in that beautiful district he appears
to have spent most of the rest of his life, writing
the poems on which his reputation mainly rests.[2]

It was at Naples between the years 37 and 30
that he composed his *Georgics*. Thereafter he
was engaged on the *Æneid* for eleven years, and he
meant to devote three years more to the revision
of that poem. But he died on 21st September
B.C. 19, leaving his task incomplete. His will
contained directions for the destruction of all poems
which he had left unpublished. But Augustus
interfered to rescue the *Æneid* from this fate, and
the poem was published soon after the poet's death.

---

[1] "Multa dantis cum laude," as Horace remarks.
[2] Suetonius mentions that Virgil made frequent visits to Sicily.

From this outline of his biography it appears that with the exception of the interval which included the period of his education and residence in Rome, Virgil spent the first thirty years or more of his life in his native district of Transpadane Gaul. During that early period he probably wrote many minor poems which have not survived, besides those which are with more or less confidence regarded as his. It was then that he composed the *Eclogues*, in the midst of the scenery and rustic life so beautifully depicted in these idylls. But his subsequent compositions, written far away in Southern Italy, show that his memory was so deeply impressed with these scenes of his youth that he could draw upon endless recollections of them and describe them with a vivid power and an accuracy of detail which could not have been excelled had they still been before his eyes. Though living among the landscapes of Campania, it seems to have been often the air and fragrance of the meadows and woodlands on the plains of the Mincius that filled his heart and warmed his imagination.

The most important influence on Virgil's poetic powers which his transference to Campania brought with it, was that of the Sea. He may not improbably in his youth have seen the Adriatic, though his references to it in his earlier poetry may have been mainly inspired by Theocritus. At least, if he ever beheld the sea while he lived in the north, its surface seems to have left

on his mind an impression of mirror-like calm,
with only a gentle murmur of breaking wavelets.
On the shores of Campania, however, he had
an opportunity of watching the sea in all its
moods, not only of calm but of storm, and this
experience gave a new feeling and a fresh set of
images and reflections to the *Georgics* and the
Æneid.

The great poem of Lucretius, which appeared
when Virgil was a young man, so powerfully
impressed him as to leave strong traces of its
influence on his poetry.   Occasionally this influence
manifests itself in direct and frank imitation.
When the younger poet, casting his eye over the
wide domain of Nature, debated with himself what
parts of it he in his turn might choose as a theme
for his verse, his first inclination, following the
path of his great predecessor, was above all to
beseech the sweet Muses, from the deep love which
he bore them, to receive him and unfold to him
the marvels of the heavens, the tremors of the
earth, and the mighty movements and pulsations
of the sea.   But should these themes prove to
lie beyond his powers, then he prayed that he
might be allowed, in more humble strains, to sing
of the country, the streams, and the woodlands
which he loved.[1]   He knew, indeed, that it would
be no easy task to give to such lowly subjects as
these the charm and dignity of true poetry ; but
he felt an ardent wish to climb the lonely heights

[1] *Geor.* II. 475-486.

of Parnassus whence no pathway trodden by former
poets led down to the Castalian spring.[1] Looking
at the poem of Lucretius, he felt how happy that
poet must have been in having been able to
discover the causes of things, in having cast
beneath his feet all fear, and inexorable fate and
the clamour of greedy death. But, on the other
hand, happy too was the man who knew the
rural gods — Pan and old Silvanus and their
sister nymphs.[2]

Whether Virgil ever made any attempt to
obey the first promptings of his muse and essay
another poem on the subjects of which Lucretius
had treated is unknown. But if he did so he
must soon have found that the task was one for
which his genius was hardly suited. There was,
at that time, no room for another didactic poem
on the philosophy of Nature. All the science of
the time would have been needed for it, and this
department of intellectual effort had already been
gone over by his predecessor. In choosing rural
scenes as his theme he took the subject which
was most familiar and congenial to him, one
which was well worthy of his ambition, and which
he loved with the deepest affection of his gentle
and meditative nature. It was well for him, for
Rome, and for the literature of all time that he
decided as he did. To the " divini gloria ruris " he
addressed himself with a devotion and enthusiasm

---

[1] *Geor.* III. 291, imitated from Book I. 922-930 of Lucretius.
[2] *Id.* II. 490-494.

and a mastery of poetic art, such as had never before appeared in the Latin tongue. He pointed out to his fellow-countrymen and to all succeeding generations in every land the endless beauties of Nature, and showed by his own immortal example the empire which these charms can obtain over an appreciative and sympathetic soul.

While indications of Virgil's character and tastes are afforded in all his works, it is in his first published poems, the *Eclogues*, that the personality of the poet comes out most clearly, as it is from the *Sonnets* that the most tangible glimpses of the personality of Shakespeare are obtainable. The *Eclogues* bring us into touch with Virgil in his early home, among the landscapes which left such a deep impression on his memory. The whole atmosphere of these poems is that of the country, and especially of the district in which the poet was born and bred. Despite the somewhat artificial conventions of the Greek models which he followed, it is easy to see that though Arcadian and Sicilian scenes were on his lips, it was his own Italian landscape that filled his eye and heart and inspired his muse. He even appeals to it by name — "hither across the meadows will the young oxen come to drink; here Mincius fringes his green banks with slender reeds, and from yonder sacred oak comes the hum of bees."[1]

[1] *Geor.* VII. 11-13.

We can picture the little farm as he traces its boundaries from where the hills begin to descend with gentle slope to the edge of the water, and the line of venerable beech-trees with their doddered tops.[1]   The landscape, although curiously compounded of Transpadane, Sicilian and Greek features, is made to stand clearly · before us where, among familiar streams and sacred springs, the old farmer would still be left in peace, with the murmur of bees in his willow hedge, the woodman's song from the foot of the neighbouring cliff, the cooing of his wood-pigeons, and the moan of the turtle-dove from the tall elm-tree.[2]   The soothing melody of these poems could not have been more aptly described than in the words of one of the personages in the fifth *Eclogue*—"Thy song, divine poet, has been to me as sleep on the grass to weary men, or as a stream of sweet water leaping forth in the heat to quench our thirst."[3]

When after the publication of the *Eclogues*, Virgil's reputation had been firmly established, and, conscious of his growing powers, the poet aspired "virum volitare per ora," it was to his native district that he longed to bring back from the haunts of the Muses the tokens of his triumph.   Though he had been driven with

---

[1] *Geor.* IX. 7-10.   [2] *Id.* I. 51-58.

[3] *Id.* V. 45-7. It was to these poems that Horace referred when he wrote that the Muses who delight in the country had bestowed tenderness and grace (*molle atque facetum*) on Virgil (*Sat.* I. x. 44). The *Georgics* had not yet appeared.

E

violence from his early home, his heart was still
there :—

> " First, Mantua, unto thee will I bear back
> The palms of Edom ; and on thy green plain
> A marble sanctuary will I build
> Beside the water's edge, where Mincius steals
> In ample curves 'tween banks of tender reeds." [1]

It was in the composition of the *Georgics* that
Virgil found fullest scope for the expression of his
joy in rural scenes and his meditative appreciation
of Nature. The subject he chose was nominally
the rules and practice of agriculture, which had
been recently discussed by Varro in the treatise
already referred to. But Virgil, while he availed
himself of information supplied by Varro's treatise
and other authorities, found the theme congenial
for poetic treatment. Illumined by his imagination, rich in his own practical experience of farming
and country-life, and affording at every turn opportunities for the expression of his sense of the dignity
of labour, his pious and reverential nature and his
abounding love of woods and fields, of meadows
and streams, and of life in every form, it became
in his hands one of the great master-pieces of
literature, wherein the varying aspects of earth and
sea and sky, and the human tasks which husbandry
involves, are depicted with the most enthusiastic
appreciation and the most consummate art.

The poet's boyhood and youth had given him
an intimate knowledge of the life of the farmer

---

[1] *Geor.* III. 12-15.

and a warm feeling for the trials which, even in so favoured a country as Italy, affected farming. In his poem he amply recognises the laborious and unintermittent toil of the husbandman, in which he himself had taken part. The struggle with Nature, wherein man is not always the victor, enlisted Virgil's heartiest sympathy, and gave the keynote to the whole poem. This sympathy formed an element in that wide affection, through the halo of which he looked out upon the world. It gave warmth and force to his love of all that was tender and beautiful in Nature, and from time to time that love seems to burst forth as an uncontrollable emotion which demands expression in his verse. Thus in the midst of his observations on the different parts of farm-routine, the suggested remembrance of some autumn or spring, some noon-tide or storm, some flower or tree, fills his soul with rapture which finds vent in words as vivid and beautiful as the vision that inspired them. These occasional out-bursts of imaginative splendour form one of the greatest charms of the poem.

Virgil was thoroughly convinced that in spite of here and there thin or ungenial soil, or inclement seasons, or insect-plagues, or other too numerous evils, there was no lot throughout all the range of human employments more to be envied than that of a man who has to till the soil or to rear flocks and herds. And to illustrate how far this lot is preferable to that of the sailor, the courtier, the soldier, the merchant, or the politician, he drew the

well-known and inimitable panegyric on the blessings of rural life and the enviable position of the
old style farmer—a passage the musical beauty of
which is lost in translation:—

"Too happy were the husbandmen did they but know
    Their bliss; on whom, far from the clash of arms,
The earth provides an easy sustenance.
If no tall mansion, through its portals proud,
Pours forth from all its halls a surging throng
Of morning clients; if no columns gleam
With tortoise-shell, nor robes with thread of gold;
If bronze from Corinth never meets the eye,
Nor white wool dyed in bright Assyrian tints;
If their clear oil no taste of casia bears,
Yet theirs is peace that knows not care: their life,
Without illusion, rich in treasures rare,
Brings restful peace upon their ample farms.
Caverns, and sparkling lakes, and valleys cool,
With lowing herds, and soft sleep under trees
Are not denied to them, nor woodland glades
Wherein the tribes of wild beasts find their home."

"With curving plough the farmer cleaves the soil,
    And from the labour of the year maintains
His land, his young grandchildren, and his herds
And labouring oxen faithful to the yoke."

"His modest home preserves its chastity;
His loving children hang around his lips;
His kine bring well-filled udders from the mead;
His plump young goats, with horn opposed to horn,
Strive with each other on the gladsome grass;
While he himself on days of festival,
Stretched on the sward, beside the altar fire,
Welcomes his friends, who wreathe the cup with flowers." [1]

---

[1] *Geor.* II. 458-471, 513-515, 523-528.

The concluding lines of this passage with their reference to the religious ceremonies that mingled with the festivities of the country-folk is characteristically Virgilian. His natural piety and conservative instincts led him to stand by the old national faith, against the spirit of irreligion so rife in the society of his day. The *Georgics* are full of indications of this piety. His was no " vana superstitio veterumque ignara deorum." Amidst his precepts for the work of the farm, and his expressions of delight in the manifold beauties of Nature there ever mingles a recognition of higher powers that watch over mankind, and to whom were owing the devout reverence and the due offerings prescribed by the established religion of the country. At the same time he was fully cognisant of the Stoic doctrine of the " anima mundi," and refers to it towards the end of the poem (IV. 219), but without positively adopting it, or giving it the solemn sanction with which he afterwards clothed it in the *Æneid*.

Intimately bound up with his piety towards the national gods was Virgil's ardent patriotism, to which allusion has already been made. Though not born a Roman citizen he had a passionate admiration for the greatness and glory of the Roman Empire, such as no one born among the Seven Hills could surpass. He loved Italy with the deepest devotion of his emotional nature. While he was keenly sensitive to the beauty of Italian landscape, and delighted in the yearly proof

of the fertility of the Italian soil, these feelings
were intensified by the fact that all this beauty and
fertility belonged to his native land.   He depicted
the scenes for their own intrinsic charm, but that
charm was heightened by the warm glow of his
patriotism.   It is as much in this ardent national
enthusiasm as in any other part of his work that
the suggested Celtic temperament may perhaps
be traced.

That this enthusiasm was thoroughly genuine
and spontaneous cannot be questioned.   At the
same time there appears to be no doubt that the
subject of the *Georgics* was suggested to Virgil
by his appreciative patron, Maecenas.[1]   The policy
of Augustus to encourage agriculture and industry
with a view towards healing the wounds caused by
the civil wars and reuniting and strengthening the
bonds of society, was loyally supported by his able
minister.   Maecenas might naturally think that a
serious poem dealing with rural life and the aspects
of the country, written as only the poet of the
Eclogues could write it, would be popular all over
Italy, and would be an influence that might
help in the fulfilment of the Emperor's designs.
Augustus also took a serious view of the growing
deterioration of the religious and moral standard of
the community, and exerted himself with great
energy to restore the national religion, building
temples, reviving rituals that had fallen into disuse,

---

[1] *Geor.* III. 41, where the poet refers to the great minister's " haud
mollia jussa."

and in other ways trying to stem the advancing
current of indifference and impiety. From this
point of view, also, Maecenas might well conceive
that the pious and conservative spirit of Virgil
might be of service if enlisted in the cause of
reform. The poet, without in the least sacrificing
any of his convictions or tastes, could honestly
devote himself to promote the laudable ends which
the Emperor had so much at heart. It might,
indeed, nerve him to higher exertion if he felt that
in giving the fullest expression to his passionate
love of the country, to his sympathy with all rural
labour, and to his reverent piety, he was at the same
time taking part in the great imperial effort to
reform and regenerate the Roman people.

The subject of the *Æneid* did not afford such
scope as Virgil's other poems for allusions to the
country and its varied aspects and interests. Yet
so full was the poet of affectionate regard for rural
scenes that they are introduced by him as episodes
even in the midst of war and battles. Some of
these episodes will be cited in later chapters. They
have a special interest in reference to the subject to
which this volume is devoted. The *Æneid* was
the last of Virgil's achievements. It was written
at Naples long years after he had quitted his
northern home, but some of the episodes here
referred to appear to be drawn, not from the
experiences of his later life in Campania, but from
the recollections of his younger days on the plains
of the Mincius. If this inference be just they bear

further eloquent testimony to the fidelity of his
early observations, the fullness and accuracy of his
recollection of them and the pleasure which he
took in recalling and describing scenes and incidents
which had been so long and so lovingly cherished
in his memory.[1] On the other hand the poetic use
which, in the *Æneid*, he makes of the varying moods
of the sea was entirely due to his experience in
Southern Italy.

As another remarkable example of the influence
of an early life in the country upon a poetic
temperament we may look at the case of Horace
(B.C. 65-8). His birthplace lay not in a luxuriant
plain, like that of Virgil, but at Venusia, in a
somewhat rugged and sterile territory on the
eastern flank of the Apulian Apennines. Of that
first home he retained some vivid impressions
which are again and again alluded to in his poems.
These recollections are of interest in showing
that the poet was not without an eye for the
features of landscape which he could felicitously
describe, often only by a happily chosen word.[2]
In those early years, too, living among the sturdy
yeomen and peasantry of Apulia, he became

---

[1] In later chapters of this volume examples will be given of this
retentive remembrance of the scenes of his youth. Of all the poets
of ancient Rome none seems to have had in the same measure as Virgil

"That inward eye
Which is the bliss of solitude"

and which can vividly conjure up the scenes and impressions of past
years.

[2] *E.g.* Celsae nidus Acherontiae ; arvum humilis Forenti ; Aufidus
tauriformis, Ustica cubans, etc.

intimately acquainted with the simple upright
lives of the old Sabellian race, for which he afterwards expressed such admiration.

Two reminiscences of the region of his boyhood, which had imprinted themselves deeply on
his mind, are referred to in various parts of
Horace's poetry — the scarcity of water in the
dry season, and the fierce impetuosity of the
river Aufidus in time of flood. He remembered
his native district as "pauper aquae,"[1] for in
summer many of the springs and brooks cease to
flow at the surface, and the drainage in large
measure finds its way towards the sea in underground passages among the limestone rocks. But
still more did he recall the one large river of
the district, the Aufidus, which while in the
hot season it may dwindle to a mere shrunken
streamlet, in seasons of heavy rain bears headlong
to the Adriatic the accumulated waters of the
greater part of Apulia. He loved to remember
that he was born near the far-resounding Aufidus.
The floods of this river remained in his memory
as a kind of type of Nature in her most energetic
mood. Every time that he takes occasion to
bring its name into his poems, he couples with
it a different epithet, indicative of its impetuosity
and destructiveness, as it rushed along with a roar
that could be heard from far. Not improbably
it was to some catastrophe which he had himself

---

[1] *Carm.* III. xxx. II. Elsewhere he speaks of "siticulosa Apulia"
(Epod. III. 16).

witnessed or had heard of, that he refers when
he speaks of men who, greedily seeking for more
than their fair share of this world's goods, are apt to
be swept away, together with the bank on which
they stand, by the fury of the "Aufidus acer."
And when he wished to picture the irresistible
onset of the Roman army against the barbarians,
he likens it to the "bull-like Aufidus as he waxes
wroth, and rushes down with dire havoc upon
the fertile plains below."[1]

Among the incidents which he thought
worthy of note in his record of the famous journey
to Brundisium, Horace includes a reference to
the part of the road where the familiar hills of
Apulia began to come into view.[2] Conspicuous
among these heights would be the lofty old
volcanic cone of the Mons Vultur, on the wooded
slopes of which he had in his childhood fallen
asleep, and, as he relates, had been covered with
young leaves by the doves of legend.[3] But the most
touching proof of his affection for the landscapes
of his boyhood is to be found in the noble envoy
with which he accompanied the publication of
the first three Books of his *Odes*. Looking
triumphantly forward to an immortality for his
verse, he was confident that his name, associated
with his Apulian home and the rushing Aufidus,
would survive the lapse of ages and would

---

[1] *Sat.* I. i. 58 ; *Carm.* IV. xiv. 25.
[2] *Sat.* I. v. 77.
[3] *Carm.* III. iv. 9.

remain ever fresh in the praise of the time to
come.[1]

In one important respect Horace was like
Virgil. He had an intelligent father who watched
over him with devoted care. A freedman in a
humble rank of life, he had been industrious
and had saved money enough to enable him
to purchase a small farm, and to give his son
the best education then procurable, first in
Rome and afterwards at Athens. The poet
owed much to this affectionate parent, and in
his poems he makes ample acknowledgment of
his debt.

Horace was living at Athens at the time of
the assassination of Julius Cæsar. When Brutus
came to that city later in the same year he induced
the impressionable young Apulian student, then
hardly twenty years old, to join the army and
to accept the important post of military tribune.
Horace, so far as we know, had gone through no
military training, but he was soon to have some
rough experience of actual warfare. He was
probably engaged in the plundering expeditions
carried on by Brutus in Thrace and Macedonia.
He was certainly present, on the losing side, in
the great disaster of Philippi, from which he
escaped with his life. On making his way back
to Italy he found himself "humbled, with his
wings clipped, dispossessed of his paternal home
and property, and driven by poverty to write

[1] *Carm.* III. xxx.

poetry."[1] He probably went through a period of some privation before he succeeded in obtaining a clerkship in the quaestor's office, and he may thus be cited as an illustration of Shelley's lines:—

> " Most wretched men
> Are cradled into poetry by wrong ;
> They learn in suffering what they teach in song."

It is at least worthy of note that not only Horace, but, as we have seen, Virgil also, and likewise Propertius and Tibullus, suffered serious loss during the political convulsions of their time.

Eventually, probably in the year 39, through his friend Virgil, Horace was introduced to Maecenas, who, after a few months, took him into special favour. In course of time the great minister bestowed on the poet a little farm (*parva rura*) in a secluded valley (*in reducta valle*) far up among the Sabine Hills (*in arduos Sabinos*),[2] and by this gift not only enabled him to live in comfort, but placed him amidst surroundings which were pre-eminently fitted to call forth his lyric powers. Thenceforth he spent his time between the capital and his country retreat. Each of these scenes had its attractions for him.

On the one hand, he became a favourite at Court and one of the cherished friends of Maecenas. The most cultivated society of Rome was thus at all times open to him. Eminently social as

---

[1] *Epist.* II. ii. 50 ; *Carm.* II. vi. 7, vii. 1, 9.
[2] *Carm.* III. iv. 21.

he was, he must have been excellent company, and a welcome guest wherever he came. A stranger introduced to him as he strolled along the Via Sacra might have taken him for a typical man - about - town (*quem tenues decuere togae nitidique capilli*),[1] well acquainted with the latest gossip of good society, and not unfamiliar with the newest tricks of the cheats and jugglers and fortune-tellers of the circus and forum. He was well known on the streets of Rome, where he was evidently not at all displeased to be pointed out by the passers-by as the poet of the Roman lyre.[2] There cannot be any doubt that he loved Rome and all that its varied life meant for him.

On the other hand, his country home gave him pleasures that could not come to him in the capital. For some years he seems to have frequently oscillated between town and country, and to have been now and then as glad to escape from the seclusion of his Sabine valley, as at other times he was to get away from the turmoil of the city.[3] In the end, however, the gay life of Rome lost much of its interest and attraction for him. As he says of himself, he had played, and knew when to break off the play. He found that in the hurry and bustle of town it was not possible for him to

---

[1] *Epist.* I. xiv. 32. Elsewhere, writing to Tibullus, he describes himself as " pinguem et nitidum," and a " porcum de grege Epicuri " (*Epist.* I. iv. 15).

[2] *Sat.* I. vi. 111-114 ; *Carm.* IV. iii. 22.

[3] See *Sat.* II. vii. 28 ; *Epist.* I. viii. 12.

write poetry.[1] Amidst the whirl of society he longed (*mens animusque*) for the quiet of his retreat among the hills, and once there he could not leave its restful seclusion without a pang of regret, when what he called "hateful business" compelled his attendance in Rome.[2] Immersed in the endless distractions of the capital, how often must he have had that longing in his mind, and on his lips, to which he gives such eloquent expression in the sixth *Satire* of his second book—"O Rus quando te aspiciam!" How many a time must he have wished to be back among the hills, in what he calls his citadel;[3] to be with his friends there, enjoying those evenings of delightful converse, worthy of the gods themselves.

The manifold attractions of the country and rural life are nowhere more pleasantly described than in Horace's second *Epode*. That the poet should have appended to that ode four lines in which the beautiful picture he has drawn is represented to be the language of a greedy money-lender, has perplexed the critics and commentators. It is certainly difficult to see what was his intention in so doing. The poem is perfect without the additional lines, and could not have been written save by one who loved the country and its simple

[1] A century later the same complaint was made by Martial (*Epig.* X. lviii. lxx ; XII. lvii.).

[2] *Epist.* I. xiv. 17.

[3] *Sat.* II. vi. 16,

"ubi me in montes et in arcem ex urbe removi."

The very mention of this retreat awakens his enthusiasm, and he asks what subject could be more fitting for his muse.

pleasures. It exactly expresses what, as shown by
the rest of his poetry, were evidently Horace's own
sentiments.

If, following the Stoic maxim, it is our duty to
live according to Nature, where, Horace demanded
of his friend Fuscus Aristius, could any place be
found preferable to the blissful country? Where
were milder winters to be met with,[1] or a more
grateful air in the hot summer? Did the grass
in the country smell less sweetly than a mosaic
pavement of Lybian marble in the city, or was the
water brought in leaden pipes purer than that which
tripped along in the murmuring brook?[2] He had
himself experienced both conditions, and he finally
gave his deliberate judgment in favour of rural life.
He declared himself to be "ruris amator," in love
with "the charming country, its rivers, its moss-
grown rocks, and its woods."[3] These delights were
all combined for him at his home among the Sabine
Hills, which to him was the choicest little nook on
the earth.[4] There he "lived and reigned" in the
midst of sunny fields (*aprica rura*) and umbrageous
woodlands that were all his own. Sitting by the
Bandusian spring or musing by the side of the
prattling brook Digentia [5] or sitting on some rocky
headland, and surveying all the wooded valley

---

[1] Yet, as we shall see, there were times when he stigmatised his
Sabine valley as "wrinkled with cold."

[2] *Epist.* I. x. 12-20.

[3] *Id.* I. x. 2, 6.

[4] "Ille terrarum mihi praeter omnes
angulus ridet"—*Carm.* II. vi. 13.

[5] "Me quoties reficit gelidus Digentia rivus"—*Epist.* I. xviii. 104.

far beyond the village of Mandela down to where
the distant little town of Varia stood perched
among the hills, he felt restored to himself and
the Muses.[1]   He has left a pleasant and throughly
appreciative picture of these surroundings in an
epistle to his friend Quinctius:—

" A chain of hills that stretches far and wide,
  Unbroken save where runs a shady vale
  Which catches on the right the morning sun,
  And on the left his last warm evening glow.
  The temperate air would gain your ready praise.
  What if you saw my brakes of generous thorns
  Laden with ruddy cornels and with plums;
  My woods of oak and ilex that delight
  My herds with fodder and their lord with shade?
  You would declare that to these Sabine hills
  The verdure of Tarentum has been brought.
  A sparkling fount that well might give a name
  To some broad-breasted stream—Hebrus itself
  That winds through Thrace is not more cool or pure—
  Pours forth its limpid waters that bring health
  To weary head and jaded appetite.
  This hiding-place, so dear unto myself,
  And, pray believe, so full itself of charm,
  Will keep me here for you in safe retreat
  Through all September's insalubrious hours." [2]

---

[1] *Epist.* I. xiv. 1.

[2] *Id.* I. xvi. 5-16. The hills around Horace's valley of Digentia
(Licenza) are composed mainly of limestone.   To the eastward they rise
up to heights of 600 to 700 metres (1,970 to 2,300 English feet), gradually
mounting higher as they go northward, till they reach a height of 967
metres (3,172 feet) just south of Orvinio.   Between the valley of the
Digentia and the plain of the Campagna the limestone country is of
greater altitude since it rises to heights of more than 1,000 metres
(3,280 feet) along the ridge that encloses the valley, and it continues
to increase in elevation further west, till it culminates in Monte
Gennaro (believed to be Horace's Lucretilis) which is 1,271 metres

The spring referred to in this poem appears to
have had a great charm for the poet.   It was
evidently in his eye one of the chief attractions of
the place.   Its perennial supply of cool, clear water
gave life and music to his little valley, afforded
grateful moisture to trees and herbage in the
hottest and driest weather, and thus preserved the
pleasant shade under which Horace and the friends
who paid him visits could enjoy refreshing rest.
His affection for it led him to dedicate to its praise
a special ode which may be almost literally translated thus :—

> " Bandusian spring that clearer art than glass—
> Worthy of richest wine and choicest flowers,
>   To-morrow thou'lt receive,
>   As grateful offering,
>
> " A kid whose forehead with its sprouting horns
> Portended love and battle : but in vain !
>   For he, the firstling bold
>   Of all my wanton flock,
>
> " Shall with his red blood dye thy limpid stream.
> The blazing dog-star cannot touch thy shade,
>   Where oxen from the plough
>   And wandering herds find rest.
>
> " Thou shalt be numbered with the famous founts,
> When I shall sing the ilex that o'erhangs
>   The caverned rocks from whence
>   Thy babbling waters leap. "[1]

(4,170 feet) above the sea, and forms the most conspicuous elevation
among the Sabine mountains as seen from Rome.   The distance
in a straight line from Horace's valley to that summit is about 8
kilometres or 5 English miles, but across a rugged tract of ground.

[1] *Carm.* III. xiii.

F

It was in such scenes that Horace found his highest inspiration. He compares himself to the Matinian bee, flitting over banks of wild thyme, by wood and stream.[1] At times he would lie stretched in reverie upon the sward near the mouldering shrine of some half-forgotten native divinity,[2] for human associations ever mingled with his delight in Nature. Thus to the varied and genial influences of this little valley among the Apennines, literature is largely indebted for the beauty of the *Odes* and the *Epistles* which have been a perennial joy to every successive generation, and have placed Horace high in the ranks of lyric poets.

[1] *Carm.* iv. ii. 27.
[2] *Epist.* I. x. 49.

CHAPTER IV

RURAL SCENES AND THE ELEGIAC POETS

THE three chief elegiac poets of Rome, Tibullus, Propertius, and Ovid chose " Love" as the main source of their inspiration—a theme which may become somewhat monotonous to the reader unless relieved by the frequent introduction of topics and allusions other than the hopes and fears of the lover. Each of the three has lightened his subject in a different manner, and has contributed his share towards the completion of the general impression which we gain of Italian rural scenes and country-life as these appeared to the imaginative writers of Rome during the years of transition from the Republic to the Empire.

Tibullus (B.C. 65 (to 60) down to 19), the contemporary and friend of Horace, was a man of a wholly different mould from the Sabine bard. Of equestrian rank, he inherited an estate in the region of Pedum, probably in the picturesque district between Tibur and Praeneste. During the political troubles amidst which his youth was passed he was deprived of some of his property, but

before the close of his short life he appears to have
been living in comfort on his ancestral land.
According to Horace, the gods had endowed
Tibullus with personal beauty, with riches, with a
mind worthy of his handsome body, and, above all,
with the true art of enjoying these blessings. He
is pictured by his brother poet sauntering in silent
meditation through his health-giving woods, conning,
perhaps, some elegy that would surpass the poems
of Cassius of Parma, and, at all events, filled only
with thoughts worthy of a wise and good man.
What more, Horace asks, can a nurse wish for her
dear foster-son who knows how to think wisely and
how to express his feelings, and to whom influence,
fame, and health have been abundantly granted,
together with a well-appointed home and a purse
that is never empty ?[1]

With these accumulated advantages, Tibullus
has left behind him little in the way of literary
remains, but that little is of singular excellence.
In his early years he served with Messalla through
his Aquitanian campaign (B.C. 28-27), and formed
with that successful commander a devoted friendship which thenceforth became a leading interest
in his life.   He was afterwards induced to set out
with Messalla for the East, but an illness which
he caught on the outward journey detained him
at Corcyra, and he had to return home invalided.
His bent, however, turned not in the least towards

---

[1] *Epist.* I. iv.   There seems to be little doubt that the Albius of this
Epistle was Tibullus.

a military career.   He was passionately devoted to
rural life.   " I sing of the country and the rural
gods " was his own description of himself.   His
gentle nature, tinged with melancholy, found its
most congenial surroundings among the meadows
and woods, and by the dells and streams, around
his home.   He took a keen interest in the work
of the farm and the vineyard.   He felt no shame
to take part in the manual labour of his dependants ; he would gladly handle the hoe, drive the
slow oxen, carry home a lamb in his bosom, or
a kid deserted by its mother.[1]   Among the day-
dreams that filled his thoughts as he mused alone
in his solitary country walks, there was one that
probably often rose before him—how he would
devote himself to the cultivation of his lands,
grow his own grapes and make his own wine ;
and how through all these pursuits there hovered
the vision of his beloved Delia, settled under his
roof as mistress of his heart and home, ruling
everything around her, while he, wrapt in his
devotion to her, would rejoice to be as nothing
in the household.   When his illustrious friend
Messalla should come to visit him, Delia would
give him welcome, and gather for him sweet apples
from their choicest trees.[2]   That pleasing picture
never came to be realised in his experience.
Delia forsook him for a richer lover.   She was
succeeded by one or two damsels, but with no
better luck to the poet, who, after pouring forth

---

[1] *Eleg.* I. i.   [2] *Id.* I. v.

his soul in passionate love-longings and tender
regrets, expressed in the most exquisitely modu-
lated verse, died probably before reaching forty
years of age.

The descriptions and images in the poetry of
Tibullus are almost wholly drawn from the rural
scenes amidst which he lived.   He delights in
the simple ways of the country - folk, and has
left some pleasant sketches of them.   He joins
with zest in the festivals of the husbandmen.
He is familiar with the humble homes of his
tenantry and dependants, where he has watched
the child catching its father by the ears to snatch
a kiss, while the old grandfather sits tending his
little grandson and prattling to him in childish
words, and the wife gets ready the warm water
with which her spouse may refresh himself when
he comes back weary from his work.[1]   Such
examples of domestic peace and happiness remind
him of the tradition that tranquil homes of this
type were to be found everywhere, when King
Saturnus ruled the land, ere it was opened up
by long lines of road.[2]   This sentiment of fond
regret for the past was congenial to the poet's
tender melancholy.   It sought in Nature those
features which awakened responsive echoes in his
heart.   When he thought of the swift course of
time it was the rapid succession of the seasons
that more particularly impressed him with a sense
of the transitory character of life :—

[1] *Eleg.* II. v. 92.   [2] *Id.* I. iii. 35.

"How swiftly does the earth put off her radiant hues!
How quickly the pale poplar sheds its lovely tresses!"[1]

Now and then he seeks a simile from some part of Nature wilder than his placid surroundings in the Pedan country, as where, in one of his fits of love-fever, he swears that, rather than suffer the pangs which he is enduring,

"I'd be a stone on some bleak mountain-side,
   Or front the tempest, like a lone sea-stack
   Which the wide ocean batters with its waves." [2]

Tibullus full of the simple piety of the olden time, was by nature as orthodox and devout a pagan as the most exacting censor of his day could desire. His poems convey the impression that his religion was less a cult which it was his duty to support and inculcate, as Virgil did, than a personal conviction influencing his life and practice. He strictly performed all the rites and ceremonies which had been handed down from antiquity, and the due observance of which constituted religion as understood by the Romans. He worshipped the old gods of Latium and would have none of the foreign divinities that were becoming so much the fashion in the city. His worship was evidently sincere and unaffected. At the due season he sprinkled milk on the altar of Pales, the shepherd's god; from his corn-crop he would twine some ears into a crown to hang

---

[1] *Eleg.* I. iv. 29.   [2] *Id.* II. iv. 8.

at the door of the temple of bounteous Ceres,
and he had in his garden a ruddy image of Priapus
to frighten away the birds with his fierce-looking
sickle.[1]   He kept the festival of his ancestral
Penates, and made the monthly offering of frankincense to his own old Lar, nor was he ashamed
to confess that the image had been carved out
of an ancient stump, for thus they lived in the
house of his old grandfather.[2]   He performed the
yearly lustration of his crops and fields according
to the rite which had come down from a remote
age.   To his guardian Lares, whom in his richer
days he was wont to honour with the sacrifice
of a calf, he could now still offer a lamb.[3]   Such
was his simple piety that he could venerate, he
says, any solitary tree trunk in the fields, or an
old stone by the highway if it were consecrated
by a chaplet of flowers.[4]

Possessing a fastidious taste and gifted with
a delicate ear for the music of language, Tibullus
raised Latin elegiac poetry to its highest perfection.   He showed that rural themes which had
inspired the hexameters of Virgil and the lyric
measures of Horace were not less appropriate to
elegiac verse.   He has brought the rich Latian
landscape with its thrifty, industrious, and pious
community most vividly before us, and his name
will for ever recall some of the tenderest and
most musical poetry of Rome.

[1] *Eleg.* I. i.   [2] *Id.* I. iii. 33, x. 17.
[3] *Id.* I. i. 19.   [4] *Id.* I. i. 11.

Contemporary with Virgil and Tibullus, but of a different poetical stamp from either, Sextus Aurelius Propertius (B.C. 50 (?)-20 (?)) was born in Umbria about half a century before the beginning of our era, probably at or near the ancient town of Assisi. He appears, however, to have lived little in the country, but to have spent most of his life in Rome. He belonged to a good family, which at one time had been in possession of considerable property, but owing, it is believed, to the confiscations connected with the provision of lands for the veterans of Octavianus, the family estate was so much reduced that Propertius, while still a mere boy, was taken by his mother to the capital, and there, with such impaired means as she could save from the wreck of their fortune, he was educated. When, after having assumed the toga virilis, the time came for him to choose a profession, he declined to study for the bar, preferring to follow his bent and cultivate his poetic faculty. His young friend Tullus, whose uncle had been Consul in B.C. 66, invited him to join in a journey to the East, but the poet by this time, when probably hardly more than twenty years of age, had become deeply attached to a lady, believed to have been some years older than himself, whom he has immortalised as the famous Cynthia. So instead of embarking on foreign travel, he remained in Rome, where for some years he poured out his soul in brilliant verse, despondent or exultant, according as the course of his amour ran troubled or smooth, but always markedly original and vigorous, and often singularly melodious.

Propertius has sketched his own portrait in drawing that of his beloved. He was obviously as indolent as he describes himself to have been.[1] Not only are there no indications of his ever indulging in or sympathising with the active pursuits of an ordinary citizen, but a number of passages expressive of repugnance to these pursuits might be cited from his poems. He was as far as possible averse from anything like patriotic activity. When the Eastern journey was proposed to him, he could only praise his friend's devotion to duty and to his country in arms; but as for himself, he confessed that he was not born for martial glory, the warfare for which the fates had designed him being that of love.[2] His writings, indeed, are full of denunciations of a military life. He wished to know why he should marry to supply sons to swell the ranks of triumphal processions, and he declared that not one of his blood should ever be a soldier. His conquest of Cynthia would be, to his thinking, a greater victory than any obtained by Rome over the Parthians. It would be to him spoils, captive kings, triumphal chariot and all. They who delighted in arms were welcome to bring back the lost standards of Crassus; the prize would properly go to those whose toil in the field of war had earned it. Enough for himself would it be to stand and

---

[1] *Eleg.* IV. vii. 72.   [2] *Id.* I. vi.

applaud the victors on the peaceful pavement of the Via Sacra.[1]

Still less did he care for sea-faring. He was sorry for any one who had to listen to the shrieks of the tempest, and hurt his tender hands with a hard rope. In his beautiful lament for the youthful Paetus drowned at sea, he records that had his advice been followed, that dear comrade would have been still alive; not indeed enriched by the profits of the voyage, but yet safe on dry land, and beside his household gods. For himself, no blast of the fierce north wind should ever fill his sail, for his lot was to be laid before the door of his mistress.[2]

In one of his day-dreams, wherein he pictures himself to be with Cynthia in the midst of the pure country, and in sight of the lonely hills, he thinks of there turning sportsman, thus exchanging for a while the service of Venus for that of Diana. But he will be cautious as to the kinds of game which he may pursue. He does not mean to attack such creatures as huge lions and wild boars, but will show his courage by catching the gentle hares, and shooting his arrows at wild fowl.[3]

This unwarlike Roman may have somewhat exaggerated the "mollitia" which he attributes to himself. There can be no doubt, however, that he was by natural preference a squire of

[1] *Eleg.* II. vii. 14 ; IV. iv. 21, v. 47.
[2] *Id.* IV. vii. 44, 71.
[3] *Id.* III. x.

dames, and never so happy as in female society.[1]
He confesses the susceptibility of his temperament,
and even boasts that his personal qualities enabled
him to reign like a king in a company of girls.[2]

But it was to Cynthia that he gave up his
heart and soul. The lustrous eyes that had first
captivated him became the twin stars that illumined
his life. For her he set aside any ambition he
may ever have had to make for himself an honourable and useful career. He was content to be
the "slave of love," and to sing of that serfdom
in tender and passionate elegies. But he was
not without ambition of another kind. Conscious
of his great poetic gifts, he was convinced that
his verse would live, and that the recital of the joys
and sorrows through which he alternately passed
in the fond worship to which he had devoted
himself, would awaken sympathetic interest in
future ages. And so, month by month, and year
after year, Cynthia continued to absorb his thoughts
and to afford the main theme for his muse. He
dwelt with delight on her personal beauty. He
was proud of her accomplishments—her music,
her poetry, the singular charm of her delightful
talk, and, not least, her appreciation of his own
verses. But his jealousy was roused by her flirta-
tions and inconstancy. Driven away in the deepest
grief and despair by her callous and imperious

---

[1] *Eleg.* III. xiii. 13, where he says that, with respect to the fair sex
as a whole, he was "tam mollis in omnes."

[2] *Id.* III. xxvi. 56.

disregard of his feelings, he could be waved back
again by a look or word of affection. After some
five years, however, of what he calls loyal service,
wearied out by her caprice and infidelities, he
cooled in his devotion, until at last he came to
renounce and curse her in language of unmanly
bitterness.[1]

The poet's health does not seem to have been
robust. His neurotic and introspective temperament was perhaps in large measure due to this
bodily weakness. One of the most obvious and
frequent symptoms of his melancholy, or even
morose, disposition may be seen in the morbid
way in which he constantly brooded over the
prospect of his early death. In elegies addressed
to Cynthia, which might be called a kind of
love-letters, he not infrequently introduces this
saddening topic. He even gives her directions
as to his burial, and recommendations as to what
he would like her to do at his funeral.[2] He
survived her, however, as he had already outlived
his affection and respect for her. In one of the
most powerful of his poems he represents her
ghost as appearing to him and addressing him in
language of mingled tenderness, reproach, and
command, such as she had probably been in the
habit of using towards him in her life time.

[1] *Eleg.* IV. xxiv., xxv.
[2] *Id.* III. v. ; IV. xvi. 23. In addressing Maecenas also, he alludes to
his approaching death and asks his patron, should he be driving near
the poet's tomb, to halt and express his pity for the untimely fate of
one driven out of life by an unkind mistress (II. i. 75).

In the prologue to the fourth Book of the
Elegies, addressed to the shades of Callimachus
and Philetas, where he reaffirms his confidence in
the immortality of his poetry, there occurs the
curious statement that Apollo had sanctioned a
provision which Propertius had made that the
tomb where his bones are to lie shall never become
a despicable place.[1]   The epitaph for himself which
he sent in one of his mournful ditties to Cynthia
has been preserved among his poems,[2] but his tomb
has disappeared, and the spot where the poet's
ashes lie, whether it be despicable now or not, is
unknown.

During the years when his poetic activity was
at its height, Propertius was too much engrossed
by his love for Cynthia to be able to spare much
room in his verse for any other theme.   In the
later years of his brief life, however, he took a
wider range of subjects, especially choosing some
of a national significance, which heighten our regret
that he did not live long enough to complete the
series of poems which he appears to have contemplated.   The charms of the open face of Nature
and of country life find somewhat scanty recognition in his extant poems.   He does not seem to
have drawn from that source, save perhaps at rare
intervals, any soothing consolation or sympathy.
Yet there are many phrases and lines in his elegies

---

[1] *Eleg.* IV. i. 37.   His tomb was to be " bustum exiguum."
[2] *Id.* III. v.   For a further reference to the tomb of Propertius see
postea p. 277.

which show that he had an eye for both the softer
and the grander aspects of the world around him.
If, as has been plausibly conjectured, his father
perished in the massacre of Perusia, and if he
himself in early boyhood witnessed some of the
tragic horrors of civil war, during which so large a
part of his patrimony appears to have been lost, we
can well believe that he may have carried with him
to Rome the saddest recollections of his first home,[1]
and that perhaps these memories may have been
in some measure responsible for his moody and
melancholy disposition.   Nevertheless he retained
his pride in his native Umbria.   He was happy in
the thought that this region would also in the
course of time be proud of him, and would even
glory in having been the birthplace of the Roman
Callimachus.[2]

There are indications that the poet occasionally
revisited the scenes of his childhood.   Not improbably it was on one of these occasions, when he had
forsaken Rome for a while on account of the treatment accorded to him by his mistress, that he
penned a fine description of a lonely retreat in
the country[3] :—

> " Here deepest solitude and silence reign ;
>   The breath of Zephyr fills the lonely grove.
> Let not the stones betray me while I plain,
>   And tell the anguish of my wounded love."

After a pathetic enumeration of the wrongs

[1] *Eleg.* I. xxi., xxii.   [2] *Id.* V. i. 63.   [3] *Id.* I. xviii.

which he has suffered at the hands of the capricious
beauty, he concludes :—

" For this devotion what has been my meed ?
    The bosky mountains with their chilly stone,
    The rough repose to which no pathways lead,
    And in this wilderness to be alone,

" Telling to chirping birds my mournful tale :
    Yet be thou whatsoe'er thou wilt, I claim
    To sing of Cynthia to the wood, the gale,
    And desert rocks that shall repeat thy name."

Another poem written in happier mood refers
also to the Umbrian country, near the Vale of
the Clitumnus, whither Cynthia had retired for
a little, and where her lover was soon to join
her. She was to be alone and in sight of the
lonely hills, surrounded with fields and flocks
and the boundary fences of the poor farmers.
There she would see bulls ploughing and the
vine shedding its leaves under the skilfully -
handled pruning - hook. There, too, she might
bring to a rude shrine an offering of frankincense, seldom to be seen in that remote spot.
He would be with her before many days had
passed, for neither solitary woods nor vagrant
brooks pouring down from mossy uplands had
charms to stay her name from being ever on
his lips.[1]

The most emphatic and detailed appeal to
Nature made by Propertius occurs in the elegy
wherein he beseeches Cynthia to discard artificial

[1] *Eleg.* III. x.

adornments and trust to the charm of her own
personal loveliness.

"Look how the Earth in beauteous tints excels !
   The ivy gains most grace when left alone,
The arbute hath most charm in lonely dells ;
   The vagrant streamlets, over moor and stone,
Know how to find their channels to the sea ;
   The shores with gleam of their own pebbles are fraught
And every bird that sings on bush or tree,
   Carols more sweetly that it ne'er was taught." [1]

Propertius repeats the praises bestowed by his
predecessors and contemporaries on the agricultural
population of the remoter districts, especially in the
olden time. He dwells with evident satisfaction
on their simple pleasures, their piety, and their
contentment. But he has to confess that these
virtues were not in his time so conspicuous and
general as they were believed to have once been.
The shrines, he says, are now silent in the forsaken
groves; piety has been vanquished and all men
now worship gold.[2] In another poem he alludes
cynically to some one who had arrived in Rome,
expecting to find there the old virtuous Tatii and
the stern Sabines, but the poet thinks it would be
as easy a task to dry up the waters of the sea, or

---

[1] *Eleg.* I. ii. 9-14. Compare Wordsworth's expression of the same
idea :—

    "How does the Meadow-flower its bloom unfold ?
    Because the lovely little flower is free
    Down to its root, and, in that freedom, bold."

and the musical couplet in the 104th of Shakespeare's *Sonnets* :—

    " The summer's flower is to the summer sweet
    Though to itself it only live and die."

[2] *Id.* IV. xiii. 47, 48.

with mortal hands to pluck down the stars of heaven, as to stem the rising tide of corruption.[1]

In one of his more thoughtful moods, when musing on the vanity of this world, Propertius resolved that when sober age should have put an end to his love-making, and his black hair should be sprinkled with white, he would then turn to the study of the ways of Nature. He enumerates some of the phenomena that he would choose to investigate, and some of the myths and legends, the credibility of which he would like to examine.[2] But the season to which he looked forward for the fulfilment of this resolution never came to him. He died when little more than thirty, and the small volume of his Elegies remains as his sole memorial.

Publius Ovidius Naso (B.C. 43 to A.D. 17), the last and most prolific of the greater elegiac poets of Rome, presents an interesting contrast to his forerunners in the same domain of Latin literature. While to Tibullus and Propertius love was the serious occupation of their lives, or at least the main source of their poetic inspiration, to Ovid it was rather a pursuit which he could watch as an outsider. His own personal love-ditties, clever as they are, want the ring of genuine feeling, and leave us in some doubt whether his Corinna had any corporeal existence, or was not rather some abstraction round which he allowed his exuberant fancy to play. His most brilliant work dealt

[1] *Eleg.* III. xxiv. 47.   [2] *Id.* IV. v.

with the art of love-making in the ignoble sense
in which he understood that term. But he had
a wide range of sympathies and interests in other
directions, and he has left a large body of verse,
whence much valuable information is obtainable
regarding the mythology, religious rites, legends,
customs, traditions, and society of Rome.

Ovid was born in the year which saw the
formation of the triumvirate of Antony, Lepidus,
and Octavian. His family was of equestrian
rank, and possessed property in the remote and
picturesque district of Sulmo, in the highest part
of the Apennine range. He records that he
began to write verses in his boyhood, and that
he tried in vain to relinquish the service of the
Muses, but that, as in the case of our own Pope,
whatever he was tempted to write shaped itself
into metrical cadence and became verse.[1] He
felt himself to be unsuited for the usual political
life of a young man in his station, and not being
under the necessity of exertion, nor spurred by
ambition, he devoted his time to the pleasures
of society and the writing of poetry. Though he
makes occasional allusion to his native region
among the distant Abruzzi, there is no satisfactory
evidence in his poems that he ever lived much
there. He had a good education in Rome, and
completed his studies at Athens. Rome had so
many attractions for him that it became his
home, where, as the chronicler of the gay life of

[1] *Trist.* IV. x. 25.

society in the capital, and as a facile, copious, and
brilliant poet, he occupied a notable place in the
pleasure-loving community.   How thoroughly he
enjoyed himself in these surroundings is abundantly
apparent in his earlier verse.   Others might lament
the decay of the simpler manners and more austere
life of the olden time, but he was happy to have
been born in a later age when the rusticity of their
old grandfathers no longer survived.[1]

It is in his relation to Nature, however, that
we have to consider Ovid here.   Above and
beyond his interest in the gallantries, frivolities,
and dissipations of the fashionable circles in which
he moved, he had a poet's eye for much of the
beauty and charm of the outer world.   Even his
amatory poetry, which includes his most brilliant
as well as his least pleasing work, contains phrases,
lines, and longer passages which indicate a love
of Nature.   In treating of the myths and legends
of Greece and Italy, and the sacred and secular
customs and traditions of Rome, he had a bound-
less field for the exercise of his peculiar gifts.
Many of these tales had been told over and
over again.   But Ovid recognised that as they
had little or no foundation in written history, it
was allowable to clothe them anew in such garb
as seemed to him most picturesque, acting on
his own maxim,

" Si poteris, vere, si minus, apte tamen." [2]

---

[1] *Ars Amat.* III. 121-128.   [2] *Id.* I. 228.

This dressing-up of old myths afforded him the opportunity to surround his personages with a background of natural scenery, and to paint little vignette landscapes that bring the quiet beauty of Nature into prominent relief. His favourite scene, if we may judge from the frequency with which he introduces it into his poems, seems to have been the popular combination of shady woodland and still or murmuring water.[1] The pictures which he draws, however, are usually of a characteristically generalised type. They seldom appeal to us as taken directly from Nature or from recollections that had deeply imprinted themselves on the poet's mind, and were recalled in their details, with something like the affection so delightfully indicated in the episodes and similes of Virgil. The various scenic features and the way in which they are grouped by Ovid suggest that they were not so much objects which he loved to think of, to allude to, and to describe, as convenient or necessary materials for the background or setting wherein he sought to place the story or legend which he desired to tell. Sometimes, indeed, it would seem that just as the grouping of the figures in one of his tales occasionally reminds us of some mythological picture or group of statuary, so these pictorial landscapes or backgrounds have a somewhat artificial or

---

[1] This preference is aptly summed up by him in two lines :—

> " Est nemus arboribus densum, secretus ab omni
>   Voce locus, si non obstreperetur aquis."—*Fast.* VI. 9, 10.

conventional character, as if suggested rather by
the recollection of pictures than of scenes actually
beheld and cherished in recollection. We do
not seem to breathe the very air of the places,
as Virgil makes us do by the light touch of a
few vivid words.

Yet Ovid was gifted with a rare power of
description. He could tell a tale with a brilliance
of fancy, an artistic faculty in the grouping of
incidents, and a skill in the choice of words such
as hardly any other poet of ancient or modern
times has equalled. This genius for narrative
was united to an unrivalled facility in verse-making.
The copious flow of his musical language rolls on
from one subject to another, not only without
apparent effort, but with the easy grace of a consummate master of his art. Its very perfection
is apt to become monotonous, while his evident
delight in the exercise of his gift of narration
sometimes makes him lose the sense of proportion and overload his pictures with a detail that
detracts from their breadth, and occasionally
becomes tedious and irrelevant.

Ovid's art is thus always conspicuous. Nowhere
is this characteristic more apparent than in the
arrangement and description of the surroundings
of the actors in one of his mythological legends.
There is generally an umbrageous wood throwing
a coolness over some spring or stream or lake.
The margin of the water is bordered with soft
turf which is kept green by the moisture. Some-

times the individual kinds of trees are noted, or the scented shrubs or flowers. A rich gallery of such landscapes is to be found in the poems. As examples of them reference may be made to the account of the sacred spring near Hymettus,[1] of the spot where Narcissus first saw his reflection in the water,[2] of the Lake Pergus where Proserpine gathered her violets and lilies,[3] of the fountain of Arethusa,[4] of the wood in which the Calydonian boar was hunted,[5] of the slaying of the dragon by Cadmus,[6] and the Cave of Sleep.[7] As an illustration, the first of these landscapes may be cited here.

> " Near to Hymettus with its flowery slopes
>   A sacred spring lies, bordered with soft turf,
>   In the low copsewood of a shady grove.
>   The arbute overspreads the verdant sward ;
>   The air around is fragrant with the scents
>   Of laurels, rosemary, and myrtles dark ;
>   Nor is the box-tree absent, with its leafage dense,
>   Nor fragile tamarisk, nor cytisus,
>   Beneath the shadow of the garden pine.
>   Stirred by the zephyrs with their balmy breath,
>   The boughs above wave gently to and fro,
>   The taller grasses quiver underneath."

The description of the Cave of Sleep is one of the most wonderful efforts of the imagination which has come down to us from antiquity. Its crowded incidents and the weird atmosphere in

[1] *Ars Amat.* III. 687-694.
[2] *Metam.* III. 407-412.
[3] *Id.* V. 385-395.
[4] *Id.* V. 585-595.
[5] *Id.* VIII. 329-342.
[6] *Id.* III. 35.
[7] *Id.* XI. 592-612.

which they are involved, show the poet at the very height of his genius for description.

When it is borne in mind that Ovid was born in one of the most picturesque tracts in the whole of Italy—the rugged highlands of the Abruzzi, not far from the highest peak of the Apennines, the huge Gran Sasso d'Italia, with its snowy covering that lasts throughout most of the year, it might have been expected that the landscapes of his native district would have evoked his enthusiasm, or would, at least, have found appreciative reference in his poetry. That he was really fond of Sulmo and the region of the Peligni may be inferred from the allusions which he not infrequently makes to them. He likes to remind the world that he is "Peligni ruris alumnus." But none of these allusions evince any strong emotion. In one of his elegies, which was actually written at his earliest home, and where the local influences should have been at their strongest, there is not the least glow of affection or fervour of admiration. He speaks coldly of Sulmo as a little place, but healthy and well-watered, never parched even in the dog-days; therefore covered with soft grass, fertile in corn, and still more so in vines, and, despite its thin soil, not without the olive. So little did he find to say about this native scenery that the references to some of the features here enumerated are given more than once in the ten lines devoted to the description. And at last, as if tired of the subject, he abruptly breaks

off in order to lament the absence of his lady-love,
on whose behalf he wishes the mountains to sink
down and the roads in the winding valleys to
be smooth.[1]

In another poem which concludes the series
of his *Amores* he again alludes to his native
district. He recalls the martial fame of the
Pelignian race, but is convinced that the little
town, covering only a few acres of ground, will
have new lustre added to it from his own poetry.
He represents some future stranger addressing
the place in these words: "Small though you be,
since you have borne so great a poet, I will call you
great." And he flatters himself that as Mantua
rejoiced in having produced Virgil, and Verona
could boast of Catullus, he himself would hereafter
be called the glory of the Pelignian race.[2] In
the misery of his exile, amongst the recollections
of his life which crowded his memory, the thought
of that Pelignian land mingled with the visions
of his other country homes and his happy domestic
life therein. He recalled his gardens on the pine-
clad hills where the Clodian and Flaminian roads
diverge, where he used to guide the water-channels
to his crops, and planted those apples which were
now gathered by some stranger whom he knew
not.[3]

Where Ovid delineates scenes that have deeply

---

[1] *Amor*. II. xvi.
[2] *Id*. III. xv. 8.
[3] *Pont*. I. viii. 41-48.

affected him, his feeling for Nature and his descriptive power are most effectively combined. Thus he has left some singularly graphic pictures of storms at sea amidst which he was himself a rueful witness of their fury. His sketches of the climate and conditions of life on the shores of the Black Sea, where he spent some ten years of piteous exile and where he finally died, are vivid representations of how that region appeared to him in his misery. They show, however, that he was led, perhaps unconsciously, to write for effect and to indulge in strong exaggeration. While every allowance is to be made for a brilliant member of a gay society, stricken with such grief as was involved in banishment to so remote a spot, it is difficult to repress a smile when we find that the poet writes of Tomi as if it lay in the Arctic regions, and speaks of hard Fate ordering him to die under the icy pole.[1] It is true that the temperature in the coldest part of winter falls there below the freezing-point, but so it does on the uplands of the poet's Abruzzi.[2] On the other hand, the summers at Tomi are as warm as in the centre of France. Ovid complains of being surrounded with naked barren plains, where neither trees nor leaves nor fruit are to be seen—places not to be approached by

[1] *Pont.* IV. xv. 36.

[2] Ovid must have been well aware of the extreme cold of his native region. He himself refers to "Sulmo gelidus" (*Fast.* IV. 81), and Horace had written of the Pelignian cold as of something proverbially severe (*Carm.* III. xix. 8).

a man who would be happy.[1] His descriptions, inspired and coloured by the misery of his exile, are pitiable enough, yet although, as far as human society went, Tomi must have been a wild and savage place on the very confines of the Roman Empire, there is no reason to believe that its climate was materially different in the first century from what it is now.

Latin literature affords no sadder contrast than is presented by the earlier and the later writings of Ovid. In the poems of his younger years written in Rome, we feel ourselves to be in the company of a lively, gay, and accomplished man of the world, who seems to have no serious convictions or employment, but to be leading a kind of butterfly existence, and playing around the outside of the problems of life. On the other hand, throughout the mass of verse which was poured out by him in banishment, the early gaiety is replaced by a heart-broken grief and a passionate impatience of exile—feelings in which he might well indulge, but which he has recorded with wearisome iteration. His old facility in versification in the end began to fail, like the spirit that once infused it, until it became mainly a means of relief from his misery, since

> " For the unquiet heart and brain
> A use in measured language lies,
> The sad mechanic exercise,
> Like dull narcotics soothing pain."

---

[1] *Trist.* III. x. 71.

There was probably nothing in the national religion which could minister to the sorrow of such a man as Ovid. No man knew the myths and legends of Greek and Roman mythology better than he, and none could trick them out with the dainty grace of so exuberant and poetical a fancy. Up to the end of his life he could quote them. But even among his earlier poems, and more decidedly in those of his exile, he now and then lets slip an expression which indicates that although, for his poetic purpose, he could treat them as veritable history, he doubted or more than doubted their historical truth. When, for example, he recounts the fable of Deucalion and Pyrrha repeopling the world with stones, he asks who would believe the tale, did not antiquity attest it.[1] In one of his lugubrious elegies from Tomi, he enumerates a list of grim popular myths, and says that he would rather believe every one of them than think that an old friend could have forgotten him.[2] In another of these melancholy poems he affirms that even the Styx itself, if there be any such place, might well be taken in exchange for the Danube in his neighbourhood, or even a

---

[1] *Metam.* I. 400. Ovid professed some respect for the authority of antiquity, but when he appeals to it in support of one of the most extravagant legends of the old mythology, his appeal suggests that he had no belief in the fable himself:

"Pro magna teste vetustas
Creditur ; acceptum parce movere fidem."—Fast. IV. 203.

[2] *Trist.* IV. vii. 11-19.

lower deep than the Styx, if the world contains any.[1]

If Ovid did not openly express his disbelief in the existence and supervision of the divinities worshipped in the religion of his country, he treated them with such disrespect as was probably more destructive to the popular faith in them than expressions of absolute disbelief would have been. He has no reverence for them, or indeed for anything. When the dim, half-mysterious outlines of some of the old myths are exchanged by him for hard realistic detail, their romantic beauty vanishes. In writing his *Fasti*, wherein he dealt with the events and customs connected with the Roman calendar of the year, he claimed to have had personal interviews with gods and goddesses, on the ground that he was a poet, or had taken sacred rites for his theme. And he certainly used this liberty to the fullest extent. He catechised the various divinities on the several subjects with which they were supposed to be especially familiar, and reported their replies with as little formality as if he had been repeating his talk with personal friends of his own. His conversation with Venus, for example, is hardly less familiar than it would have been had his interlocutor been his own Corinna.[2] When he is visited by a company of goddesses and finds Juno among them, he professes to have trembled on recognising her. But he records that his

---

[1] *Pont.* IV. xiv. 11, 12.   [2] *Fast.* IV. 1-16.

agitation was soon dispelled by the good-natured
Queen of Heaven, who gave him the information
of which he was in quest.[1]   The picture which
he gives of old Silenus stung by a swarm of
hornets and laughed at by the Satyrs with Bacchus
at their head, who recommends him to daub his
wounds with mud, might have been taken from
some frolic of the poet's rakish young friends at
Rome.[2]

There is no evidence in Ovid's poetry that he
had fortified his mind with any of the consolations
which were offered by the philosophy of the day.[3]
If neither religion nor philosophy could minister
balm to the crushed and despondent spirit of
the poet, no more could he draw support from
Nature.   He had never loved her with whole-
hearted devotion, even when she appeared before
him in her fairest guise.   And now in this remote
spot on the shores of the Euxine, she seemed to
him to have lost every charm.   He could find no
beauty in the clear skies by day and night, the
keen frosty air, the wide mantle of pure snow,
and the broad expanse of frozen sea that mark
mid - winter in that region.   Nor did summer
bring him any solace, though it duly came with
its leaves and flowers, its sweet scents and its
birds.   His eyes refused to see anything around
him but one universal pall of desolation.   In the

---

[1] *Fast.* VI. 17 *seq.*   [2] *Id.* III. 745-760.
[3] In the 15th Book of the *Metamorphoses* he shows himself to be
acquainted with the natural philosophy of that time, a sketch of
which he puts into the mouth of Pythagoras.

heyday of his prosperity at Rome, and when writing the poem which was the ostensible cause of his disastrous downfall, he could say in the gladness of his heart: "Let others praise the olden time; I bless myself that I was born thus late; this age suits my tastes."[1] While his sun shone he was enabled to indulge these tastes to the full, and their gratification was the main pursuit of his life. But when they could no longer be enjoyed he had no more solid ground on which to support his mind, or worthily to exercise his poetic faculty. He could then only repine at his fate, and entreat his friends in Rome to intercede with the Emperor for his restoration, or at least for some amelioration of his misery.

[1] *Ars Amat.* III. 121. He repeated the opinion in later years, "Laudamus veteres, sed nostris utimur annis."—*Fast.* I. 225.

CHAPTER V

FLOWERS IN ROMAN LIFE

THE love of flowers may be regarded as one of the earliest and simplest stages in the development of the love of Nature. Their beauty of form and colour, the charm of their fragrance and the profusion with which they deck the fields and woods, year after year, at their appointed seasons, appeal to childhood, and this appeal is strengthened by degrees, in races as well as in individuals, until it awakens a devoted affection. From the earliest ages of human history down to our own day, flowers have been the accepted tokens of sympathy, alike in joy and sorrow. Among the Greeks and Romans, however, they played, perhaps, a more prominent part in the life of the people than they do among most modern nations. They were connected with many of the religious observances of these ancient communities, they constituted some of the highest rewards for military service and for eminence at the public games, they figured as important accessories in innumerable social habits and customs, they found an honoured place in art, and they often gave a touch of tenderness to literature.

From an early time in the history of Rome,
flowers and sprays of trees, twined into garlands,
appeared in various religious rites.   They were
worn by priests officiating at sacrifices, and by
the victims that were to be offered up.   Among
an agricultural people like the Romans, it was
natural that the most ancient form of crown
should be one of ears of corn (*Corona spicea*)
which was dedicated to Ceres, and was worn by
the Arval priesthood as their most honourable
distinction.[1]   The images and altars of the gods
alike in public places and in private houses were,
on festive occasions, decorated with garlands.
The domestic hearth with its Lares was crowned
with flowers on the kalends, ides, and nones, and
on other festal days.[2]   At first, and for a long time,
these offerings were of the simplest kind.   A little
spelt and sparkling salt was enough to propitiate
the domestic deities; the simple altar smoked
with familiar Sabine herbs, while laurel leaves
crackled in the flames.[3]   If there was any one
who could add violets to the chaplets made out
of the flowers of the meadow, he was accounted a

---

[1] Pliny, *Hist. Nat.* XVIII. ii. 2.

[2] Cato, *De Re Rust.* CXLIII.   It was the duty of the Villica to attend
to this service.   In the plays of Plautus the crowning of the domestic
Lares with flowers at the hearth is again and again referred to.   The
domestic Lar is even brought on the stage and speaks a prologue in
which he refers with satisfaction to the offerings and wreaths with
which he is honoured.   In the *Aulularia* (II. viii. 16), the master of
the house orders a little frankincense and floral crowns to be placed
in foco nostro Lari.

[3] It was a good omen when the laurel crackled well (Tibullus
II. v. 81).

H

rich man.[1] Horace could assure his humble Phidyle
that she need not seek for costly gifts as her offering; it would be enough if she crowned her little
gods with rosemary and a branch of fragile myrtle.[2]
Myrrh, frankincense, and sweet-smelling spices had
not in early days found their way from the East,
and even when these materials became available in
Rome, they were long in being common in the
country districts. Hence Propertius, as we have
seen, could tell his Cynthia that in Umbria her
offering of frankincense on a rustic altar would be
a rare sight to the simple country-folk. A hundred
years later, when foreign spices had become more
familiar, the little Lares could be placated with a
tiny bit of frankincense and a modest wreath.[3]

[1] Ovid, *Fast.* I. 345.
[2] *Carm.* III. xxiii. 13.
[3] Juvenal, IX. 137. From an early period in the history of Rome,
the crowns offered to the greater or national gods, especially to
Capitoline Jove, were sometimes of gold. Livy records the
increasing costliness of these offerings. In old days, he says,
the crown was of little weight, " for riches were scanty, and the worship
of the gods was conducted with greater piety than splendour" (II. xxii. ;
III. lvii. ; IV. xx. ; VII. xxxviii.). With characteristic irreverence
Ovid makes Janus affirm that though the gods still approved of the
antique simplicity, they preferred golden temples, as more consonant
with their divine majesty. In old days the shrines of the Capitol had
been garnished with branches, but now they were adorned with gems
(*Fast.* I. 203, 223). On high holidays the statues and shrines of the
gods, even in the open country and on the high roads, were included
in the floral decorations. Propertius represents the gardener's god
Vertumnus as saying through one of his statues (which had been a log
of maple-wood before the days of Numa) that there was not a flower
blooming on the meadows but would droop becomingly from its fore-
head (*Eleg.* V. ii. 45). We learn from Ovid that the image of the god
Terminus which, whether a stone or a stump sunk into the ground,
marked the boundary between two properties, was crowned by the two
proprietors, each bringing his garland and his cake (*Fast.* II. 641).

The practice of conferring crowns as rewards for military successes, and for athletic, literary or other eminence was adopted from Greece by the Romans. As with the other garlands, these crowns were at first of the simplest and most modest kind. The highest honour a man could receive from his fellow countrymen was a chaplet of green leaves. The most valued of all the Roman military crowns and the most difficult to gain, the *Corona obsidionalis*, was made of grass, weeds, or wild flowers gathered from the ground on which an army had been beleaguered. Such was the simple but coveted decoration presented by a grateful soldiery to the general who relieved them. The *Corona triumphalis* worn by a victorious general at his triumph was composed of laurel and bay leaves. The commander who gained the lesser distinction of an ovatio had the *Corona ovalis* which was of myrtle. The *Corona civica*, made of oak-leaves, was another prized military honour. In course of time, however, these crowns, like those offered to the gods, came to be made of gold, and thus lost the charm of their original simplicity. An ivy crown was the conventional decoration for poets.[1]

In the family life of the Romans flowers took a conspicuous place. Over and above the requirements of religious customs, they appeared on every occasion of joy or sorrow, and at many other times in the daily intercourse of families and friends. One notable employment of them was in the form

[1] Horace, *Carm.* I. i. 29.

of chaplets that were worn at the evening meal. In early times these adornments were of the simplest kind—sprays of some evergreen or other verdant plant, such as ivy, myrtle, olive, privet, or parsley, or wreaths of garden flowers. The variety and richness of the materials increased with the growth of wealth and luxury. The practice of using fragrant and diversely-coloured flowers is said to have been introduced at Sicyon, one of the great centres of Greek art, by the celebrated painter, Pausias and the flower-girl Glycera, whose artistic floral combinations Pausias was fond of painting, and who, to stimulate him, continually varied the material of her wreaths, thus, as Pliny remarks, giving rise to a contest between Art and Nature.[1] Among the flowers most in request in Rome were violets, lilies, and, still more, roses.[2] It was one of Cato's directions respecting gardens that materials for garlands (*coronamenta*) should be grown in them,[3] so that a household could supply itself with its own chaplets. But as the demand eventually far exceeded this source of supply, flower gardens sprang up around Rome and in other favourable districts, such as Praeneste and Paestum.[4] Blooms were likewise imported in large quantities from

---

[1] *Hist. Nat.* XXI. iii.

[2] Pliny states that very few kinds *Coronamenta* were grown in Roman gardens in his day, and that they were almost only violets and roses. Lilies were reckoned next in beauty after the rose. Of this last flower Pliny enumerates twelve different kinds (*Op. cit.* XXI. x.).

[3] Pliny, *Op. cit.* XXI. i.

[4] Martial enumerates some of the various places from which flowers were brought to Rome (*Epig.* IX. lx.).

the valley of the Nile. / In the early days of
the Empire floral decorations became increasingly
elaborate and costly, vast sums of money being
sometimes lavished by the fashionable and frivolous
society of Rome, even for the garnishing of a single
feast.   Such large quantities of flowers, especially
violets and roses, were thus brought into the city
for sale, that the streets were said to be sometimes
red from the abundance of garlands displayed.[1]   It
would seem that even the resources of the rose-
gardens in Italy and Egypt were not always able
to supply the demand for flowers in the height of
winter, and that recourse was had to the use of
green-houses.[2]

The custom of wearing chaplets of flowers at the
evening meal became so common that dinner-time
could be referred to as " the hour when the rose
reigns." [3]   So long as the practice remained simple
and inexpensive it was a pretty usage, to which
not even the sturdiest moralist had reasonable
ground of objection.   Horace, for instance, who,
when he liked, could speak bitterly enough against
the growing luxury of his time, saw no harm in

[1] Martial, *Epig.* VI. lxxx.   There appears to have been a well-known
maker of garlands near the Temple of the Lares at the top of the Via
Sacra (Ovid, *Fast.* VI. 792).

[2] This practice called forth a characteristic vituperation from Seneca.
He dwelt on the unnatural life of men who so lusted after roses that
they must needs make use of artificial heat, and gather spring flowers at
the winter solstice (*Epist.* cxxii. 8).

[3] Martial, *Epig.* X. xix. 20.   The same poet gives us a glimpse of the
extravagancies of the practice when, in his fulsome flattery of Domitian,
he himself orders ten wreaths of roses to be twined round his head
(" sutilis aptetur decies rosa crinibus," IX. xciii.), one for each letter of
the emperor's name.

having his grey hairs perfumed with roses, as he
lay sipping his wine beneath the shade of his
favourite pine-tree.[1]   There were occasions of
special jubilation, indeed, on which even he could
indulge in ampler floral displays.   When, for
instance, he wished Torquatus to share his modest
supper in honour of Cæsar's birthday, he promised
him good company, and undertook that he himself
would start the drinking and the strewing of flowers,
even if he ran the risk of being deemed a madcap.
Again, in a still more hilarious mood, anticipating
his programme for a feast in honour of Murena,
the new augur, and protesting his delight to play
the fool at times, he calls for music and bids
the boy scatter the flowers.[2]   But usually his
floral display was of a simpler kind.   He denounced
the ostentatious decoration in which wealth and
extravagance delighted — " Persian magnificence "
as he called it, wherein the costly wreaths of
rich blooms were twined together with strips of
linden bark.   He would not have the last linger-
ing rose of the season carefully searched for in
order to deck his chaplet, enough for him would

---

[1] He tells that he had often done this with his old comrade in arms,
Pompeius—

"Cum quo morantem saepe diem mero
   Fregi, coronatus nitentes
      Malobathro Syrio capillos."—*Carm*. II. vii. 6-8.

[2] *Epist*. I. v. 14 ; *Carm*. III. xix.   *See* also I. xxvi. 7, 8.   Horace's
floral display could be varied, if not ostentatious (*Carm*. I. xxxvi. 15).
It included roses, lilies, myrtle, and parsley.   He shared the universal
love of roses.   Propertius too refers to " facilis spargi munda sine arte
rosa " (V. viii. 40).

be a spray of plain myrtle.[1] And when he invited his friend Phyllis to help him to celebrate worthily the birthday of his generous patron, Maecenas, he took care to let her know that she would find in his garden plenty of parsley and ivy wherewith to wreath her hair.[2] The gentle Tibullus, too, solaced himself with flowers and the juice of the grape. When thrown over by his lady-love, he determines not to make himself miserable on that score. " Go boy," he exclaims, " fetch some stronger wine. I ought long ere now to have bedewed my head with Syrian nard and encircled my hair with a garland."[3]

Originally every guest brought his own chaplet with him to a party, but afterwards these were supplied by the host,[4] who would naturally be under the temptation to outvie his neighbours and rivals in the beauty and cost of his garlands. Not only were chaplets put round the head, but wreaths were also worn round the neck, a custom which appears to have been in use as far back as the time of the kings.[5] It was not improbably to satirise by exaggeration the extravagant luxury in floral adornments of the person that at Trimalchio's feast slaves are represented as binding the legs, ankles, and feet of the guests with garlands on which they poured liquid perfumes.

Following the Greeks in their anthropomorphic

---

[1] *Carm.* I. xxxviii.   [2] *Id.* IV. xi.   [3] *Eleg.* III. vi. 62.
[4] Ovid, *Fast.* I. 403.   [5] Ovid, *Op. cit.* II. 739.

treatment of the celestial hierarchy, the Romans
pictured their gods as crowned with flowers at
their banquets.   Even the drunken Silenus is
represented to have been surprised in a cave,
lying fast asleep, not having yet recovered from
his usual debauch of the evening before, while
at a distance lay the garlands that had slipped
from his head.[1]

But over and above the personal decoration
and the copious display of flowers inside the house,
a family that was holding high festival made the
fact known to the outside world by garlands or
branches of evergreens hung at the door, and by
sounds of rejoicing which were heard afar off in
the streets.[2]   At a wedding, for example, while the
bride and bridegroom were crowned with flowers,
the guests likewise wore chaplets, while floral
festoons and garlands were conspicuous all over
the house to which the bride was to be conducted
as her future home.   In his epithalamium for
Mallius and Junia, Catullus binds the brow of
the bride with blooms of the sweet - scented
marjoram, and as she stands radiant in the
bridal chamber, he can find no fitter emblem for
her beauty than that of a white lily or golden
poppy.[3]   One of the incidents at the marriage
of Peleus and Thetis, so charmingly described

[1] Virgil, *Eclog.* vi. 16.
[2] When Propertius instructs Cynthia how her birthday is to be kept,
he entreats her not to leave her head without flowers, and to take care
that " publica vicinae perstrepat aura viae " (*Eleg.* IV. x.).
[3] *Carm.* lxi. 190.

by the same poet, is that of the centaur Chiron
bearing sylvan gifts—

" all kinds of flowers that deck the fields, or are
found on the huge mountains of Thessaly, or spring
to life under the pregnant breath of the balmy
west wind—all these he bore twined together and
blended into garlands, and the house, charmed
with the pleasant fragrance, smiled."[1]

Long before a lover could think of his wedding
wreaths he had ample occasion to make much use
of flowers during the time of his courtship. One
of the accepted forms of paying his addresses
consisted in hanging wreaths at the door of his
lady-love, and this was all the more imperative if
his advances should not have been favourably
received ; he might even smother her threshold
with flowers, and hang at her gate-posts the roses
from his own head.[2]

On public holidays, when the populace streamed
out of Rome by road and river to enjoy itself
in the country, garlands were naturally in great
request. While the statues and shrines of the
gods were everywhere crowned with flowers, the
boats that bore the excursionists down the Tiber
to celebrate the festival of the goddess Fors
Fortuna, were similarly adorned.[3] In the course

---

[1] *Carm.* LXIV. 278-284.

[2] Lucretius, IV. 1177 ; Tibullus, I. ii. ; Ovid, *Ars Amat.* II. 527.
Propertius avers that the lover's own personal chaplets were sometimes
" turpes corollae" (I. xvi. 7).

[3] Ovid, *Fast.* VI. 775.   The poet recommends the merry-makers not
to spare the wine on their trip upon the river, seeing that on such an
occasion as a religious festival they need not be ashamed of going

of triumphal processions the streets were strewn with flowers.

It was not only as symbols of happiness that flowers entered so fully into the social life of ancient Rome; they were likewise used to express sorrow and mourning, and certainly no outward token of affectionate sympathy appeals more directly and feelingly to a human heart crushed with grief over the death of one who was ardently beloved. At funerals garlands were placed on the bier, and on the pyre. Flowers were offered to the manes of the dead, and where a lost one was long and sincerely lamented, the tomb was faithfully decked every year with flowers. When Ovid in the deep despondence of his exile sent his wife the epitaph which he wished to have cut in large letters on his tomb outside Rome, he entreated that his ashes should be brought back from Tomi, in order that he might not still remain an exile when dead, and he prayed that she would then perform his funeral rites, placing on his grave chaplets wet with her tears.[1] So also Tibullus, in one of the tenderest of his elegies, refers to a young maiden who, since her death, had become sacred to him, and on whose tomb he would offer gifts:—

"Et madefacta meis serta feram lacrymis."[2]

---

home tipsy. The same opinion is also expressed and still more explicitly even by the more reverent and orthodox Tibullus with reference to the celebration of rustic festivals,

"Non festa luce madere
Est rubor, errantes et male ferre pedes"
Eleg. II. i. 29; *see* also V. 87-90.

[1] *Trist.* III. iii. 82.   [2] *Eleg.* II. vi. 32.

In another poem he alludes to an amiable girl on whose grave her old lover would place a yearly wreath, praying that she might rest in peace and that the earth might lie lightly on her quiet bones.[1]

Familiar as the wearing of chaplets became in Rome, there was a time, during the earlier and sterner Republican days, when the manners of the people were much more strictly looked after, and when it was accounted a serious offence to be seen crowned with flowers in the daytime and in public. Pliny relates an anecdote of a certain Lucius Fulvius, a banker, who during the second Punic War was incautious enough to look out from his booth into the forum, with a garland of roses on his head. By order of the Senate he was sent to prison, and was kept there till the end of the war. The same writer records also the case of P. Munatius, who took a floral crown from the image of the god Marsyas and put it on his own head. He was promptly sent to jail by the triumvirs, and though he appealed to the tribunes of the people, they would not interfere on his behalf. Pliny contrasts these proceedings with the licence allowed at Athens, where a company of young men, crowned as for a procession, made their way in the morning into a school of philosophy.[2]

In Latin literature the love of flowers is abundantly displayed. Even a matter - of - fact

---

[1] *Eleg.* II. iv. 45-50.

[2] *Hist. Nat.* XXI. vi. We are told by Ovid that no business was transacted when the heads wore their chaplets (*Fast.* v. 341).

naturalist like Pliny the Elder, could not begin
his natural history of plants without an eloquent
exordium on the indescribable delicacy and wealth
of beauty wherewith Nature has painted flowers,
and how she seems wantonly to delight in
their varied fertility. Such kinds of vegetation,
he says, as are required for human needs she
takes years or even centuries to mature, but
flowers and perfumes she pours forth from day
to day.[1]

It is naturally among the poets that the
appreciation of flowers finds fullest expression.
To Catullus they suggested pathetic emblems of
human sorrow. When, broken - hearted at the
faithlessness of his beloved Lesbia, he thought of
quitting Italy in despair, the image that seemed
most fitly to symbolise his own blighted affection
was that of "a flower on the edge of the meadow,
which has been caught by the passing plough-
share."[2] So, too, in a familiar ode, he compares
a maiden before and after marriage to

" a flower that has grown sequestered in a fenced
garden, unknown to cattle, upturned by no plough,
caressed by the breeze, strengthened by the sun,
nourished by the shower, and coveted by many
a youth and many a maiden. But after it has
been culled from its slender stalk, it fades away,
and is then coveted neither by maidens nor
youths." And again: "As an unwedded vine,
born on bare ground, never raises itself up, never

[1] *Hist. Nat.* XXI. i.
[2] Catullus, XI. 22.

bears a mellow grape, but, letting its weakly frame bend prone under its own weight, touches with its root the furthest spray, no husband-men, no youths have tended it : yet should the same vine chance to be wedded to an elm, many a husbandman and many a youth then cherish it ; so the maiden, while she remains untouched, grows old, neglected ; but when at the ripe age she has made an equal marriage, she is dearer to her spouse and less disliked by her parent." [1]

In another simile Catullus speaks of a bride " binding her mind fast with love, as the cling-ing ivy, spreading hither and thither, firmly clasps a tree." [2]

Flowers bloom luxuriantly almost everywhere in the poetry of Virgil. Like his own bees (*tantus amor florum*) he loved to linger among the banks of wild thyme and violets, noting by name and affixing some appropriate epithet to each plant that had given him pleasure—the scented anise, the late-flowering narcissus, the white lily, the bee-haunted saffron, the bending acanthus, the lowly broom, the soft hyacinth, the yellow marigold, the wan-coloured ivy, the shore-loving myrtle, the silver-grey willow, and the generous, long-lived olive, fosterer of peace. [3]

---

[1] Catullus, LXII. 39-58.   [2] *Id.* LXI. 33.

[3] The poet's affection for a plant, sometimes leads him not to be content with a passing epithet but to add a few words of commendation, as in his allusion to the olive above cited. The most notable example of this treatment is to be found in his reference to the Italian starwort or aster. " There is in the meadows," he says, " a flower to which the

In his *Eclogues* and *Georgics*, where he was
singing of country scenes, it was natural that
Virgil should dwell with evident joy upon the
floral charms which so strongly appealed to his
sense of beauty. But like Catullus, and, indeed,
sometimes with that bard's music in his memory,
he felt too their pathos and recognised how well
their frailty could express the eclipse of youth,
vigour, and beauty at the hand of death. We
seem indeed to gain a clearer conception of how
deep a hold flowers had upon the poet's sympathies
and imagination when we find that even in the
Æneid, where he had to depict scenes of carnage,
it is to the realm of flowers that he turns for
images that may heighten our realisation of the
untimely fate of a young, comely, and brave hero.
Thus, he compares the dead body of the youthful
Pallas, slain by Turnus, to "a blossom plucked
by a maiden's hand from tender violet or drooping hyacinth, which has not yet lost its radiance
and beauty, though it can no longer draw sustenance from its mother earth."[1] The same
simile, slightly varied, is applied to Euryalus,

country-folk have given the name of Amellus, a plant easily to be
recognised by those who seek for it, seeing that from one turf it bears
quite a forest of leaves. It is itself golden in colour, but in the leaves
which are abundantly grouped around there gleams the purple of a
dark violet. Entwined in garlands it often adorns the altars of the
gods. It has a bitter taste. Shepherds gather it in valleys that are
cropped, and also by the winding streams of Mella" (*Geor.* IV. 271-
278). No one would have introduced this minute description into a
discourse on bees unless he loved the plant and welcomed the
opportunity of dwelling on its features.

[1] *Æn.* XI. 68.

another youthful warrior (*ora puer prima signans intonsa juventa*) who was slain on the field of battle. He is likened to "a purple flower struck down by the plough and fading away as it dies, or to poppies which the rains have weighted down till their heads hang upon their drooping necks."[1]

Following the example of his illustrious predecessors, Ovid also has employed a floral image to heighten the impression made by the tragic death of a handsome and vigorous youth. But his use of it is less simple and brief. In depicting the fatal blow given by the rebound of the quoit thrown by Apollo, he tells how the strength of the hapless Hyacinthus rapidly fails

"as if in a well-watered garden one were to break down violets or poppies or lilies; the frail flowers, clinging to their yellow stalks, would speedily hang their heavy blooms, and their heads would fall prostrate on the ground: so lies the dying youth and his head sinks upon his shoulder."[2]

Propertius, who shows in so many ways the originality of his mind, employs flowers as images to express two of his predominant sentiments. In his choice of similes to convey his enthusiastic admiration of female beauty, especially of that of the lady to whom he had given his affections, he compares her complexion of mingled pink and white to "rose-leaves floating in pure milk."[3]

---

[1] *Æn.* IX. 181, 435.　　　[2] *Metam.* X. 190.

[3] *Id.* II. iii. 12. Virgil had compared the complexion of Lavinia to a nosegay wherein white lilies blush amid a profusion of rose-blooms (*Æn.* XII. 68).

More characteristic of his melancholy temperament
is the image which he takes from the fading
flowers of the festal board to show the shortness
and uncertainty of life.

> " As petals from our fading chaplets fall,
>   And scattered, float upon the cups of wine,
> Even so, on us, though eager for love's call,
>   To-morrow's sun may haply never shine." [1]

---

[1] *Eleg.* III. vii. 57.

CHAPTER VI

ROMAN GARDENS

" A GARDEN," says Bacon, "is the greatest refreshment to the spirits of man,"[1] and the Romans fully realised the truth of the aphorism. In the early days of the Kings to each Roman citizen were allotted two jugera of land (not quite an English acre and a third) as his "heredium." On this land he lived and maintained his family, the wife and children sharing in the work of cultivation. The hortus or garden was a little farm on which, besides the crops, live-stock of various kinds was raised. It was the peasant's surety to the State, seeing that he depended on its yield for his sustenance. One of its advantages, according to Pliny, was that much of its produce being of a vegetable kind, which was ready for the table without cooking and could be eaten and digested with the help of a little vinegar, fire was little needed, and thus a great economy of wood was secured.[2] In later times, when property was more unequally divided, the husbandmen looked upon

[1] " Essays," No. XLVI.
[2] *Hist. Nat.* XIX. xix.

I

the hortus as their second flitch of bacon.[1] In
course of years, as the population increased and
wealth and luxury grew apace, the two jugera, which
had satisfied even the veterans of the Punic wars,
were not thought large enough by men who, a
short time before, had been the slaves of Nero,
but who now looked with contempt on such
limited space, as quite inadequate to provide
their pleasure-grounds, fish-ponds and other requirements, and not even large enough for a
mere garden.[2]

The love of flowers led naturally to the cultivation of them, and this taste became widely
diffused through all classes of society in Rome.
Among the urban plebeians who had no ground
on which to plant or sow, the custom was followed
of growing flowers at their windows in pots or
boxes, and thus, as Pliny remarks, they brought
the country sights daily before their eyes until
the ruthless robberies of an increasing population
compelled them to block up all outlook.[3] It
must have been a thankless task to keep plants
alive and flourishing during a hot summer in the
narrow, dark, and dusty streets where the poorer
inhabitants congregated. Those who could command a few feet of bare earth were often glad to
make of it such a garden as was possible. Even

---

[1] Cicero, *Cato Major*, XVI. Cato was of opinion that in acquiring a
property, while vine-growing might be a first consideration, a "hortus
irriguus" should come second (*De Re Rust.* I. *ad init*).

[2] Pliny, *Hist. Nat.* XVIII. ii.; Juvenal, XIV. 161-172.

[3] *Hist. Nat.* XIX. xix.

within the enclosing walls of small town-houses room was often found for more or less greenery —little plots of flowers or shrubs, a group of trees or even a single tree. How integral a part of the household economy such intramural gardens might become is well seen at Pompeii. Enclosed within the open courts of unpretentious dwellings, they might be no larger than one of the rooms, but yet of size enough to enclose a few flower-beds or a group of bushes or trees, and thus to supply a pleasant and even shady open-air room in the middle of the house.

From the modest window-boxes of the urban populace, every gradation of horticulture could be traced up to the vast pleasure-grounds with which some of the wealthiest citizens succeeded in surrounding not only their country villas but even their mansions in Rome.[1] Pliny remarks that under the name of gardens, charming places (*deliciae*)—fields and villas, had been formed even within the city itself, and he adds that Epicurus, whom he sarcastically calls *otii magister*, was the first to introduce such town-gardens into Athens.[2] This fondness for living vegetation gave rise to the extravagance of planting orchards on the very

---

[1] The "magni Senecae praedivitis horti," and those of Sallust, Maecenas, Nero, and others were famous examples of such extensive town-gardens. The grounds of Lucullus, close to Rome, were accounted of more than regal splendour (Plutarch, *Lucull.* xxxix.), and they were made still more magnificent after his death.

[2] *Hist. Nat.* XIX. xix.

roof—a custom denounced by Seneca as altogether unnatural.[1]

An interesting account of a garden within Rome has been preserved in one of Martial's epigrams.[2]

"A few acres lying along the ridge of the Janiculan Hill have been turned into a little domain, more blissful than the gardens of the Hesperides. Broad hollows that shelve down the slopes are surmounted by the smooth, gently-swelling summit which enjoys a serene sky and its own gleam of light, while a fog lies over the winding valleys. The graceful roofs of a tall villa rise gently towards the clear heavens. Thence can be seen the seven hills, lords of the world, and the eye can take in the whole of Rome, likewise the Alban and Tusculan heights and every cool spot around the city—old Fidenae, and little Rubrae, and the orchard grove of Anna Perenna. Thence, too, the traveller is plainly visible as he takes the air on the Flaminian and Salarian Roads, but the sound of his chariot does not reach so far. Sleep, therefore, is here not disturbed by wheels, nor, though the Mulvian Bridge (Ponte Molle) is so near, by the cries of the skipper and the shouts of the men who haul the barges. The boats on the sacred Tiber can be watched as they glide swiftly along."

It was round the country villas of wealthy proprietors that the most extensive tracts were turned into pleasure-grounds and gardens, where ample scope was found for ornamental or landscape gardening on the one hand, and for the

[1] *Epist.* cxxii. 8. [2] *Epig.* IV. lxiv.

cultivation of vegetables and fruit on the other. Detailed accounts of such country retreats, are to be found in the letters of the younger Pliny. As already mentioned, this accomplished aristocrat owned a number of villas and estates in different parts of the country.   He has left descriptions of two of them, one on the coast, not far from Ostia, a favourite winter residence of his;[1] the other far up the valley of the Tiber, in the Tuscan region, where he loved to spend his summer vacation.   The latter estate occupied a commanding position at no great distance from the main range of the Apennines, and far enough from Rome to afford the most perfect seclusion and freedom from intruders.   The enthusiastic picture which he has left of the general external and internal arrangements of the house and grounds gives probably a fair representation of the country residence of a man of wealth, culture, and taste in Italy during the first century of the Christian era.[2]

Sheltered by higher ground behind, and placed on a southern slope whence a wide view could be had down the fertile vale of the Tiber, the spacious villa was surrounded with grounds laid out according to the fashion of the time, where Nature was on every hand controlled and supplemented by Art—a style which may be commonly seen in the Italy of to-day. Walks bordered with box or rosemary, or enclosed between trimmed

---

[1] *Epist.* II. xvii.   [2] *Id.* V. vi.

hedges of evergreens or roses, led in straight or winding courses through the vineyards to all parts of the estate. The central portion was kept open and was surrounded with leafy plane - trees, up whose stems ivy clustered thickly and was thence extended in festoons from tree to tree, while a grove of laurels afforded a thick screen behind. Further protection from the heats of summer was furnished by the deep shade of a semi-circle of cypress-trees. The prevailing green of the place was relieved by the gleam of white marble. Besides the colonnades round the house, there was in one place a large semi-circular marble seat resting on four Carystian pedestals and over-shadowed by a vine. From beneath the seat water gushed out so as to fill a marble basin in front. On the opposite side rose a large two - storey summer-house, resplendent in white marble and embowered amidst verdure.

From the copious employment of box-wood for hedgerows and in isolated bushes, abundant scope was afforded for all the vagaries of the topiarian art, then so much in vogue. When the visitor descended the gentle slope from the violet-scented terrace in front of the house, he passed between a row of box-wood bushes on either side, clipped into the forms of different animals facing each other.[1] At another time he might find himself between

---

[1] Bacon, in his essay on gardens already cited, remarks : " I, for my part, do not like images cut out in juniper or other garden stuff ; they be for children."

hedges of evergreens trimmed into various shapes.
Emerging upon a little meadow, he was next
confronted by a still more extraordinary display
of topiarian invention, where the box had been
cut into a thousand different figures, sometimes into letters indicating the name of the
proprietor or that of the landscape gardener who
had designed them.   Further on he would notice
a row of little obelisks alternating with fruit-trees,
and then, of a sudden, in the midst of all this
elaboration of ornamental horticulture (or as Pliny
calls it, this *urbanissimum opus*), he would find
himself in an area wherein an attempt had been
made to imitate Nature, presumably by leaving
her as much as possible to herself, and excluding
the knife and the pruning hook.[1]

From the position of Pliny's garden, in the
midst of higher ground and with hills beyond,
good use could be made of the abundant water-
supply which was available.   At one part of the
domain a cascade, shooting from a height, was
caught in a marble basin, whence the water was
conveyed in pipes all over the grounds.   Scope
was thus afforded for the construction of fountains
and rills of clear and cool water, which kept the
grass green.   The whole gardens and pleasure-
ground were fenced in with a boundary wall, which
on the inside was concealed from view by a box-
hedge cut into steps.   Outside of that wall lay

---

[1] Bacon also, in his design for a princely garden, would have a
heath "framed as much as may be to a natural wildness."

the meadows, woods, and copses of the open
country, which, as Pliny truly remarks, were
beholden for their beauty to the hand of Nature
not less than his garden was to that of Art.
Even those modern readers, who may most
strongly object to his artificial tastes in horticulture, must at least admit that he was an
enthusiastic gardener and an ardent lover of the
country. That he also had a keen eye for the
natural charms of the scenery amidst which his
home was placed, is clearly shown in the same
letter from which the foregoing particulars have
been culled.

In this letter, so full of detail as to the external
features of his villa and its surroundings, there is
no reference to what we should call the kitchen-
garden. But this essential portion of the establishment of a country-house was certainly not omitted
by Pliny from his Tuscan home, though he did
not think that it required description to his friend.
The provision for the table was no doubt amply
arranged for. In another letter of this correspondence, the writer's seaside villa at Laurentum is
spoken of as merely a house and garden in the
midst of the sand, yet small though the establishment may have been, it included a "hortus
pinguis et rusticus." [1]

The use of ivy in pleasure-grounds had been
long in fashion before Pliny's time. Cicero, for
instance, gives an amusing account of how it was

[1] *Epist.* II. xvii. 15 ; IV. vi.

being carried out at his brother's villa near
Arpinum. Writing to Quintus after a visit to
the place, he says :

"I praised your landscape-gardener ; he has
clothed everything with ivy, both the foundation-
wall of the villa and the interspaces between the
columns of the walk, so that, in short, those
Greek statues of yours seem to be landscape-
gardeners crying up their ivy." [1]

Vitruvius recommended that the interspaces of
the open porticoes at the theatres should be orna-
mented with greenery (*viridibus*), seeing that such
hypæthral walks are very healthy, first from the
beneficial effects of the plants on the eyes
(probably by mitigating the glare of strong sun-
light), and secondly from the excellent results of
bodily exercise in the open air.[2]

The characteristic artificial style of Roman
gardening was displayed also, though, of course,
on a much more modest scale, in the restricted
spaces available in the intramural courts of town
houses. Even in those of a small town like
Pompeii, we find the surrounding portico with
its white stuccoed columns, the flower-plots with
the little gravelled walks between them, and the
statuettes, hermae, vases, and other works of art.
The leaden pipes remain, but the water that once
kept up a pleasing murmur in these courts is gone.
Doubtless even within such narrow confines there

[1] *Ad Quint. Frat.* III. i. 5.
[2] *De Architect.* V. ix. 5.

were bushes of box-wood clipped into fantastic shapes. In judging of this horticultural taste we must remember how dominant in the Roman mind was the idea of mastery; Nature must be subdued not only to the needs but to the fancy of man. The more labour and expense that were spent in transforming a piece of ground from its original natural condition into one of these varied but formal gardens, the greater was the praise due to the owner. Amusing illustrations of how this praise was sometimes lavished by flattering friends may be found in Latin poetry. Statius, for example, had an acquaintance who had made considerable transformations of natural scenery at Tibur, and another who had worked even greater marvels on the coast near Sorrento. In recounting their triumphs of landscape - gardening the poet speaks of Nature bowing to the work of a true artist, and he praises the genius of a man who, evidently at a vast expenditure of thought, labour, time, and money, had obliterated the natural charm of a portion of the coast, and had created in its place a villa and grounds, with the usual accompaniments of statues in marble, bronze, and wax, arcades, and all the other artificial splendours of a rich man's home.[1] Here and there a voice was raised in favour of leaving Nature to her own devices, and enjoying what she so

---

[1] *Silv.* I. iii. ; II. ii. ; III. i. The poet admits that some of the scenes he refers to were full of natural beauty before the hand and art of man had touched them (I. iii. 15).

bountifully supplies without cribbing and maiming her to suit the narrow limits of Roman taste. Propertius, for instance, in a passage already cited (p. 97), when urging Cynthia to give up the artificial adornments in which she indulged, appeals to the vegetable world, where plants grow so much better and attain so much more beauty when allowed to spread at their own sweet will.

There is an interesting reference to gardens towards the end of the *Georgics,* where Virgil alludes to the combination of the useful and ornamental which a simple peasant could achieve on his modest piece of land. Discoursing on the management of bees, and dwelling on the importance of planting near the hives the trees, shrubs, and flowers which these insects particularly frequent, the poet suddenly breaks off from his subject in order to indulge in an expression of regret that as he is nearing the end of his poem, he cannot now sing of the various charms of a garden, but must leave the theme to those who will come after him. Among the topics on which it would have given him special pleasure to dwell, he mentions the rose-gardens of Paestum with their double blossoming in the year, and he singles out a number of flowers of which he would fain have sung—the narcissus, the acanthus, the ivy, and the myrtle. Nor does he forget the homely vegetables that minister so kindly to the wants of man in a country where plant-food counts for so much in daily life—" the endive as it gladly

drinks from the rills, the parsley on its green
banks, and the cucumber creeping along the grass
and swelling as it goes." The thought of this
commingling of plants cultivated for their beauty
or fragrance with those grown for their use as
food, brings to the poet's remembrance a scene
that he had himself once witnessed in Southern
Italy, where a sturdy old Cilician settler lived
on a few acres of unappropriated land, as happy
as a king. The soil was poor, unfitted for corn
or pasture or vines, and covered with the wild
flowers, briars, copsewood, and scattered trees of
the district. Nevertheless with plodding industry
the man had planted his pot-herbs here and there
in sheltered nooks, between the brambles, where
the white lilies and vervain and poppies grew.
Returning home late in the evening from his daily
toil, he could load his table with a supper which
he did not need to buy. His roses were the first
to bloom in spring, and his apples came soonest
to ripening in autumn. While winter elsewhere
was still splitting the rocks with frost and bridling
the brooks with ice, he would already be cutting
his tender hyacinths. His bees always throve
and gave the earliest honey. The trees of various
kinds which he had planted in rows flourished
apace, and among them the plane-tree, under
whose grateful shade men drink their wine.[1]

[1] *Geor.* IV. 125-146.

CHAPTER VII

TREES AND WOODLANDS

FROM the infancy of mankind, trees have been regarded with mingled feelings of admiration and of awe. The combined majesty and grace wherewith they tower above the soil that supports them; their infinite variety of individual forms and colours, whether carrying their foliage all the year, or at one season clothing themselves with tender leaf and blossom, at another flaming in the varied glories of autumn, and thereafter, bare and leafless, stretching their giant arms and delicate branches to all the winds of heaven; their immemorial age; their calm endurance and seeming defiance of the vicissitudes of time, in pathetic contrast to the short and troubled span of human life; their varied music under the changeful moods of the weather, from the faint whisper awakened by the gentlest breath of summer to the loud roar or moaning wail aroused by the fury of a wintry tempest; the grateful shelter which under their canopy of leafy boughs they provide for man and beast; the endless services which they render to man's daily life in their yield of timber or leaves or fruit — these features give to trees a high place among the charms and bounties wherewith Nature teems.

A single noble tree is always an impressive sight. But it is where trees are massed in woodland and forest that they exert the full measure of their fascination. Crowded together, they may lose something of the breadth and unconstrained dignity which any one of them can attain when free in the open to fling its arms to every quarter, but their venerable, mossy, or lichen-crusted trunks rise straighter and taller, one behind the other, in seemingly endless succession. Their multitudinous interlacing branches, that shut out the sky, throw a twilight gloom upon all below. Solitariness and silence brood over the scene. No wonder that, from the earliest childhood of the human race, these places have been regarded with a feeling of awe, and that still to-day they attune the mind to solemn thoughts, such as hardly any other part of the material world so powerfully inspires.[1]

Such sylvan influences have had ample scope for their development in Italy. In ancient times all

---

[1] Keats, who could enter so deeply into the spirit of the antique world, adds this sylvan influence to his vivid picture of the dethroned Saturn and his surroundings :—

> "Upon a tranced summer-night,
> Those green-robed senators of mighty woods,
> Tall oaks, branch-charmed by the earnest stars,
> Dream, and so dream all night without a stir."

As an illustration of the modern spirit Wordsworth's lines may be quoted :—

> "One impulse from a vernal wood
> May teach you more of man,
> Of moral evil and of good,
> Than all the sages can."

the higher grounds of the country and much of the
plains were clothed with wood. Only by slow
degrees was this primeval forest cleared away from
the lower grounds. In his graphic narrative of
the progress of early man Lucretius has sketched
in a few picturesque lines the progress of this
conquest of wild nature :

"One kind of culture after another did men
try on their dear little fields. They saw that
the earth tames wild fruits by fostering and
fondly rearing them. Day by day did they
force the woods to retire further into the
mountains and resign the lower land to tilth,
so that on hills and plains they might have
meadows, ponds, brooks, crops, and happy vineyards, and that the blue-grey belt of olives
might run conspicuous between them, spreading
over hillocks, hollows, and plains. Thus it has
come that you now see all the land marked
out with varied charms, where men adorn it by
planting it with sweet fruits and surrounding it
with plantations of other kindly trees." [1]

From time immemorial, therefore, Italy has been
a land not only of fertile plains and flowery pastures,
but also of abundant glades and woodlands. The
pine-clad slopes of the Alps, the forests of chestnut,
walnut, and oak, and the groves of olive trees that
stretch along either side of the Apennines have
each its own variety of impressive charm. The
dwellers in this land have thus from early times
had before them a wide range of wooded scenery.

[1] *De Rer. Nat.* V. 1367-1378.

As far back as their history can be traced
the Romans appear to have felt the solemnising
influences of such scenery and to have associated it
with their religious observances. Thus, following
the Greeks, they assigned particular species of
trees to different gods ; the oak being held sacred
to Jupiter, the laurel to Apollo, the ivy to Bacchus,
the myrtle to Venus, the olive to Minerva, and the
poplar to Hercules. Moreover, as a stately tree
was one of the most glorious things their eyes
could rest on, the country - folk, faithful to the
traditions of their ancient faith, continued in
successive generations to dedicate the finest
example to some god.[1] Lucan gives a graphic
picture of one of these sacred trees and the
devotion with which, in spite of its age and
failing strength, it continued to be regarded.
It was a tall oak, which time out of mind had
received the veneration and pious offerings of
the district. Dead and leafless, it still stretched
its bare branches to the winds, and though
clinging to its decaying roots, was upheld mainly
by its own weight. The wide shade which it
could once afford was now narrowed down to
what was supplied by the massive trunk which
seemed tottering to its fall, as if the next
south-east gale would level it with the ground.
And yet, although all around there were younger
trees that towered aloft in full vigour of growth,
this venerable patriarch of the woodland main-

[1] Pliny, *Hist. Nat.* XII. ii.

tained his time - honoured spell, and was alone
the object of worship.[1]

Where for any reason a shrine had been erected
on open ground, trees were planted round it, so
that the worshippers could bring their offerings
and hold their service under the shade of green
leaves. This association is frequently observable
in the Pompeian frescoes. But it appears to have
been more usual from the first to select a site for
such a shrine in some wooded place. Hence arose
the numerous sacred groves which helped so
powerfully to strengthen and perpetuate the belief
that the divinities loved to haunt sylvan recesses,
and were pleased to be worshipped there.[2] Thus,
besides being affected by the solemnising influences
which forests naturally exert upon the mind, the
ordinary Roman citizen, under the sway of the
state-religion and the nature-worship out of which
that religion came, could not readily divest himself of the traditional feelings and prepossessions
of his forefathers. How fully these hereditary
influences were felt may be judged from a remark
of Pliny the Elder, who could hardly be called
a sentimental man. "The images of the gods,"
he says, "resplendent in gold and ivory, do
not inspire us with more veneration than do

---

[1] *Phars.* I. 136-143. The poet employs his description of this tree
as a simile in allusion to Pompey at the beginning of the campaign that
ended at Pharsalia.

[2] Lucretius admitted that all over the world, shrines, lakes,
groves, altars, and the images of the gods were held sacred (*De Rer.
Nat.* V. 47).

K

the groves; there we worship the very silence itself."[1]

The allusions to sacred groves, which occur so often in Latin literature, would bring a crowd of associations to the mind of a Roman reader which we at this day fail to realise. Now and then, indeed, we seem to catch a glimpse of how the sanctity of a holy place may have come to be established and confirmed. Thus Virgil, in describing the aspect of the site of the future Rome, when Aeneas came to see it under the guidance of Evander, tells that the Capitoline Hill and the Tarpeian Rock were then covered with rough woods and thickets, and that a deep religious awe hung about the place and filled the timid country-folk with fear. The King assured his guest that some god must dwell there. Which of the immortals it might be, had not been discovered, though Jupiter himself, it was thought, had been seen gathering a storm around the height.[2] This pristine sanctity pre-eminently fitted the site for its future greatness. In course of time, as Rome grew, the woods and thickets were cleared away, but the sacred associations still clung to the spot.[3] The unknown divinity of Evander's days became none other than Jupiter Capitolinus, best

---

[1] *Hist. Nat.* XII. ii. Quintilian also remarks that men reverence the ancient sacred groves where the massive and antique oaks are not so much distinguished for their beauty as for their religious awe (*religionem*). *Inst. Orat.* X. i. 88.

[2] "Tarpeiusque pater nuda de rupe tonabat."—Propertius, V. i. 7.

[3] "Romulus infami complevit moenia luco."—Lucan, *Phars.* VII. 437.

and greatest of the gods, the tutelary guardian of
the commonweath, in whose honour the Capitol
was crowned with a splendid temple. Thus the
holiest place in the national religion and the heart
of the mighty Roman dominion were traced back
by the poet to the piece of wild Nature which
had called forth the awe-struck veneration of the
earliest inhabitants. It may be added that tradition had also handed down the memory of a grove
which clothed the Aventine Hill and had so
strikingly solemn an aspect that no one could see
it without feeling sure that some divinity must
dwell there.[1]

The choice of places to be set apart as sacred
groves was often determined by some striking
topographical features that heightened the weirdness of the dense woodland. The most obvious
examples of this selection are to be found among
the extinct volcanoes of Italy. The bottoms of
the now silent craters had become, probably before
the Latins occupied the country, receptacles for
surface water, and were thus converted into tarns
or lakes, while their shelving sides were clothed
with brushwood and trees. Here and there steam
and mephitic vapours still hung about such places
and added to their impressiveness.[2] Such deep,
dark, mysterious hollows were admirably fitted for

[1] "Lucus Aventino suberat niger ilicis umbra,
Quo posses viso dicere, 'numen inest.'"—Ovid, *Fast.* III. 295.

[2] These mephitic localities have a special interest in regard to the
Roman conceptions of the underworld. They are more particularly
dealt with in chap. xvi.

selection as sacred groves, and a number of them
rose to fame as places of great religious sanctity.
One of the most remarkable of them came to be
known as pre-eminently the Nemus (grove), and
was dedicated to Diana.[1] The traveller who now
visits it as the "Lake of Nemi," can be at no loss
to understand the impression which its surrounding
circle of wooded cliff and slope and its deep seclusion
must have made upon the pious worshippers
of the "Montium Custos nemorumque Virgo."
The Vadimon Lake, in the vale of the Tiber, so
well described by the younger Pliny, was likewise
one of these holy places. The blue-green water
covering the floor of this crater gave forth in his
day a sulphureous odour, and, as he remarks, no
vessel of any kind was to be seen on it, for it had
been declared sacred.[2] Another retreat of a similar
kind, which lay among the volcanic hollows near
the ancient town of Caere, is mentioned by Virgil
in the impressive passage where, passing abruptly
from the famous hexameter line that recalls the
sound of horsemen galloping over a plain in all
the panoply of war, he leads us at once to the
solemn silence of a vast grove embosomed among
hills and girt round with dark fir - trees — a
place renowned far and near for the sanctity with
which it had been invested ever since in days of
yore it was dedicated by the old Pelasgians to
the god Silvanus.[3]

[1] " Vallis Aricinae silva praecinctus opaca
      Est lacus, antiqua religione sacer."—Ovid, *Fast*. III. 263.
[2] *Epist*. VIII. xx.   [3] *Æn*. VIII. 597.

From his allusions to them, Ovid seems to have had a particular affection for these sacred groves, in the sequestered silence of which he could indulge in undisturbed reveries. Thus, when debating as to his future poetical career, he represents himself as sauntering within the shade of an ancient grove that had not been felled for many years, and where it was easy to believe that some divinity must dwell. In the midst rose a sacred fountain; there was a cavern in the overhanging rock, and on every side the birds were warbling their tender plaints. In these appropriate surroundings he pictures a colloquy between his favourite Muse of Elegy with her perfumed hair wreathed in flowers, and the stern Muse of Tragedy, who was impatient to know when the poet meant to leave off his love-making and essay a worthier task.[1] Again, in another poem, he refers to an ancient and gloomy grove on the heights above Falisci, which from its very look would be recognised to be a sacred spot. It contained a simple altar, built in old artless days, and there the offerings of pious pilgrims were made to Juno.[2]

Outside of the region in which their own national religion flourished, the Romans found that the surrounding barbarous races likewise had their sacred groves, whereto some strange features of pagan worship added another horror. One of the most notable of these was the Gaulish grove

---

[1] *Amor.* III. i.   [2] *Id.* III. xiii.

near Marseilles, of which Lucan has left such a gruesome description. Its relics of human sacrifices, its flames, dragons, and other reputed terrors struck dismay into the hearts of the bravest Roman soldiers, who shrank from obeying Cæsar's orders to cut the trees down, until he himself, seizing an axe, dealt the first blow, exclaming at the same time : " Let none of you now hesitate to level the wood, but lay the impiety on me." [1]

Apart from their religious associations, the obvious usefulness of trees, from the welcome shade and shelter which they afforded, led to extensive plantation in all parts of Italy. The plane-tree, introduced from Greece, was more especially made use of towards the end of the Republic on account of its heavy foliage and the depth of its shade.[2] The elm was everywhere planted as a support for the vines. The pine, the poplar, the beech, the cypress, the ilex, and other trees have their praises sung by the poets for the pleasant shade which their leafy branches afford in sunny weather.[3]

It was not only among the pleasure-grounds and gardens in the country, where ample space for

---

[1] *Phars.* III. 399-437.

[2] Virgil, *Geor.* IV. 146. Pliny relates that this tree was so much prized as to be sometimes watered with wine. Ovid calls the tree "genialis."

[3] Ovid, describing the effects of the music of Orpheus gives a characteristically detailed, but not very poetical, catalogue of some two dozen trees and shrubs that were drawn to the musician. It has an interest as indicating the kinds of plants most familiar in Rome. The epithets which the poet applies to them contain allusions to their characters, uses, or legendary history (*Metam.* X. 86-105).

arboriculture could be obtained, that the planting
of trees was carried out. In the city and even
within the open courts of town-houses this practice
was also followed. Sometimes, instead of the
flower-plots, already referred to as frequently to be
found in these places, a single tree would be set in
the atrium, like the plane-tree planted at Corduba
by the hands of Julius Cæsar, and celebrated by
Martial as in his time grown so tall and densely
foliaged as to overshadow the whole surrounding
mansion.[1] When a new villa was erected in the
country, care was sometimes taken by a man of
taste to preserve special trees in his general clear-
ance of a wooded site. Thus amid the fellings that
preluded the construction of a mansion at Tibur,
Vopiscus saved a single tree in the very centre of
the house, and allowed it to mount above the roof
into the clear air, to the intense admiration of his
friend, the poet Statius, who has immortalised the
incident.[2]

In other cases, even within the city, room was
found for a "nemus," or group of trees within the
enclosing outer walls of a house, and thus, as already
mentioned, another apartment was obtained, open
to the air, yet under the shade of green leaves.
Horace alludes to such a "grove," planted within
the beautiful courts of Lyce's house, and to the
howling of the northern blasts through its trees.[3]
Among the tokens of wealth for which Tibullus

[1] *Epig.* IX. lxi.　　　　[2] *Silv.* I. iii.
[3] *Carm.* III. x. 5.

had no desire, he mentions "woods inside houses, imitating sacred groves, together with gilded beams and a pavement of marble." [1]

One of the most widespread pleasures which the Romans owed to trees, and to which many allusions are made in their literature, was the grateful shade wherein, near a clear spring or babbling brook, they could rest and sleep, or sip their wine with friends.   Lucretius sympathetically paints the delight wherewith

"men lie stretched on the soft grass beside some stream of water and beneath the branches of a tall tree, where at but little cost they pleasantly refresh themselves, above all when the weather smiles and the season has strewn the green sward with flowers." [2]

Probably no one enjoyed this convivial companionship more keenly than Horace, whose lyrics contain various references to it.   But in the little pictures of it which he draws, the sketches of the scenery are so full and so vivid that we can have little difficulty in believing that his surroundings on these occasions gave him not less pleasure than the friendly intercourse :—

> "Where giant pine and poplar pale
> Unite their boughs to wrap the vale
>   In friendly shade ;
> While the clear stream that toils below
> Trips onward with a winding flow
>   Adown the glade:

---

[1] *Eleg.* III. iii. 15.
[2] *De Rer. Nat.* II. 29.

" Thither thy wines and perfumes bear,
  With roses, though their beauty rare
        Too soon is fled :
  So live while wealth and years remain,
  Ere the three sisters snap in twain
        The fatal thread." [1]

But apart from allusions to such *al fresco* convivial pleasures, the Latin poets exhibit also a genuine appreciation of the varied charms of woodland scenery.   Juvenal indeed affirms that one of the characteristics of a true poet is that he shows himself to be " cupidus silvarum."   And certainly in the writings of his poetical predecessors he had good ground for the statement.   It is above all in the works of Virgil that the woodlands find their fullest and most joyous appreciation.   In his early days, as already mentioned (p. 62), this poet felt an ambition to choose lofty themes, perhaps even to follow in the footsteps of Lucretius, and sing of the wonders of Nature.   But if he ever seriously contemplated such a task, he abandoned it in favour of the rural scenes which were so dear to him.   He was content, as he said, ingloriously to choose the rivers and the woods, where his muse did not blush to dwell.

How largely Virgil drew his poetic inspiration from sylvan scenery is manifested in many passages throughout his poetry from its earliest to its latest parts.   He confessed that as every one is drawn by his own special affections, he above all

---

[1] *Carm.* II. iii. 9.   *See* also I. i. 21 ; xvii. 17-22 ; II. xi. 13.

other things loved the woods. In a few words, often only by a single epithet, he gives to each tree the character that more particularly appealed to his observant eye and his poetic imagination. The very first line of his first *Eclogue* brings us to a wide - spreading beech - tree, and as we accompany him through the various country scenes which he so faithfully and affectionately describes, we are led by blossoming bee-haunted willows to the stream where the marsh-loving alders grow, past scented groves of laurel, copses of hard hazels and prickly briars, and plantations of the silver-grey olive. From the boughs of the tall, richly foliaged elms comes the croon of the turtle-dove. We find ourselves in the shade of thick woods of high chestnuts, broad-leaved æsculus and oak, huge ash - trees, white poplars, and umbrageous plane-trees. We hear the varied music of the winds as they pass through groves that whisper and pines that speak. The ilex rustles in the breeze. We are taken up to the hills to see the barren mountain-ash among the rocks, and higher still to the dark firs that clothe the heights, and the yews that love to grow in the path of the chill north winds.

The poet's eye was caught by the sombre tints of the coniferous trees and their deep shadows, in strong contrast with the lively greenery and mottled shade of the deciduous kinds. He refers to the *nigra abies*, the *picea nigrans*, the *juniperi gravis umbra*, and the *feralis cupressus* with its

frondibus atris. Even the individual plants in
the tapestry of verdure that hangs over rocky
scarps meet with Virgil's appreciative recognition.
Thus he calls special attention to the sprays of
wild vine clustering round the mouth of a cave.
And from the shade of such a cool recess he
could scan the varied vegetation that clothed the
face of a neighbouring cliff.[1] Some of his detailed
sketches of sylvan scenery afford interesting proofs
at once of his accuracy as an observer, his poetic
sympathy, and his skill in felicitous description.
As an instance of this graphic power reference
may be made to his picture of the aspect of a
venerable æsculus tree :—

> " High as his branches rise towards the sky
> So deep his roots descend to Tartarus.
> Thus neither wintry blast, nor storm, nor rain
> Can e'er dislodge him : steadfast he remains,
> While many generations come and go.
> Still bravely doth he spread his giant arms
> To all the winds, and standing in the midst,
> Bears up the burden of his ample shade." [2]

Again, a little sylvan vignette is given in the
Æneid, where, if great events can be rightly
illustrated from small, the gloom of the recital of
the destruction of Troy is for a moment relieved
by a woodland simile. The imagination of the
poet recalls a scene which he had doubtless himself

---

[1] *Eclog.* I. 76 ; V. 6.
[2] *Geor.* II. 291-297. Part of this description is repeated in the
Æneid, where it is applied to the oak (*quercus*) (IV. 445).

witnessed on the flanks of the Apennines, and
he likens the fall of the luckless city to that of

" A mountain-ash, which, perched among the hills,
   The husbandmen are earnest to uproot.
   Their two-faced axes fall with frequent stroke
   Upon the trunk which trembles to the roots ;
   The foliage on its crest begins to nod,
   Until sore weakened by its wounds, the tree
   Gives its last groan and, sundered from the ridge,
   Drags down a mass of ruin in its train." [1]

A woodland scene by night is introduced as a
prelude to the weird journey of Aeneas through
the empty halls of Dis into the underworld :—

" Beneath a fitful moon, through forest glades,
   With scanty light, the traveller seeks his way,
   When Jove has spread a curtain over heaven,
   And night has robbed all colour from the earth." [2]

Familiar with the usual varieties of aspect in
the woods amidst changes of the seasons and
fluctuations of the weather, Virgil had experience
also of the characteristic incidents of sylvan life,
such as the forest fire of which he has introduced
a description among his directions for the planting of vines :—

" Oft careless shepherds let a spark escape,
   Which, lurking first beneath the juicy bark,
   Ere long attacks the trunk, and rushes up
   With a loud roar among the higher leaves ;
   From branch to branch, even to the topmost spray,
   The flames victoriously pursue their course,

---

[1] *Æn.* II. 626-631.   [2] *Id.* VI. 270.

Spreading around till all the grove takes fire,
And clouds of pitch-black smoke ascend to heaven.
The worst befalls when, from above, a storm
Sweeps down upon the wood, for then the wind
Gathers the fire into a fiercer blaze."[1]

While Virgil stands out pre-eminent in his enthusiastic appreciation of the woodlands, the same feeling in varying degree is manifest in the works of the other poets of the golden age. It is strongly displayed by Horace, not merely where he pictures the pleasure of convivial gatherings under trees, but still more where he expresses the charm of the cool woods, far from the crowded city.[2] He well knew the delight "tacitum silvas inter reptare salubres."[3] A goodly list of the trees specially noted by him could be compiled from his poems. He seems to have had a particular regard for the pine. Not only does he single out this tree by name in several of his sylvan landscapes, but, in a graceful ode, he dedicates to Diana the pine that overhung his own country villa :—

"Guardian of the hills and woodlands
    Virgin Goddess, hear this prayer :
Let the pine that shades my dwelling
    Henceforth be thy special care.
Gladly then, as each year closes,
    Shall I in thy praise bestow
Blood of youthful boar, still dreaming
    Of his earliest sidelong blow."[4]

---

[1] *Geor.* II. 303-311.   [2] *Carm.* I. i. 30.
[3] *Epist.* I. iv. 4.   [4] *Carm.* III. xxii.

One of the tenderest passages in the poems of Horace is that in which, addressing his friend Postumus, he alludes to the cypress: "thou must leave this earth, and thy home and thy dear wife; nor of all the trees which thou art planting will any follow its short-lived master save the hateful cypress."[1] This tree from its sombre foliage came to be especially associated with funereal ceremonies, and was planted beside tombs.[2]

When composing the epistle to Tibullus already referred to (p. 84), Horace tries to picture what at that moment his friend would be doing. He thinks of him as perhaps engaged in the occupation of which he himself was so fond—"Sauntering silently through the health-giving woods, and musing on whatever is worthy of the thoughts of a wise and good man." Tibullus in one of his elegies gives his own account of himself—"As for me I am content to live on little, to avoid being always upon long journeys; and shunning the sultry dog-star, to rest under the shadow of a tree by the banks of a passing stream."[3]

---

[1] *Carm.* II. xiv. 21. Horace was here imitating the passage in Lucretius already cited (*antea* p. 56).

[2] Virgil's allusion to the "ferales cupressos" has been already mentioned. Lucan states that the cypress did not make its appearance at plebeian mournings (*Phars.* III. 442). The melancholy associations of this tree have lasted down to our own time. In his list of trees and their uses Spenser includes "the cypresse funerall" (*Faer. Qu.* I. i. 8), and Byron prolongs the same note in his *Giaour* :—

> "The very cypress droops to death—
> Dark tree, still sad when others' grief is fled,
> The only constant mourner o'er the dead."

[3] *Eleg.* I. i. 25-28.

Propertius, too, felt the charm of woodland scenery and moving water. Among his memories of his native Umbria he recalled the lovely Clitumnus winding beneath its over-arching grove, the solitary woods, and the wandering streams which in that region pour down from mossy uplands. And he records his desire that his tomb should not be on one of the great high roads, amid the traffic of the crowd, but that his bones should rest in some remote spot, beneath the branches of a tree, or be buried among the sand-dunes of some unknown shore.[1]

That the woodlands exert an inspiring influence in literary production was affirmed by the younger Pliny in an amusing letter to the historian Tacitus.

"You will laugh," he says, "and well you may, when I tell you that I, Pliny, whom you know so well, have taken three most splendid wild boars. 'What? Pliny!' you enquire. Even I. But that I might not altogether leave off my usual inactivity and love of rest, I sat down beside the nets. There was neither boar-spear nor lance near me, but in their place I had my stilus and writing-tablets. I was thinking and jotting down my thoughts, so that, should I come back with empty hands, at least my note-books would be full. You need not despise this way of studying. It is wonderful how the mind is excited by the activity and movement of the body. And further, the woods on all sides, and the solitude, and the very

[1] *Eleg.* III. x. 25 ; IV. xvi. 28.

silence itself involved in hunting, are great incite-
ments to thought.   Hence when you go to hunt,
let me recommend you to take with you not only
your basket and flask, but also your tablets.   You
will find that Minerva can ramble about the hills
as well as Diana." [1]

[1] *Epist.* I. vi.

CHAPTER VIII

FLOWERS AND FOLIAGE IN ROMAN ART

In all that relates to Art, the debt of Rome to Greece was so overwhelmingly great, and the superiority of the Hellenic sculptors and painters who came to Rome continued for generations to be so incontestible, that for a long time little room was left for the development of a native school. The Romans were not naturally an artistic people, eager to embody in concrete shape their conceptions of the beauty of form and colour that surrounded them in their own country. Acknowledging the pre-eminence of Greek art, they took every opportunity of acquiring examples of it for the adornment of their temples and of their mansions in town and villas in the country. The large number of Greek sculptures, either originals or most frequently copies by Greek hands, which, notwithstanding the revolutions and devastations of centuries, now crowd the public and private galleries of Italy, and the countless works which have found their way from Italy to the collections of all civilised countries afford some indication of the extent of the accumulation of these artistic

L

treasures on Italian soil. Greek artists were
invited to settle in Rome, where they multiplied
copies of Greek masterpieces, and also made statues
and busts of living men. At the end of the
Republic, however, the Hellenic influence was
affected by a movement towards a more dis-
tinctively Roman type of conception and work-
manship. This change is indicated in the sculpture
of the Augustan age, wherein a keen appreciation
is shown of the human body as the embodiment
of strength and dignity, while at the same time
a recognition is manifested of the grace and
delicacy of various forms of vegetation.

But it is not chiefly from sculpture that we
can, in some measure, estimate the extent and
direction of the Roman feeling for Nature as
expressed in works of art. The masterpieces of
painting in the ancient world, whereof Pliny and
others have handed down descriptions, have all
long since perished. The accounts of them that
have reached us, valuable and interesting as they
are for the light which they throw on the history
of figure-painting, are of little aid in enabling us
to trace the rise and progress of the treatment
of landscape, which is what more especially con-
cerns the subject of the present volume. The
only direct evidence now available regarding the
Roman style of delineating natural scenery is
supplied by the fresco wall-paintings and decorations which have fortunately been preserved under
the *débris* of centuries, and which, in their fading

tones, still remain as visible relics of Roman pictorial art towards the close of the Republic and in the first century of the Empire. These precious memorials have been disinterred in the course of excavations in and near Rome, but most abundantly at the buried cities of Campania, where they have been preserved under the volcanic material thrown out by Vesuvius in the memorable eruption of A.D. 79.

Among the wall-paintings which have thus come again to light, no feature is more prominent than the profusion of flowers, leaves, and fruit in the decorations of the rooms and courts. Although much of the vegetation thus depicted has been conventionalised to suit the recurrent festoons and garlands that stretch their graceful curves along the walls, it can easily be recognised that the plants must often have been copied directly from Nature. Their forms and colours, together with the individual characters and mode of growth of each kind, are rendered not only truthfully but even with considerable artistic feeling. In perhaps the most finished example that has been recovered, that of the villa of Livia at Prima Porta, a garden scene is represented with extraordinary detail and fidelity. The drawing and colouring are there so carefully finished that to the various plants their botanical names can generally be assigned. We may not be disposed to rank as noteworthy art this faithful reproduction of vegetable forms and tints; but it must be admitted that the patient and

accurate study of the plants indicates an affection
for them which can hardly be excelled among
modern flower-painters. And it is as witnesses
of this affection, more than for their artistic merit,
that I cite them here. They are further interesting and valuable as they enable us to see what
were the favourite trees, shrubs, and flowers, and
the manner in which they were grown in the
garden of a wealthy horticulturist of ancient Rome.
Other examples of the effective use of floral subjects for wall-decoration may be seen in the House
of Germanicus, on the Palatine Hill, where some
of the rooms are adorned with graceful festoons of
luxuriant flowers, foliage, and fruit.

That the delicate beauty and charm of this
style of mural decoration were much appreciated
during the early decades of the Empire may be
inferred from its occurrence not only in Rome
but in the country. Its prevalence may be
plausibly taken as a further proof of the love of
flowers throughout the whole community. While
the most artistic examples of it have been exhumed
in and near Rome, where the most accomplished
painters, perhaps mostly Greeks, would naturally
fix their headquarters, the taste for floral wall-
painting would soon be transported to the country
villas of the wealthier classes. Pliny the Younger,
who was so typical an example of the cultured
country gentleman of his day, has left on record
that among the numerous embellishments of his
favourite Tuscan home, one of the bedrooms,

which was kept in cool green shade by a plane-tree planted near, had its walls partly covered with slabs of marble and partly with what he thought not less pleasing—a painting of branches with birds perched upon them.[1] A good instance of this mode of decorating the country residence of a rich man was unearthed some years ago at Bosco Reale, not far from Pompeii.

A fashion which was the vogue in Rome and among the rural villas of the landed gentry, was sure to find its way into the smaller country towns. More especially would it be adopted in the coast-towns where well-to-do city-men had houses in which they resided during some part of the year. Pompeii, for example, though only a little Campanian sea-port and walled town, had a population that consisted not merely of sailors, fishermen, and traders.   Wealthy citizens of Rome were fond of the place.   Cicero had a villa there, and a century after his time it was still a favourite seaside resort.   Seneca calls it a famous town,[2] and Tacitus describes it as populous.[3] From this buried city hundreds of pictures have been exhumed and removed to the Museum in Naples, over and above those which have been allowed to remain on the walls of the houses.

This large collection of mural paintings possesses extraordinary interest.   It brings vividly before our

---

[1] *Epist.* V. vi. 22.
[2] *Quaest. Nat.* VI. i. 1 ; *see* also *Epist.* xlix. 1; lxx. 1.
[3] *Ann.* XV. 22.

eyes the domestic decoration in the midst of which cultivated Romans of the first century lived their daily lives. One of the first impressions which it makes on the mind is a realisation of the continued potency of the art of Greece on Italian soil. The figure subjects chosen for delineation are predominantly Greek, and mostly represent well-known incidents in the Hellenic mythology. Some of these subjects, perhaps copied from original Greek paintings, were evidently favourites, for they are found repeated in different houses. But it is not the figures in the pictures so much as the accessories that concern us at present, for it is from these that we can best form an idea of the kind of objects and of scenery that appealed most to the artists of the time and to the owners of the houses who selected subjects for the permanent adornment of their walls. Landscape art, as we now understand it, can hardly be said to have any place in these paintings, for a knowledge of perspective was wanting. The background of the large figure-pictures is for the most part sketched in so vaguely and roughly as to suggest that the main object of the artists was to tone down the whiteness of the stuccoed walls and to set off the forms and colours of the human or divine personages, rather than to trace any very definite surroundings. But in many smaller paintings or vignettes, introduced to fill panel-like spaces in the scheme of mural decoration, distinct landscapes are portrayed, which supply illustrations of the kind of scenery that

seems to have been most appreciated at the time
of the painting of the walls.   These landscapes,
evidently Italian and probably Campanian, are for
the most part shore-scenes.   They will be further
noticed in chapter xiv.

Passing to the floral decoration of the Pompeian
houses we are at once struck by its profusion.
At every turn we meet with elegant scrolls of
leaves of acanthus, plane, ivy, or vine with clusters
of grapes and delicate tendrils intertwined among
the foliage, or festoons of the leaves of the olive or
myrtle, or garlands of wild thyme in bloom, or
wreaths of roses with buds peeping out from
between them, while various kinds of fruit are
often intermingled with the leaves and flowers.
When first uncovered to the air, after their
seclusion of so many centuries, the colours
appear as fresh as when they came from the
painter's hands, and even after years of exposure
on the walls or in the Museum, some of them
retain enough of their vividness to enable us
to realise the remarkable brightness with which
they must have lit up the somewhat darkened
rooms of which they formed the chief adornment.   The noteworthy deftness with which the
artist has caught the varying tints of the foliage
of the same plant can still be recognised, as where
he has here and there, on the sprays of the vine,
introduced a fading yellow leaf amid the full green
of the fresher foliage.   Besides their richness in
plant-life, many of the floral decorations are

enlivened with little gaily-coloured birds perched among the leaves.

It is worthy of remark that this kind of decoration is not confined to the larger houses in Pompeii, which no doubt were tenanted by the richer members of the community. Some even of the smaller dwellings are similarly adorned, where the inmates were probably by no means wealthy. We may thence infer that the fashion for floral decoration had become widespread through the different classes of society before the last quarter of the first century.

Not less conspicuously did the artistic treatment of vegetation for decorative purposes find expression in sculpture during the Augustan period. The truthfulness of detail and the charming grace with which leaves, blossoms, fruit, and branches are carved on the Ara Pacis and other monuments of that time have called forth the most unstinted praise from modern artists. Exquisitely modelled spirals, bearing leaves and blooms of acanthus, wind across the surface of the marble, ending in rosettes or delicate blossoms of different flowers, and throwing off slender curling tendrils. There are likewise abundant fruits of various kinds, symbolic of the rich fertility of that " magna parens frugum, Saturnia tellus." Amidst this luxuriant plant-growth further sympathy with living Nature is shown in the many forms of animal life which are introduced. Insects hover among the leaves, birds are perched on the branches, lizards and snakes creep among the flowers. Not only in sculpture but also in the singularly graceful stucco-reliefs that adorn interior walls and ceilings and even some of the vaulted tombs of the same period, the love of floral decoration may be seen, expressed with the same remarkable taste and skill.

It has been well remarked by Mrs Strong that while

"plants appear in Greek art only to be conventionalised into architectural forms; in Roman art the love of natural form conquers the stylistic tendency. To those who are familiar with the conventional forms of the lotus in Egyptian art or of the acanthus in Greek art, it is almost a surprise that even the political Imperial plants, the symbolic laurel, the oak, and the olive, were never conventionalised, but showered their shapely leaves and fruit over every space artistically available."[1]

[1] "Roman Sculpture from Augustus to Constantine," 1907, p. 76.

CHAPTER IX

THE ANIMAL WORLD IN ROMAN LIFE

In an enquiry into the relation in which the Romans of the Augustan age stood towards the world of animated nature, we are met at the outset by the appalling spectacles of the Circus and the Amphitheatre. If the men and women of that time could watch and applaud the butchery of human beings and of noble beasts of the forest, what amount of sympathy and affection, it may be asked, can they be supposed to have had for the animal world, whether wild or domesticated? The modern mind, which for centuries has grown accustomed to respect the sanctity of human life, and is slowly learning to detest and to punish cruelty to animals, finds it hard to account for the long-continued popularity and wide prevalence of gladiatorial shows and combats with wild beasts among a people like the Romans, and perhaps still harder to explain the absence of any outspoken condemnation of these horrors in the writings of the cultivated men of successive generations. The inference has not unnaturally been drawn that,

170

with all their good qualities, the Romans must have been essentially a cruel and bloodthirsty race.

It must indeed be sorrowfully admitted that, on this side, their moral standard was extraordinarily low. The existence of such atrocities among them, the universal popularity of these debasing shows, and the continued toleration of them for nearly seven hundred years, fill a black page in the history of the Republic and the Empire. But when this admission is made to the fullest extent, there are certain considerations which, while they cannot be pleaded in extenuation of the practices, help us in some degree to understand how the evils arose and how it came about that they lasted so long and enjoyed such wide prevalence and popularity. Originally, and for many years, the gladiators were taken from the ranks of criminals, prisoners of war, and slaves. The lives of such men were not by Roman citizens regarded as of much account. Some of them certainly deserved the punishment of death, and it would in those days seem immaterial by what means the punishment was inflicted. The accomplishment of the execution in the amphitheatre would be thought to have the advantage of gratifying a large assemblage of onlookers. Prisoners of war who had not been sold as slaves were sometimes got rid of by being made to fight in the arena, and thus again the populace was pleased. As for slaves, they were

mere chattels who had no rights, and whose death
was of little moment, except where their services
were of value to their owners.   When such were
the sources whence the amphitheatre was supplied
with combatants it can be partly understood why
a Roman audience had no compunction in witnessing the spectacles.[1]

It must also be remembered that these
spectacles, at least in Rome, were given on a
scale of extraordinary magnificence.   Everything
was done, alike by magistrates and generals during
the Republic, and by the heads of the State under
the Empire, with all the resources of art, to
enhance their splendour and attractiveness.   The
mere sight of so many thousand spectators as
could be assembled within the amphitheatre,
especially within the Flavian building in Rome,
must have been one of the most impressive sights
that human eyes could behold.   When pairs
of trained gladiators encountered each other in
mortal combat, and the vanquished appealed to
the audience for their fate ; when the tragedies of
a battlefield were reproduced by numerous bands

[1] Strabo tells an anecdote which illustrates how the Romans
combined capital punishment with the excitement of the arena.
When he was in Rome, a certain Selurus, a captain of robbers, who
was known as the "Son of Aetna," from having made his headquarters
on the mountain, had been caught and sent up to the capital.   He was
taken to the arena and set upon a platform made to represent Aetna,
which, being suddenly unfastened and collapsing, the robber fell among
a company of wild beasts, assembled for the occasion.   Strabo relates
that he was present himself and saw the man torn to pieces by the
animals.   All this had been preceded by a contest of gladiators.   The
geographer makes no comment on what he saw (*Geog.* VI. ii. 7).

of combatants on the arena which was drenched
with gore and covered with wounded and dying;
when men were pitted against the fiercest beasts
of prey and had to fight for their lives; or when
hundreds of wild animals, gathered with infinite
labour and expense from distant countries, were
mustered in the amphitheatre and made to attack
each other, or were slaughtered with spear and
sword, the tense excitement of the spectators
must have been something to which there has
been no equal since those days.

The extraordinary fascination of these scenes,
and its influence even on young and cultivated
minds, are strikingly illustrated by the instance
recorded by St Augustine, when one of his friends
and fellow-students, who had always hated and
avoided the arena, was carried thither against his
will by some of his companions. Firmly closing
his eyes, the youth determined to be no witness
of the performances. But at some incident in
the fighting, which drew forth vast applause from
the audience, he opened his eyes. Instantly he
was overcome by what he saw. Like one of the
crowd, he gazed and shouted, and became as
excited as those around him. Thereafter he
returned again and again to the amphitheatre, and
even brought others to share in the excitement.[1]
It can hardly therefore be matter for surprise
that a callous populace, eager for amusement
and accustomed from childhood to the scenes

[1] *Confess.* VI. vii.

of the arena, should long have clung to such spectacles.

But the question may be asked: Is it conceivable that no voices were raised against these orgies of blood? Are we to believe that even among the educated and thoughtful part of the community no protest was made against such cruel and debasing exhibitions? The Latin literature which has survived is only a portion of what originally existed, and in that portion which has perished there may have been here and there a condemnation of these practices. But in the part that remains to us, though the gladiatorial combats and the wild beast hunts (*venationes*) are frequently alluded to, we search in vain for any vigorous denunciation of the exhibitions in the arena, or even the indication of a disposition publicly to disapprove of them and to plead for their abolition. They are treated as matters for current gossip in society; the relative merits of different gladiators are canvassed, much in the same way as race-horses are among us before the Derby; or the whole subject is put aside, as if too trivial for the attention of serious men. As an illustration of the light-hearted way in which these matters could be treated even by so great and humane a man as Cicero, let me cite a passage from one of his letters written at Rome in the month of October, B.C. 55, to M. Marius, in which he refers to his own presence at the great games given by Pompey in the autumn of that year.

" Why should I suppose you to care about missing the athletes, since you disdained the gladiators? in which even Pompey himself confesses that he has lost his time and his trouble.   There remain the two wild-beast hunts, lasting five days: magnificent—nobody denies it.   And yet what pleasure can it be to a man of refinement, when either a weak man is torn by an extremely powerful animal, or a splendid animal is transfixed by a hunting-spear?   Things which, after all, if worth seeing, you have often seen before; nor did I, who was present at the games, see anything the least new. The last day was that of the elephants, on which there was a great deal of astonishment on the part of the vulgar crowd, but no pleasure whatever. Nay, there was even a certain feeling of compassion aroused by it, and a kind of belief created that that animal has something in common with mankind." [1]

The subject is also referred to in the Tusculan Disputations where Cicero thus expresses himself:

[1] *Ad Fam.* VII. i. (Mr Shuckburgh's translation).   At these great *venationes*, given by Pompey in order to regain his influence with the people, 500 African lions are said to have been killed, while or 18 elephants most were slaughtered by Gaetulian huntsmen.   Pliny gives a more serious account of the disposition of the crowd at the sight of the wounded and dying elephants, for he relates that when the animals, finding that they could not escape by flight from the deadly swords of the huntsmen, seemed by indescribable gestures to implore the pity of the onlookers, so great was the compassion of the people that, forgetting the imperator and the munificence of the entertainment which he had prepared in their honour, they in tears rose up as a body and heaped curses on Pompey, for which he was not long in paying the penalty (*Hist. Nat.* VIII. vii.)   That there could be sometimes a limit even to the popular delight in the gladiatorial bloodshedding seems to be indicated by the remark of Tacitus that Drusus, who presided at an exhibition of gladiators given in honour of Germanicus, displayed such pleasure in blood, even though it was only that of slaves, as to displease the populace (*Ann.* 1. 76).

" By some the exhibition of gladiators is thought to be a cruel and inhuman spectacle, and I do not know whether it is so, as now conducted. But when criminals used to fight with real swords there could not be a more effective training for the eye, though perhaps there might be many for the ear, in the enduring of pain and death."[1]

This passage is of interest as an indication of the existence of a feeling against gladiatorial shows at the time of the publication of the philosopher's treatise (B.C. 44). But the feeling was one in which he does not seem to have shared. Rather more than a century after Cicero's time the view of a humane and cultured member of Society was expressed by the younger Pliny, who wrote as follows to a friend that had lately lost his wife and had followed an ancient usage in offering to her memory a gladiatorial exhibition in the amphitheatre of Verona :—

" You did well in promising a gladiatorial show to our friends in Verona, by whom you have long been loved, respected, and honoured. It was from that city that you received your dear and admirable wife, to whose memory some monument or spectacle was due ; and this which you chose was above all appropriate from its funereal character. Besides, the request to you was made by such a general consent that to decline it would have seemed to show not constancy but rather unfriendliness. Moreover, you granted the favour as readily as you have carried it out liberally, for even in such

[1] *Tusc.* II. xvii. 41.

matters a great mind may display itself. I wish
that the panthers, of which you had purchased a
large number, had arrived by the appointed day, but
though they were delayed by bad weather, you were
equally deserving of thanks, since it was not your
fault that you exhibited less than you intended."[1]

The same writer, however, records that he was
present at a Council held by the Emperor Trajan
when a case came up for consideration as to
whether certain gymnastic games (*gymnicus agon*)
at Vienne on the Rhone, which the Triumvir had
abolished, should be revived. When the assessors
were asked for their opinions Junius Mauricus
declared against the re-establishment, and added:
" I wish the games could be abolished in Rome also."
Besides athletic contests and racing at gymnastic
exhibitions, gladiatorial combats were sometimes
introduced. Pliny adds that it was decided to
suppress the games in question

" which had corrupted the morals of the Viennese,
as ours at Rome have depraved the morals of all
men. For the vices of the Viennese remain with
themselves, but ours are spread far and wide. It
is with the State as with our bodies; the most
dangerous disease is one that spreads from the
head."[2]

The only Roman writer within the historical
period with which we are here concerned, who, so
far as I am aware, has been quoted as one that
declared his abhorrence and condemnation of the
performances in the amphitheatre is the philosopher

[1] *Epist.* VI. xxxiv.   [2] *Id.* IV. xxii.

Seneca. It would appear that in his earlier years
he had no dislike of these exhibitions, for in his
consolatory discourse to his mother Helvia, written
during his exile in Corsica, he speaks without
disapprobation of attendance on games and gladiatorial shows as one of the accepted means of
diverting the mind from grief.[1] But later in life
he came to look on these exhibitions with detesta-
tion. His trenchant denunciation of them is to
be found in one of the letters, or rather moral
essays, which he addressed to his friend and
pupil Lucilius. He there, in his usual somewhat
rhetorical style, states his opinion that what above
all should be avoided in this life is the crowd
(*turba*).

" Assuredly," he says, "nothing is so destructive
to good morals as to sit through a public spectacle,
for the evil creeps in all the more easily on account
of the pleasure that attends it. Let me tell you
that I return more avaricious, more luxurious, nay,
even crueller and more inhuman, because I have
been among men. By chance I dropped in to the
mid-day performance at the amphitheatre, expecting some amusement as a relief to one's eyes from
the sight of human blood. But on the contrary,
the fighting which before had been merciful, was
now sheer murder. In the morning men were
thrown to the lions and bears, at mid-day to
the spectators."

He gives some revolting details as to what he
saw. Even during the intervals the survivors had

[1] *Dial.* XII. xvii. 1.

their throats cut, "lest nothing should be going on." He supposes himself to be remonstrating with one of the onlookers as to the proceedings, who remarked in their justification that one of the victims had been guilty of murder.

"What then," exclaims the philosopher, "because he has been guilty of murder does he deserve to suffer thus? And you, miserable wretch, what have you deserved that you look on at it all?"[1]

Seneca expresses here the sentiments of the modern world. But if it be asked what influence his condemnation of the arena had upon the world of his day, we have to admit that his fervid denunciation was probably written in his old age, that it was not a manifesto to the Roman public to reform its ways, but together with many other praiseworthy sentiments was enshrined in his studied correspondence with a friend.[2] It must be

[1] *Epist.* I. vii.

[2] It is difficult to decide at what period of Seneca's life this letter was written. It has been ascribed to his latest years, and this ascription is probably correct. But if one sentence in the letter has been rightly regarded as containing a reference to Nero, an earlier date might be claimed. The philosopher, supposing himself to be addressing the crowd in the amphitheatre, exclaims, "Give thanks to the immortal gods that he whom you are teaching to be cruel cannot learn to be so." It is difficult to believe that even Seneca could in his last years carry flattery so far as to write thus of Nero. And yet when we remember that in his *Quaestiones Naturales,* in which he lectured Lucilius on the evils of flattery, he himself committed some signal instances of the vice in his allusions to the Emperor, we must confess that an argument as to the date of any of his writings can hardly be based on his flattery of Nero. (*Quaest. Nat.* IV. pref., and I. v. ; VI. viii. ; VII. xvii., xxi. This treatise was probably his latest work.)

In another letter to Lucilius which comes later in his correspondence,

remembered that he had been for a number of years one of the two powerful ministers of Nero, having the administration of the Empire largely in their hands, and that in course of time he amassed a colossal fortune, so as to be styled by the satirist "praedives." Yet with all this political power and vast wealth, there is no evidence that he ever stirred a finger to lessen the evils which he denounced to Lucilius. That he could have succeeded in effecting any reformation of an institution so long established and so overwhelmingly popular is not probable, but it would have been to his honour had he made the attempt, or at least had he proclaimed to the world how keenly he resented the horrors of the arena.

If, then, the Romans, as a people, had so little conception of the sanctity of human life, and so little remorse at the infliction of needless suffering and death upon the noblest animals as well as upon their fellow-men, our modern instincts might tempt us to the conclusion that this people was utterly destitute of any trace of kindliness of nature. But the history of mankind assures

and may belong to a subsequent date, the philosopher again alludes to the subject of the amphitheatre. He was at that time in Naples, where for some days he had been attending the disputations in a philosopher's school. Referring to this return to the pursuits of his youth he playfully remarks that "though an old man, he will go to the theatre and be carried to the circus, while no pair of gladiators will fight it out without having him as a spectator" (*Epist.* LXXVI. 2). His words are not to be interpreted as conveying his real intentions, but they have an interest as indicative of one of the favourite pursuits of the youth of Seneca's time.

us that such an inference would be unwarranted. Communities and individuals that have been marked by ruthless cruelty, are well known to have also had their affectionate side both for man and for animals. The fashionable matrons who took such keen pleasure in the combats of the arena were often kind-hearted and careful mothers to their children. Many of them who sat as interested spectators through prolonged scenes of carnage and death would shed tears over the illness of some favourite bird or dog. Among the male spectators too, there were many who in private life were as humane and considerate as any cultivated gentlemen of the present day. So hard is it for us to realise how centuries of familiarity with some form of cruelty can deaden the mind to the perception of its inhumanity, while at the same time the heart may remain in other directions responsive and affectionate.

We may be sure, therefore, that in every generation at Rome, there were tender-hearted members of the community who possessed and cultivated the love of animals. It may indeed seem strange that there is in Latin literature more evidence perhaps of sympathy with the brute creation than with mankind at large, outside the circles of kinship and friendship. Whether or not as a revulsion from the searing influence of the amphitheatre on the human conscience, the Roman poets evince a sympathy with bird and beast which is as genuine and spontaneous as can be found in any literature, and which doubtless was shared by multitudes of their fellow-countrymen.[1]

By none of the Latin writers, among the closing decades of the Republic and the first century of the Empire, does the love of animals appear to have been more sincerely felt than it was by Lucretius. His capacious mind and warm heart welcomed within their embrace the whole animal world, domesticated and wild—

"the race of men, and the dumb scaly brood that swims the deep, the joyous herds and wild beasts, and the various birds that haunt the delightful watering-places by the banks of rivers and springs and meres, with those that people the woods and flit far away."[2]

Out of all this ample domain of living creatures the poet would seem to have chosen dogs as worthy of his more special affection. He refers to them again and again in his poem, and always with some kindly epithet to mark his personal regard for them. His close observation of the ways of animals, and his affectionate recognition of the

---

[1] Francis Bacon acutely remarks: "The inclination to goodness is implanted deeply in the nature of man; insomuch, that if it issue not towards men, it will take unto other living creatures; as it is seen in the Turks, a cruel people, who nevertheless are kind to beasts, and give alms to dogs and birds; insomuch as Busbechius reporteth, a Christian boy in Constantinople had like to have been stoned for gagging in a waggishness a long-billed fowl" ("Essays," No. XIII., On Goodness).

[2] De Rer. Nat. II. 342-346.

habits of dogs in particular, are well illustrated in the following quotation.

"When huge Molossian hounds are angry and begin to snarl, showing their hard teeth between their large soft lips, they threaten in a far different tone than when pleased they bark and fill all the place with their noise; and when they try gently to lick their cubs with their tongue, and toss them about with their paws, seeking, as it were, to bite them and actually to swallow them, they fondle them with a growl very different from that which they utter when, left alone in the house, they bark gently, or when they piteously whine and cringe to escape a beating."[1]

The races of wild animals, Lucretius says, have been furnished by Nature with the means of self-preservation. The lion has its bravery, the fox its cunning, the stag its swiftness.

"But the lightly-sleeping dog with its faithful heart, the whole race of the beasts of burden, the fleece-bearing flocks, and all the breeds of horned cattle are placed under the tutelage of man."[2]

Every lover of dogs to-day will recognise the truth of the following picturesque lines :

"Often hunting-dogs, in the midst of their soft sleep will suddenly toss their legs, utter cries, and keep snuffing the air with their nostrils, as if they were following the tracks of game which they had found; and even when awakened, they often follow the empty visions of stags, as if they saw them taking to flight, until, shaking

---

[1] *De Rer. Nat.* V. 1063-1072.   [2] *Id.* V. 864.

off their phantasy, they come to themselves again."[1]

The scent of dogs is noted by Lucretius as one of their faculties of more particular interest and value to man, and he quotes it as an illustration of how in his opinion the investigation of Nature should be pursued :

" As dogs in roaming over mountains very often scent out there the lairs of game hidden under the greenery, when once they have set foot on sure tracks, so you, Memmius, will be able to see one thing after another, penetrate into all the lurking places, and thence draw forth the truth."[2]

Perhaps the reference which most forcibly brings before us the affectionate regard of Lucretius for these animals is to be found in his description of the ghastly horrors of the plague at Athens. Following the narrative of Thucydides, he mentions the dogs, but brings them into special prominence, and characteristically does not forget to add an allusion to their faithful nature :—

" Many inhabitants, stricken with the malady, were

---

[1] *De Rer. Nat.* IV. 991. Tennyson in his *Lucretius* has not omitted to notice this characteristic observation of the poet :

> "As the dog
> With inward yelp and restless forefoot plies
> His function of the woodland."

Scott, another keen lover of dogs, noted this canine habit as a feature that added to the vividness of his picture of life in Branksome Hall :—

> "The staghounds, weary with the chase,
> Lay stretched upon the rushy floor,
> And urged, in dreams, the forest race
> From Teviot-stone to Eskdale-moor.
> —*Lay of the Last Minstrel*, I. ii.

[2] *De Rer. Nat.* I. 404.

dying. Foremost were the faithful dogs that gave up their lives with difficulty, and their bodies lay strewn in all the streets, for the virulence of the disease forced the life from their bodies." [1]

From the variety of types of dogs which the Romas bred, some for the chase, others for protecting the flocks and herds, especially on the high hill-pastures, and some as household pets, the dog evidently held a favoured place among their domesticated animals. [2] Its fidelity, to which Lucretius so often alludes, was widely recognised as one of its most admirable qualities and was frequently commemorated in art. Thus among the wall-frescoes of Pompeii the dog is often introduced into the figure subjects. In one of the paintings of Mars and Venus, seated at the foot of a rugged rock, with trees in the distance, their attendant dog lies beside them. In another of these pictures, where Narcissus is represented resting on a rock beside a calm pool and looking at his reflection on the surface of the water, while the background shows various conventionalised types of trees, his dog is his only companion. Another subject is that of Venus with the dying Adonis on her knees. She looks on him in an agony of grief, while Cupid

---

[1] *De Rer. Nat.* VI. 1222.

[2] Varro gives an account of various kinds of dogs (*De Re Rust.* I. xxi. ; II. ix. ; *also* Pliny, *Hist. Nat.* VIII. lxi.-lxiii.). Martial's epigram on the little pet dog of his friend Publius affords good evidence of the mutual affection between master and animal that could be met with in the Roman society of his day (*Epig.* I. cix.).

weeps, and a third mourner, as sincere as the other two, lies in front of the group in the shape of his favourite dog.   In a painting of Diana and Endymion, the goddess appears in the air floating towards the sleeping youth, but his trusty dog, which has been watching by his side, descries her and barks at her furiously, to warn and protect him.   It will be remembered, too, how frequently the dog, as a symbol of fidelity has been sculptured on ancient tombs.

The same kindly feeling with which dogs were regarded was extended to other domestic animals, and even to some with which most men do not come into personal contact.   Here again the muse of Lucretius shows the tenderness of his sympathy, as where he pictures the distress of a cow that has been deprived of her young calf :—

" Often before the fair shrines of the gods a calf has fallen in sacrifice at the incense-bearing altars, spirting from its breast a warm stream of blood. But the bereaved mother, as she wanders over the green glades, recognises the prints left on the ground by the cloven hoofs, scanning all places, if she can but catch sight of her lost youngling ; and when she halts, she fills the leafy grove with her plaints.   Many a time she returns to the stall, pierced to the heart with a yearning for her calf, nor can the tender willows, and the grass freshened with dew, and the brimming streams divert her thoughts, or suddenly turn aside her care ; nor can other calves among the gladsome pastures distract her mind or lighten her sorrow ; so long does she seek for something which she knows and which is her own." [1]

In the poetry of Virgil the love of the whole world of animated nature finds even fuller and more frequent expression than in that of his great predecessor. Bird, beast, and insect were scanned by his closely observant eyes, with all the sympathy of his gentle and kindly heart. He makes us feel how keenly he realised that each living creature is a sentient being, with habits and instincts worthy of our attention, and subject to sufferings that appeal to our compassion. As an example of how these sufferings could call forth his pity, reference may be made to his account of the effects of a plague that had befallen Italy in autumn. Every kind of cattle and wild beast had died, and the waters and pastures were tainted with infection. The poet gives an example of how suddenly and fatally the disease struck down the animals, even in the midst of their work :—

> " Lo ! at the toilsome plough the reeking bull
> Drops down ; spirts from his mouth a mingled stream
> Of blood and foam : then heaves his latest groan.
> Sadly the ploughman now unyokes the steer
> That mourns his brother's fate, leaving the plough
> Fixed in mid-furrow, and the work half-done.
> No shade of deepest grove, nor pasture soft
> Can move him now ; nor yet the stream that rolls,
> Clearer than amber, o'er its rocky bed
> To seek the plain. His deep flanks are relaxed,

---

[1] *De Rer. Nat.* II. 352-366.

> While stupor steals into his leaden eyes,
> And heavily his neck sinks to the ground.
> What now avails his service and his toil?
> What, to have oft upturned the heavy glebe?
> And yet no Massic grape nor plenteous feasts
> E'er harmed these creatures : leaves and simple grass
> Are all their fare ; their cups the limpid spring
> And hurrying streams ; nor is their healthful sleep
> Disturbed by care." [1]

With the various animals employed on a farm Virgil would make full acquaintance in his youth, and his references to them have the vividness of personal reminiscence. Among them the horse meets with due appreciation in his verse. In enumerating for the farmer's guidance the good points of the animal, he alludes to its instinct for military sounds, and he gives as one of the marks of an excellent steed that "should he hear the distant sound of arms he cannot stand still; he pricks up his ears, his limbs quiver, and he rolls the fire from his nostrils." [2] The thought of the horse brings the animal's galloping movement before the poet's mind, and he breaks at once into dactylic hexameters, as in the famous line—

" Quadrupedante putrem sonitu quatit ungula campum." [3]

The contests of rival bulls were probably familiar enough on the pastures around the Mincius. Virgil has sketched them with his usual picturesque touch, and sometimes not without a trace of sympathy for the vanquished hero, whom he follows into his

---

[1] *Geor.* III. 515-530.   [2] *Id.* III. 83-85.
[3] *Æn.* VIII. 596 ; *also* VI. 614, 615.

retirement, until the animal can renew the contest
and obtain the mastery of the field.[1] Such incidents
supplied similes, at one time to illustrate the duels
between great chiefs on the field of battle,[2] at
another to represent the fury of a mountainous
wave as it rushes against the shore.[3]

Of all wild creatures, birds have secured the
surest place in the affections of the mass of mankind
in every age and country. Their annual pairing
and nesting, their rearing of their fledgelings, their
endlessly diverse forms and colours, their marvellous
variety of notes, their regular appearances and dis-
appearances with the succession of the seasons, and
the familiarity of so many of them with man, have
given them a fascination all their own. Their
praises have been sung in the literature of all
lands. In that of Rome they received much
appreciation, though of a more restrained kind
than that which has been so enthusiastically
bestowed upon them by our own bards. The
Latin poets, like those of modern days, have
especially associated birds with spring, and in
their descriptions of that season, how brief
soever, the voices of birds are seldom absent.
Virgil, with his abounding affection for living
things and his keen poetical instinct, evidently
delighted to watch the habits of birds which
he has so graphically depicted. The *Eclogues*
and *Georgics* are naturally full of references to

---

[1] *Geor.* III. 220-236.

[2] *Æn.* XII. 715. [3] *Geor.* III. 237.

birds and their ways, but even in the *Æneid* the poet's interest in these subjects has supplied him with some of the similes used in that epic. His most varied pictures of bird - life are to be found in the first *Georgic*, where, in considerable detail and with great charm of language, he gives the portents of the weather which popular observation had drawn from the movements of birds.

The Greeks, who were active sailors and traders, and therefore constrained to watch the signs of the sky, had in the course of centuries accumulated a considerable store of weather-lore, drawn partly from inanimate nature and partly from the movements of animals, especially of birds. This popular meteorology was made use of by the philosophers, Aristotle and Theophrastus in their treatises, and by Aratus in his poem on the *Diosemeia*. This latter work had been turned into Latin verse by no less a literary man than Cicero. Hence in Virgil's time a good deal of published information on the subject was ready to his hand, and of this he largely availed himself, imitating or quoting freely from Aratus.[1]

---

[1] With reference to Virgil's indebtedness to Aratus, the opinion of Mr Warde Fowler is of great value as that of one who is entitled to speak both as a scholar and a naturalist. "Let any one," he says, "compare the translations of Aratus by other Roman hands, by Cicero, Festus, and Germanicus, with Virgil's first *Georgic*, and he will not fail to mark the difference between the mere translator and the poet who breathes into the work of his predecessors a new life and an immortal one" ("A Year with the Birds," chap. vii. on the birds of Virgil).

The subject is introduced in the first *Georgic* with the following brief prelude :—

" That we might learn from certain signs to guard
   Against the coming heat or cold or rain,
   The Father has himself ordained for us
   What portents should the moon give month by month ;
   What sign should bode the sinking of a gale ;
   What oft-repeated signal should the farmer warn
   To keep his cattle nearer to their stalls." [1]

The poet then proceeds to enumerate the various portents which were popularly accepted in his time as indications of coming weather. We shall here deal only with those taken from the habits of animals, leaving the meteorological signs to be considered in the next chapter.

By far the most numerous presages were those supplied by birds, both for fine and bad weather. At the approach of a gale, we are told

" Back from mid-ocean swiftly fly the gulls,
   And raise a clamour as they near the strand.
   The sea-coots sport on shore ; the heron, too,
   Forsakes his marsh to soar above the clouds." [2]

The coming of rain is heralded by noteworthy bird-signs :—

" The cranes above the misty valleys soar ;
   The twittering swallow skims around its mere ;
   Quitting their feeding-ground in dense array,
   The rooks fly off with din of rustling wings.
   And now the many sea-fowl and the birds
   That search Caÿster's pools by Asian meads
   Delight to splash their shoulders with the spray,

---

[1] *Geor.* I. 351-355.   [2] *Id.* I. 361-364.

Now diving down, now running to the waves,
Full of the wanton pleasure of the bath.
The villain raven calls aloud for rain
As by himself he stalks along the sand." [1]

Sunshine and clear weather have likewise their feathered prophets—

" No more the halcyons, loved of Thetis, stand
   Sunning their outspread wings upon the shore ;
   The owl on roof-top views the setting sun,
   And aimlessly repeats his nightly song.
   High in the limpid air Nisus [2] appears
   And Scylla, punished for that purple hair ;
   Where'er she cuts the ether with her wings,
   Her foe fierce Nisus, whirring through the breeze,
   Pursues ; where Nisus mounts into the breeze
   She swiftly cuts the ether with her wings.
   Then twice or thrice the rooks, from narrowed throats,
   Repeat their liquid cries, and often perched
   Upon their lofty roosts among the leaves,
   Most gleeful over some unwonted joy,
   Caw to each other, pleased that now at last
   The rain has ceased, and that they see again
   Their little brood, and nests to them so dear.
   I claim not that to birds the gods have given
   Reason or foresight into destiny :
   But that when weather and the fitful sky
   Change mood, when dense grows rare, and rare turns dense,
   The minds of birds are moved in sympathy :
   And hence they make such concert in the fields,
   The herds rejoice, and rooks exultant caw." [3]

---

[1] *Geor.* I. 374-389.

[2] Legend represents Nisus, King of Megara, as having purple hair, on which his life depended. His daughter Scylla cut this off. On his death he was changed into an eagle, while she was transformed into the bird called Ciris.

[3] *Geor.* I. 398-423. Some of these popular signs are still current among country - folk in many lands. They were cleverly em-

The presages of weather afforded by birds are also alluded to by Horace, who urged his friend Aelius Lamia to get in his wood dry while this was possible, for on the morrow, unless his augur, the old raven, was mistaken, an easterly gale was approaching that would strew the groves with leaves and the shores with useless seaweed.[1]

The autumn migrations of birds were noted by Virgil and referred to by him in simile. When he depicts the crowd of departed spirits that rushed towards Charon by the waves of Tartarian Acheron he represents them to be numerous

> "As leaves that fall when the first autumn chill
>   Touches the woods, or as the birds that flock
>   From the deep sea to shore, when winter comes
>   And drives them far away to sunnier lands."[2]

The most familiar birds, more especially those that build their nests near the dwellings of man, awakened kindly feelings among the poets. In the *Eclogues* and *Georgics* these feelings find frequent expression. Above the hum of bees we hear the crooning of the wood-pigeon, and the

---

bodied in verse by Dr Jenner from whose lines those that refer to birds may be here quoted.

> "Loud quack the ducks, the sea-fowl cry,
>   The distant hills are looking nigh,
>   Low o'er the grass the swallow wings
>   The cricket too, how sharp he sings !
>   The sky is green, the air is still,
>   The mellow blackbird's voice is shrill.
>   Behold the rooks, how odd their flight !
>   They imitate the gliding kite,
>   And seem precipitate to fall
>   As if they felt the piercing ball."

[1] *Carm.* III. xvii. 9.   [2] *Æn.* VI. 309-312.

N

murmur of the turtle-dove. . The nightingale
receives a sympathetic mention, as

> "Grieving beneath the poplar's shade, she mourns
> Her stolen brood, seen by some callous swain
> Who tore her fledglings from the nest : she weeps
> The livelong night, and sitting on a branch,
> Renews her melancholy song that fills
> The whole wide woodland with her sad complaints." [1]

To this quotation, as a further proof of the
poet's keen sympathy with the sorrows and
sufferings of the brute creation, may be added
another passage which seems to be reminiscent
of some scene of agricultural improvement which
he had himself regretfully watched in his younger
days, when

> "A wrathful husbandman has cleared the wood,
> Levelling the groves that stood for many years,
> Uptearing by the roots the trees that bore
> Full many an ancient nest ; the hapless birds
> Driven from their fallen homes take to the sky;
> Now a rough plain lies trim beneath the plough." [2]

In the *Æneid*, birds have supplied a number
of similes, in some of which the details of bird-
movement are singularly vivid. Take, for example,
this picture of a rock-dove :—

"Suddenly startled from her cave, where within
the shady rock are her home and dear nestlings,
she flies off and makes for the fields, in her fright
loudly clapping her wings as she escapes from her
abode; but soon, gliding through the still air, she

---

[1] *Geor.* IV. 511-515.   Cf. *Odyssey* XIX. 518.
[2] *Geor.* II. 207-211.

skims along on her liquid way, nor ever moves her swift wings."[1]

Virgil must have attentively watched this bird ere he could have given so accurate a description of the contrast between its frightened and fluttering course, when first aroused from its shady covert among the rocks, and the later floating movement when, freed from danger and hardly waving a wing, it makes for some place of rest until the disturbance is past and the nest can be revisited. Another charming bird-simile occurs in the twelfth Book where the warrior-maid Juturna, as she raced to and fro among the host, is compared to

"a black swallow that flits about in the great mansion of some rich lord, and as she speeds on her wings through his lofty courts, picks up little crumbs of food for her chattering nestlings, and twitters now in the empty arcades and now around the ponds."[2]

The owl is referred to more than once in the *Æneid*. Thus the Fury sent down by Jove to confront Juturna is said to have shrunk into "the shape of the little bird that oft at night, sitting on tombs or lonely roofs, sings in the dark its late and lamentable ditty."[3] An incident which heightens the weirdness of the scene in the palace

---

[1] *Æn.* V. 213-217. It is impossible to convey in a translation the imitative music of the last line—

"Radit iter liquidum, celeris neque commovet alas."

[2] *Id.* XII. 437-477.   [3] *Id.* XII. 862-864.

of the disconsolate Dido is added when through the darkness of the night the only sound that breaks the silence is the frequent sepulchral song of the owl on the house-top, with its long-drawn melancholy notes.[1]

Among birds of prey the hawk appears in the *Æneid*, swooping from a lofty cliff, overtaking in the air a dove which it tears to pieces, while the blood and feathers fall earthward from aloft.[2] The eagle supplied the poet with some apposite comparisons. Thus Turnus, tearing down Lycus from the wall, reminds him of the armour-bearing bird of Jove seizing a hare or white swan.[3] In another instance chase is given by all the birds to an eagle that has carried off a swan. Assaulted on all sides and unable to defend himself and yet keep hold of his prey, the huge bird flings the swan from his talons into the river and flees far within the clouds.[4] Again, when Tarchon, on horseback, charged down upon Venulus and bore him and his arms from the field, his deed is likened to that of

"a golden eagle which, mounting aloft with a captured snake, entwines it in her feet and holds it fast with her talons; the wounded serpent twists its winding coils, bristles with its erected scales, and hisses with its mouth as it rises upward; but the bird none the less presses her struggling prey with

---

[1] *Æn.* IV. 461-463.
[2] *Id.* XI. 721. This and the following bird-similes in the *Æneid* have been partly suggested by passages in the *Iliad* and *Odyssey*.
[3] *Id.* IX. 563.　　　　　　　　　　[4] *Id.* XII. 247-256.

her curved beak while with her pinions she beats the air; in such wise does Tarchon bear away his spoil in triumph from the ranks of the Tiburtines."[1]

The birds that frequented a poet's little country home are enumerated by Martial from his Nomentan farm. He writes to a friend that if he could supply him with fattened field-fares or choice fish, he would gladly send him a birthday present. But his fields could hear only wretched starlings, and complaining finches, and the shrill-chirping sparrow, with here a magpie chattering to the ploughman, and there a kite soaring into the sky. All he can furnish is only some small gifts from his little court-yard.[2]

Some of the commoner birds were caught by the Romans and domesticated as household pets. Of these the most memorable example is Lesbia's " passer," to the memory of which Catullus dedicated two of his most charming sonnets. There is some doubt as to what was the species of this bird. We can hardly suppose the capricious beauty to have given her affections to the most impudent, pugnacious, greedy, and shrill-voiced of all European birds—the house-sparrow. It was probably one of the thrushes. At all events it was exceedingly tame, would never leave its mistress, to whom only it would sing its little song, and who when it died wept with red and swollen eyes for her loss.[3]

---

[1] Æn. XI. 751-758. [2] Epig. IX. liv.

[3] Catullus, Carm. II., III. Ovid composed an elegy on the death of Corinna's parrot (Amor. II. vi.). It is in his characteristic style, full of conceits. The birds are invited to come in numbers to the burial

Among the birds which were kept in confinement and taught to imitate human speech were the nightingale, starling, raven, magpie, and parrot.

The Romans were noted bee-keepers. Virgil, who could see much more of interest in these insects than the honey they yielded, has given the fullest and most vivacious account of them and their ways, which may still be read with profit, even though it mistakes the sex of the queen-bees and represents them as kings. Especially graphic is his account of the battling at the hives, and there is a touch of human pathos in his remark that all this display of passion and these mighty conflicts may be stilled by the throwing of a handful of dust.[1] Virgil also extended his insect observations to ants, and we could wish that he had put on record as ample and entertaining a statement of their habits as he has given of those of bees. He makes effective use of his acquaintance with these insects when he introduces them as an illustration of the hurrying to and fro and ceaseless industry of the Trojans in the preparation of their fleet to depart from Carthage.[2]

Among the blessings that Nature has showered on Italy, which called forth unstinted praise from the poet of the *Georgics,* was the absence of savage tigers and of fierce lions from all the borders of

of the parrot, and are bidden to beat their breasts with their wings and to scratch their tender cheeks with their sharp claws — a strange contrast to the simplicity and pathos of Catullus.

[1] *Geor.* IV. 86.

[2] *Æn.* IV. 402-407.

the land.[1] The largest and most important wild beasts in the country were wolves, bears, and wild boars. All these animals required a good deal of attention from the husbandman in country districts. In the early days of the Republic wolves were probably numerous among the wooded hills near Rome. From these retreats they came in winter to prowl round the farms and carry of such of the live stock as they could reach. Their numbers were gradually thinned as agriculture crept up into the hills. But they still survive in the remoter parts of the peninsula. The wolf was in ancient times disliked and feared by the country people, as it still is to-day.[2] It appears in Virgil's *Eclogues* as one of the enemies of the farmer, for it was "triste stabulis." But a fuller picture of its prowling habits is given in the *Æneid* as a simile for the conduct of Turnus and his warriors around the Teucrian walls. They are likened to

"a lurking wolf at a well-filled sheep-fold, when braving wind and rain he howls round the cote at midnight, while safe beneath their mothers the lambs keep bleating; fierce and angry and wearied with long hunger and thirst for blood, he rages at the prey which he cannot reach."[3]

The *Lupus montanus* or wolf of the mountains was a fierce animal, and when collected in

---

[1] Lucan gives a gruesome catalogue of the beasts and birds of prey that hurried from all quarters to the field of slain at Pharsalia (*Phars.* VII. 825-846).

[2] "Odimus acciptrem, quia vivit semper in armis,
     Et pavidum solitos in pecus ire lupos."—Ovid, *Ars. Amat.* II. 147.

[3] *Æn.* IX. 59-64.

companies, was a serious menace to the flocks
and herds on the high - lying pastures.   These
distant tracts required a race of specially stalwart
shepherds and a powerful breed of dogs.[1]   But
not only were the flocks liable to be plundered by
the voracious wolves ; sometimes even a shepherd
would lose his life from their attack.   Such an
incident is alluded to as an appropriate simile for
the conduct of Arruns at the death of Camilla :

" When a wolf has slain a shepherd or a stout
young bullock, conscious of his audacious deed,
before hostile arms pursue him, he straightway
hides himself far off among the hills, and drooping
his coward tail beneath his belly makes for the
woods." [2]

Horace, in recording his adventure with a wolf,
has held it up in his inimitably playful manner as
a proof of the safety enjoyed by a virtuous man in
the presence of danger.   He tells how once when
wandering beyond the usual limits of his rambles,
unarmed and carelessly singing the charms of his
Lalage, a wolf met him in a Sabine wood and fled—
such a monster as was not to be found in the oak
forests of Daunia, nor even in Mauretania, so
famous for its lions.[3]   The wolf was probably as
much surprised and alarmed at the sight and voice
of the poet, as the poet was at the appearance of

[1] Varro, as already quoted, *ante* p. 26.

[2] *Æn.* XI. 809-813.   In this and the previous simile from the *Æneid*
Virgil has taken the idea from the Greek, but has worked it out more
fully.

[3] *Carm.* I. xxii. 9.

the wolf. But, recovered from his fright, Horace welcomed the adventure as another prodigy of the higher powers in his favour, for it showed that whether or not virtue is always safeguarded, a votary of the Muses may certainly count on their protection.

The brown bear was also probably common enough in some parts of Italy during at least the earlier centuries of the Republic, before its numbers were thinned by the spread of agriculture and the demands of the amphitheatre. Virgil alludes to the season when "the shapeless bears deal most death and destruction in the woods."[1] Ovid mentions the shaggy bears that haunt the higher mountains.[2] It was another of the half-serious, half-playful boasts of Horace that even in childhood he had the protection of the Muses, for on the occasion, already referred to, when he wandered to the foot of Mount Vultur and fell asleep there, he was not only covered with leaves by the doves, but was also protected from the vipers and bears that infested the glades of that mountain.[3] When in one of his despondent moods about the future destiny of Rome, he counselled the people to forsake their native country and emigrate to the blessed isles of the Western Ocean, which had been reserved by Jove for a worthy race, he enumerated as one of the attractions of that happy region, that there "no bear at eventide

[1] *Geor.* III. 247.

[2] *Metam.* XIII. 836.　　　　[3] *Carm.* III. iv. 9-20.

growls around the sheepfold, nor is the teeming soil raised up by vipers.[1]

The wild boar abounded in all the wooded parts of Italy. Besides running free in the forests, it was also preserved on large estates, for it afforded one of the favourite kinds of hunting. Catullus calls it *aper nemorivagus*, and couples it with the *cerva silvicultrix* as creatures with which Attis feared to spend his life among the peaks of Phrygia.[2] Boar-hunts involved some personal danger when the huntsmen came to close quarters with the infuriated animal, which was driven towards a space partially enclosed with nets. Some courage was needed to approach it, for to fail with the spear might let the boar rush forward and deal that sidelong blow (*obliquus ictus*) which gives such a ghastly wound. Descriptions of various boar-hunts are to be found among the poets. Virgil gives one in a few lines as an illustration of the conduct of the warriors who feared to close with Mezentius.[3] Ovid relates at some length the hunting of the Calydonian boar — a story which afforded him ample scope for his fancy and power of narration.[4] Hunting, which Cicero admitted to be a respectable form of athletic exercise,[5] had the advantage of taking men into the wilder parts of the country, especially into the fastnesses of the hills and the depths of the

[1] *Epod.* XVI. 51.　　　[2] *Carm* LXIII. 71.
[3] *Æn.* X. 707.　　　[4] *Metam.* VIII. 329 *seq.*
[5] *De Off.* I. xxix.

forests. It showed them Nature in her freest and most unchanged guise, and it braced them to endure the hardships of weather beneath the open sky by night as well as by day.[1]

With regard to the preserves in which wild animals were enclosed, an interesting account has been given by Varro, of one that belonged to the orator Q. Hortensius. It lay among the sandy flats and dunes of Laurentum, close to the site where afterwards the younger Pliny had the villa already referred to.

" A tract of more than fifty jugera was surrounded with a fence so as to be an enclosure for wild beasts rather than a warren for hares. There was one part of it, raised above the rest, on which a dining-room had been erected and where we supped. A musician was ordered to attend. When he came in his long gown, holding his cithern and was bidden to play, he blew his horn, whereupon we were surrounded with such a multitude of stags, wild boars and other quadrupeds that the spectacle seemed to me not less fine than the *venationes* of the Aediles in the Circus Maximus, on occasions when the performance includes no African beasts." [2]

---

[1] As Horace tells,
    " Manet sub Jove frigido
      Venator."—*Carm.* I. i. 25.

[2] *De Re. Rust.* III. xiii. 2.

CHAPTER X

DAY AND NIGHT

FROM the infancy of mankind no part of Nature
has been so constantly watched as the face of
the sky—that "corslet of heaven"[1] as Lucretius
picturesquely calls it, which with all its glories
and its mysteries clasps the earth. From dawn
to dusk, day after day, and season after season,
man has scanned its changing aspects, now with
hope and now with fear, as its look has seemed
to him to presage calm or storm, peace or war,
prosperity or disaster. How varied soever his
creed, he has realised his dependence and that of
all living things, upon the light, warmth, and
moisture which come to him from the sky. In
that upper region, far above the stir and din of
earth, he has placed the dwelling-place of his
gods, and has fondly trusted that there, too, he
will himself find an eternal home. The splendour
of the day he has seen to be succeeded by the
brilliance of the night. In the clear air of southern
climes he has fancifully mapped out the nocturnal
firmament into constellations. Far back in pre-

---

[1] "Caeli lorica" (*De Rer. Nat.* VI. 954).

historic time he had observed that the stars seem
to be moving across the sky, that they have
their risings and their settings, and that year
after year they follow the same route.   Thus
watching, his first vague wonderment was exchanged for admiration and for an assured confidence that he could count on the movements of
sun and stars as faithfully marking out for him
the progress of the seasons and the length of
the year.

In such a climate as that of Italy, where "the
witchery of the soft blue sky" is so powerful, these
diurnal and nocturnal aspects of the heavens appeal
with fullest force to the human imagination. They
were well appreciated by the Romans, and have
found ample recognition in Latin literature.
Lucretius, in a graphic passage, enumerates some
of the more imposing features of the celestial
regions—the clear, pure, blue sky, the splendour of
the sun, the stars that wander across the firmament,
the moon in her course—and he asks whether
if all these marvels were suddenly and for the
first time brought before our eyes, we could have
dared beforehand to believe that such wonders
could exist. Assuredly nothing else in the world
so marvellous could be presented to us.   And
yet, he continues, because we are tired of having
seen these sights so long, nobody deigns to look
up at the shining circuit of heaven.[1] The poet,
however, was well aware that in spite of its

[1] *De Rer. Nat.* II. 1030-1039.

familiarity the fascination of the heavens can
never become stale. Certainly no man was more
keenly alive to that fascination than Lucretius
himself. Throughout his poem many scattered
allusions and descriptions record the impressions
made on his own mind by different aspects of
the heavens. He hails the æthereal sun as our
bountiful fountain of liquid light, which continually
floods the sky with new splendour, ever replacing
with fresh light the light which comes to us and
then disappears.[1] Perhaps the most remarkable
passage wherein he deals with this subject is
that in which, considering the reason why men
placed the abodes of the gods in the serene region
of the sky, he seems to be actually swept onward
by the enthusiasm of his contemplation of the
universe—

"the sun and moon are seen to roll along their
paths through the heavens, with day and night,
and the stern constellations of night, and the night-
wandering torches of heaven, and the flying flames,
the clouds, the dew, the rain-storms, the snow, the
winds, the lightnings, the hail, and the rapid roar
and mighty murmur of heaven's menacings."[2]

The changes in the aspects of Nature during
the course of a day from dawn to dusk have
awakened many responsive notes from the Roman
poets. Lucretius dwells on the charms of sunrise,

[1] *De Rer. Nat.* V. 281.
[2] *Op. cit.* V. 1189. The poet's love of alliteration lends an effective
touch to the close of this passage—

"rapidi fremitus et murmura magna minarum."

"when the golden rays of morning fall with ruddy glow on the grass begemmed with dew-drops," and "the dawn strews the land with new light, while the many-coloured birds, flitting in the soft air through the pathless woods, fill the scene with their liquid notes."[1]

Virgil, too, cherished the memories of early morning at his youthful home among the meadows of the Mincius, where at the call of the west wind, the glad summer sent the flocks to their glades and pastures, and the shepherds betook themselves to the cool fields at the first peep of the morning star, while the grass was hoar with rime and the dew on the tender blade was pleasantest to the cattle.[2] Even in the *Æneid*, amid the din of arms, the poet now and then intercalates an allusion to the quiet beauty of early dawn, as where at the close of the struggle wherein Euryalus and Nisus fell, the day which was to renew the carnage is ushered in with a reference to the saffron dawn that was besprinkling the land with new light.[3] And again, another contrast is introduced where the narrative transports us from the cave of the Cyclopes, with its blazing forge and thundering anvils, to the humble home of Evander on which the fostering light of dawn was then falling, while the birds under the eaves were carolling

---

[1] *De Rer. Nat.* II. 145 ; V. 461.
[2] *Geor.* III. 324 ; *Eclog.* VIII. 15.
[3] *Æn.* IX. 459.

their morning songs.[1]　Ovid's touch is characteristically more diffuse—

"lo the vigilant Dawn, from the golden east, throws open her purple doors, and her halls filled with roses.　The stars fade away whose ranks Lucifer marshalls, and he himself vanishes last from his place in the sky."[2]

The heat of an Italian noon in summer, and the languor which then falls upon the landscape are vividly brought before us in Virgil's second *Eclogue*, when even the cattle take to the cool shade, the green lizards hide themselves among the thorns, the reapers are weary with the fierce heat, and under the burning sun the trees resound with the hoarse notes of the cicala.　Each successive touch in this picture heightens the impression made by the scene, until when all visible sign of animal life has retreated from the hot glare, the twittering of the cicala is left as the only sound to reach the ear.[3]　Another sketch of a similar scene is given in the second *Georgic* :—

"the fierce Dog-star scorching the thirsty Indians was blazing in the sky, and the fiery sun had run half his circuit, the grass was withering and the streams in their parched channels were being dried up, down to the very mud on their floors."

---

[1] *Æn.* VIII. 455.　　　　　　　[2] *Metam.* II. 113.

[3] With this passage we may compare the appeal made by a similar scene to a poetic spirit of modern times :—

> "The poetry of earth is never dead :
> 　When all the birds are faint with the hot sun,
> 　And hide in cooling trees, a voice will run
> From hedge to hedge about the new-mown mead ;
> 　That is the grasshopper's."

It was only at such a sultry time, "when the sun had kindled his noontide heats, when the herbage was athirst and shade was most welcome to the cattle," that there was any chance of catching and securing the many shaped Proteus.[1]

Horace in his cool and shady upland valley thoroughly appreciated his escape from the heat and glare of the Dog-days, and often took occasion to refer to that trying season

> " When Procyon and Leo's star
> Are raging, and the sun
> Brings back the days of drought :
> Now the tired shepherd with his panting flock
> Makes for the shade of rough Silvanus' glades,
> Where flows the quiet stream
> Unruffled by a breath." [2]

The charms of evening found a responsive echo in Virgil's heart. They have their recognition both in the *Eclogues* and in the *Georgics*. How delicately the feeling of the close of day is implied rather than expressed in the last two lines of the first *Eclogue*—the aspect of sundown and the return of the wearied labourers to their modest homes, where their wives are lighting the fires to prepare their welcome evening meal !

> " Now the far cottage roofs begin to smoke
> And longer shadows from the mountains fall." [3]

---

[1] *Geor*. IV. 401, 425.   [2] *Carm*. III. xxix. 18.
[3] *Eclog*. I. 82. Another evening scene occurs in II. 66, 67.

An ampler picture of the various features that make the delight of evening is given in the third *Georgic*.

> " The sun is set ; and the cool evening star
> Tempers the air ; while now the dewy moon
> Brings freshness to the woodland pasturage.
> The halcyon's notes resound along the shores ;
> The brakes are loud with warblings of the finch." [1]

As daylight goes and darkness comes on how vividly one feels the beauty and the force of Virgil's striking phrase that " the stars are leading forth the night." [2]

It was a primitive belief that when the sun sets he sinks beneath the sea. Long before the Augustan age, however, more correct notions regarding the relations of the earth to the heavenly bodies had been arrived at by philosophers. Yet allusions to the old notion continued to be made for poetic effect, sometimes even with such definiteness of language as to suggest that the primitive conception was not yet wholly abandoned ; as where Statius expresses the opinion that Italy was blest in that she " sees the courses of Hyperion sink beneath the ocean waves, and hears the hiss of his descending chariot wheels." [3]   In his *Ulysses* Tennyson appropriately introduces an allusion

----

[1] *Geor.* III. 336.

[2] " noctem ducentibus astris."—*Geor.* III. 156.

[3] *Silv.* II. vii. 25.

to the early belief when he makes the hero
resolve

> "To sail beyond the sunset, and the baths
> Of all the western stars." [1]

The changing aspects of the sky, as shown
in the shapes and movements of the clouds, seem
to have greatly interested Lucretius. By no
other Latin poet have such vivid pictures of
cloudland been drawn. He watched the sky
with the eager attention and curiosity of a man
of science, as well as with the rapture of a poet.
Nor was he content to study clouds as they
can be seen from the plains. He climbed
mountains and had there an opportunity of
observing them as they grow and disappear. He
noted how, on the higher crests, vapours are
gathered into clouds and are borne away by the
winds till they burst in a fierce storm.[2] But he
appreciated also their beauty and grandeur, and
found in them fit subjects for poetic treatment.
In one passage he gives a graphic description of
their movements and changes of shape :—

"Sometimes we see clouds massing together
aloft, overcasting a serene sky and gently moving
through the air. Often they seem to take the form
of giant faces that fly across the heavens and cast

---

[1] Milton makes the angel Raphael teach this philosophy to
Adam in Eden.

> "The sun. . . . at even
> Sups with the Ocean."—*Par. Lost* V. 423.

[2] *De Rer. Nat.* VI. 459.

their shadows far and wide, or like vast mountains and rocks borne away from the mountains, they go on in front and mount past the sun, or they shape themselves into the likeness of some huge beast that drags forward other rain-clouds." [1]

In another picture he shows the clouds gathering for a thunderstorm :—

" Look when next through the air the winds shall sweep clouds shaped like mountains, or when you shall see them piled up one above another upon lofty mountains, and when from above they are pressing downwards on the places where they are at rest, and the winds are everywhere buried. Then will you be able to perceive their huge mass and to mark their caves, seemingly built up of hanging rocks. When a storm has risen, the winds which have filled the openings and are shut up within the clouds wax wroth with loud tumult, and threaten like wild beasts in their dens, roaring through the clouds, now on this side, now on that, and wheeling all round in search of an outlet, they roll up the seeds of fire from out the clouds, and thus driving many of these together, they whirl the flame within the hollow furnaces, until, bursting the clouds asunder, the lightning flashes forth." [2]

The theory here expressed that thunder and lightning are due to the violent struggling of winds to escape from caverns in the clouds where they have been imprisoned and where they " roll up the seeds of fire," had been formulated in Greek philosophy long before the poet's time,

[1] *De Rer. Nat.* IV. 133.   [2] *Op. cit.* VI. 189-203.

and it held its place in the general belief of mankind for many centuries. Nor could any more satisfactory explanation have been proposed until the existence of electricity was discovered, and the science of meteorology took definite shape.

Lucretius appears to have often watched, as it gathered far away at sea, such a thunderstorm as he has sketched in another part of his poem:—

" Many a time over the sea a black cloud, filled from afar with darkness, like a stream of pitch falling from the sky, descends upon the waves, dragging along a dark tempest big with lightnings and hurricanes, itself filled full of fires and winds, in so much that even on land men shudder and seek refuge beneath their roofs." [1]

In connection with the Lucretian cloud-pictures it may be mentioned that not only do they include studies of thunderstorms, when the landscape is involved in such darkness as to suggest that all the gloom of Acheron has risen into the sky,[2] but they also show the poet's observation of cloudland at night. He has recorded an appearance that is familiar enough in northern more cloudy climates, when

" in the night season, winds sometimes carry scattered clouds athwart the heavens, and then the brilliant stars seem to be gliding across the rack and moving aloft in a direction far different from that in which they are really travelling." [3]

[1] *De Rer. Nat.* VI. 256-261.
[2] *Op. cit.* VI. 250.   [3] *Op. cit.* IV. 443.

No phenomena in Nature are more familiar and at the same time seemingly more capricious and inexplicable than the various movements of the air by which we are surrounded and continually affected.   There are times when these movements would appear to have entirely ceased.   We speak of a calm when not a leaf is quivering, when

" The water stretches smooth and still
And all the murmurings of the breeze have sunk." [1]

The solemn quietude that sometimes precedes a thunderstorm is not the least impressive of the features of a summer day.   But as may be seen when any minute particles, such as those of smoke, escape into the air, the atmosphere is really always in motion, and for the most part its movements are sensibly felt by us.   The gentler of these may be audible when they cause vibrations in trees or other objects.   From hardly perceptible whispers endless varieties of sound may be heard up to the moan or wail or loud roar of the forest in a gale.   The attentive ear may detect distinctions in the notes according to the character of the foliage and the strength of the wind that blows through it.   Virgil seems to have been specially sensitive to these various cadences of Nature.   He has noted the rustle or murmur of the ilex and the speaking voice of the pines.   And when the gale blew strongly he heard the wail of the forest.[2]   Ovid compared the

[1] Virgil, *Eclog.* IX. 57.
[2] *Eclog.* VII. 1 ; VIII. 22 ; *Geor.* I. 334.

timid shuddering of Ariadne, surprised by the
Satyrs and Silenus, to the quivering of barren
corn-ears as the wind stirs them, or the slender
reed that trembles in the watery marsh.[1]

To these natural voices Lucretius traced back
the earliest form of instrumental music :

" The whistling of the zephyr through the
hollow stems of reeds first taught the rustics
to blow into hollowed hemlock-stalks. Thence
by degrees they learnt the sweet laments which
the pipe pours forth when struck by the fingers
of the players, and which are heard among the
trackless groves and the forests and glades, amidst
the lonely haunts and the divine resting-places
of the shepherds." [2]

The Romans had a separate name, generally
euphonious, for each wind ; not only those which
blow from the cardinal points, but for certain of
those that come from the intermediate quarters.
Some of the names belonged to the old Latin
language, while others had been adopted from
Greece. It sometimes happened that the Greek
name had not wholly supplanted the native term,
and the same wind might have two appellations.
Thus the old word Favonius and the Greek
Zephyrus were both names for the west wind.
The poets found this enlarged nomenclature convenient for metrical purposes. Besides Favonius,
among the old native names for the winds which

---

[1] *Ars. Amat.* I. 553.
[2] *De Rer. Nat.* V. 1382-1387 (*pastorum otia dia*).

held their place in current use, were Aquilo the
north wind, Auster the warm south wind, and
Vulturnus the south-east wind.[1]   The gentle airs
of the balmy Favonius with their heralding of
spring, and the music they make as they pass
through the woodlands, find frequent eulogy among
the poets of Rome.   Virgil evidently took pleasure
in listening to the rustle of the coming Auster.[2]
Ovid, too, knew the charm of the pine-woods when
the wild Eurus (south-east wind) whistles through
them.[3]

The ancient habit of clothing the forces of
Nature with the personal attributes of supernatural
beings that could be incorporated into the
national mythology, found special scope for its
exercise among the winds, which were often spoken
of as if they were conscious intelligences.   Thus,
when Horace wished the poetaster Maevius every
kind of bad luck on his proposed voyage to Greece,
he prayed Auster to remember to lash both sides
of the vessel with angry waves.   Dark Eurus was
enjoined to scatter her rigging and broken spars
over the upturned sea ; Aquilo was to mount as

[1] The Latin writers of verse, in their allusions to the winds, were in
much better case than their English successors.   For not only had they
distinctive and euphonious designations ready to hand, but these
naturally lent themselves to personification and thus an added
picturesqueness was obtainable.   Our English " north-easter," " sou'
wester," east wind, west wind, etc., have geographical precision, but no
musical charm.   Hence in our poetry, though the winds fill an ample
space, they have not that distinctive character which they wear in the
poetry of Rome.

[2] *Eclog.* V. 82.   [3] *Metam.* XV. 603.

high as when he breaks down the ilexes on the
lofty mountains.   And if the wretched victim
escaped from all these assaults, the poet hoped that
the Ionian gulf, roaring before the rainy Notus,
would tear the ship asunder.[1]

By none of the Latin poets was the personification of the winds more graphically carried out than
by Ovid.   As he loved to make the personages in
his tales as life-like and picturesque as possible, he
employed all the resources of his brilliant fancy in
a picture of the south wind with which, as he
narrates, Jupiter had resolved to destroy the human
race.   The father of gods and men, having first
shut up, under the Æolian Islands, the north wind
and all the other breezes that blow away the clouds
and bring fair weather, then let out Notus, the
south wind, as the special blast that would gather
the rain-clouds together and precipitate a deluge.

> " With soaking wings the south wind issues forth,
>   His hideous face in pitchy darkness wrapped,
>   His beard all heavy with downpouring rains,
>   The water streaming from his hoary locks ;
>   Thick clouds around his head ; his wings
>   And every vesture-fold adrip with wet.
>   His broad hand, pressing on the pendant clouds,
>   Evokes a crash, when from the livid sky
>   The pent-up torrents swoop upon the earth." [2]

That the winds should have been fabled to be
imprisoned in a vast cave underneath the Lipari
or Æolian Islands, no doubt arose from the conspicuous volcanic activity of that district.   The

---

[1] *Epod.* X.   [2] *Metam.* I. 264-269.

rumblings, earthquakes, and eruptions of the islands
were regarded throughout antiquity as manifestations of the movements of subterranean winds
struggling to find an escape to the surface, but
kept in order by their regent Æolus.[1]   It is to this
subterranean potentate that Virgil represents Juno
having recourse in order to obtain the storm
wherewith she meant to wreck the Trojan fleet.
At the request of the goddess he smote the hollow
mountain with his spear, whereupon the winds, like
an army in battle array, poured out through the
opened gateway and swept over the land and sea.

> " Eurus and Notus and the stormy Africus
>   Rushed out together ; to its utmost depths
>   They stirred the sea, and rolled vast waves ashore."[2]

The Greeks and Romans had a profound
sense of the force of a tempest.   They realised that
it was the greatest display of physical energy in
their experience, or of which they had any conception. Not unnaturally, therefore, the Romans
in their deification of abstract qualities and of
the powers of Nature, included storms among

[1] *See postea* chap. xvi.

[2] *Æn.* I. 81-86.   Seneca in quoting this passage remarks that such
a collocation of winds is a physical impossibility (*Quaest. Nat.* V. xvi.).
Virgil of course saw no difficulty in supposing that, as the different winds
were imprisoned together, they might also escape together by the opened
gate.   But, curiously enough, from one point of view the order in which
Virgil mentions the winds is that in which they follow each other in
one of our normal cyclones in Europe.   A gale which may begin blowing
from the south-east gradually shifts round by south to south-west, and
may finally be coming from the north-west before the whole vortex has
passed on.

their divinities, who had to be propitiated and to whom gratitude was due from men who had escaped from the perils of the deep. The "Tempestates" accordingly had their shrines and their rites.[1]

Lucretius, to whom the elemental forces of Nature were a subject of supreme interest, has left some vivid allusions to the tumult of a great gale and the havoc which it works on sea and land. He speaks of its piercing shrieks and angry roar as it rushes along with rapid whirl, breaking down the woods on the mountains, strewing the fields with the largest trees, wrecking the great ships at sea, and sweeping along the clouds in the sky.[2]

Catullus, in the course of his varied wanderings by sea and land during his short life, saw a good deal of Nature in her different moods, and he has left a few all too brief reminiscences of his experiences. Some of these which refer chiefly to the sea will be dealt with in chapter xv. His poem on the marriage of Peleus and Thetis is especially rich in allusions and short descriptive passages, which lightly but vividly sketch various scenes and landscapes. One of these passages traces in a few

[1] Cicero, *Nat. Deor.* III. xx. 51. Lucius Scipio, who was Consul in B.C. 259, and in that year narrowly escaped with his fleet from a great gale, had inscribed on his tomb that he took Corsica and the town of Aleria, and dedicated a temple to the Tempestates. Horace, after heaping maledictions on the voyage of Maevius (*ante* p. 216), concluded his imprecations by vowing that if the body of that wretched poet should be cast ashore as a dainty repast for the sea-fowl, a goat and a lamb would be offered in sacrifice to the Tempestates.

[2] *De Rer. Nat.* I. 271-276.

lines the work of a cyclone among the mountains, as a simile to heighten the effect of the picture of Theseus and the Minotaur.   The hero is represented prostrating the monster :—

> " As when a raging hurricane assails
>   An oak that waves its boughs on Taurus' crest,
>   Or pine-tree with its cones and sweating bark ;
> The blast with whirling fury straight tears up
> By its far-stretching roots the giant trunk,
> Which, falling prone, comes crashing down the crags." [1]

Virgil has drawn from his own experience a detailed picture of the summer storms which, even in so genial a climate as that of Italy, sometimes burst upon the cultivated lands and spread dire ruin all along their track.

> " In autumn time, when to the golden fields
>   The reapers have been mustered for their task,
>   And the first swaths of barley have been cut,
> Oft have I watched the winds in battle fierce
> Tear, even from the roots and fling aloft,
> Whole breadths of heavy corn, and, swirling round,
> Sweep blade and stubble through the darkened air.
> Full often at such times a vast array
> Of sombre rain-clouds gathers in the sky,
> And the foul tempest, rolling from the deep,
> Descends in torrents that soon wash away
> The farmer's smiling crops, and bring to naught
> The labours of his oxen in the fields.
> The dykes are filled ; the rivers in their beds
> Swell with the spate that loudly roars along,
> While ocean boils among its seething firths.
> Throned in the midnight of the clouds, great Jove
> Wields in his red right hand the flaming bolts

---

[1] *Carm.* LXIV. 105-109.

That make the huge earth shudder to the core ;
The wild beasts slink away, and mortal hearts
Through all the nations tremble with dismay.
And as the flashing levin strikes the peaks
Of Athos, Rhodope or Ceraunian cliffs,
The wet south-winds redouble their turmoil,
The rains fall denser still, while now the groves
And now the shores lie wailing 'neath the blast." [1]

In Latin prose two narratives of storms are
specially noteworthy for their graphic details of
the feeble resistance that can be offered by man
to the uncontrollable energy of the elements.
One of these descriptions is that given by Livy of
the prolonged and diversified tempest encountered
by Hannibal and his army in their attempt to cross
the ridge of the Apennines; [2] the other is the
narrative in which Tacitus so vividly describes the
gale that dispersed the fleet of Germanicus in the
North Sea. [3] Both accounts are too long for quotation here, and they are familiar to readers of the
classics. But they may be referred to as excellent
examples of how a historian may effectively interrupt the current of his human story in order to
dwell for a moment on some extraordinary display
of the forces of Nature.

The pleasure and fascination of listening to or
watching a storm from a safe and comfortable
shelter is more than once referred to by the
Roman poets. Besides the famous passage with

---

[1] *Geor.* I. 316-334.   [2] *Hist.* XXI. lviii.
[3] *Ann.* II. xxiii., xxiv.

which Lucretius begins the second Book of his poem—

"Suave, mari magno turbantibus aequora ventis,
  e terra magnum alterius spectare laborem,"

the sentiment is more fully expressed by Tibullus who, wrapped in luxurious repose, exclaims : " How pleasant it is to hear the pitiless winds when one lies abed, or, when the wintry south wind pours out its icy waters, to prolong one's secure slumbers, lulled by the plash of the rain." [1]

Besides the weather portents derived from the habits of animals, as referred to in the foregoing chapter, the Greeks and Romans, in the course of the experience of many generations, had noted a number more in the aspect of the sky, in the appearance of sun, moon, and stars as influenced by the varying conditions of the atmosphere, and in the sounds uttered by the sea or by woods. These, whether well founded or not, are interesting as further indications of the close watch which in ancient times was kept upon the changes that supervene on the face of Nature, and of the real or fanciful relations which were inferred to exist between these changes and the variations in the weather. Virgil, in musical language, tells how a coming gale is heralded on sea and land, how the ocean - straits begin to heave, how a dry crackling sound is heard coming from the mountains, how the shores give forth a mingled

[1] *Eleg.* I. i. 45.

long-resounding noise, and the murmur of the
woodlands waxes louder. As for rain, he holds
that never does it injure us without first having
warned us of its advent, and he gives that
picturesque list of portents, already cited, wherein
beasts and birds all conspire to make known its
approach. To these signs from Nature outside,
he adds one from the domestic hearth, where
"even the girls as they spin the nightly wool, are
not unaware of the coming storm, when they see
the oil sparkle in the lighted lamp, and crumbling
soot gather on the wick." [1]

Virgil, following Aratus, lays, much stress on
the value of the indications of weather-changes
furnished by the variable aspects of the sun and
moon, as the conditions of the atmosphere vary.
Especially important were the warnings furnished
by the sun believed to be. Trusting to the
prognostics of that great luminary, we shall not be
deceived; the treacherous snares of a calm night
will never catch us unprepared. Are we eager to
know what kind of skies the evening has in store
for us? Do we ask whence the wind will bring
us fair weather, and what the moist south is
meditating for us? The sun will give us sure
forecasts of what we may expect. And who shall
say that the sun is false? [2]

[1] *Geor.* I. 390.

[2] *Id.* 424, 461. The physical portents in the poem as well as those
from animal life are selected from the fuller list in Aratus. Pliny
has much to say about weather prognostics; he culls freely from
previous writers, Greek and Latin (*Hist. Nat.* XVIII. lxxviii.).

Who that has ever enjoyed it can forget the beauty of an Italian night, when the languor of the day has gone, and in the cool fresh air life revives, while the stars in a sky of darkest blue shine with a brilliance and in a visible multitude such as the dweller in a mistier clime can hardly ever see ? These features could not but impress and delight the Roman poets. Lucretius appears to have been especially struck by the darkness and silence of night, for he refers to them again and again. He alludes to dreams wherein we seem to be actively engaged, yet we are really lying still "in the blind darkness of night," and though we think we hear sounds and believe we are answering them, "the stern silence of night" encompasses us all the while.[1] The starry sky must sometimes have awakened in his mind doubts as to the foundations of his Epicurean philosophy. In the wonderful fifth Book of his poem he writes :

"When we look up at the celestial spaces of the great world, and the steadfast ether above the twinkling stars, and it occurs to us to think of the courses of the sun and moon, then into our hearts, already weighed down with other ills, this doubt also begins to raise its awakened head, whether there may not perchance be some vast power of

---

Lucan's peasant boatman gives a list of weather presages unfavourable to the attempt to boat across the Ægean, which Cæsar was determined to do (*Phars.* V. 540-559).

[1] *De. Rer. Nat.* IV. 455-461. Shakespeare's noble line may be quoted :

"In the dead vast and middle of the night."

He more than once uses the expression "the deep of night."

the gods over us, which whirls the stars along in their various motions."[1]

To many minds the silence of night is oppressive, and the mere barking of a dog or the cry of a hooting owl is felt by them to be a relief from the stillness that seems to lie as a crushing weight upon the dark and death - like face of Nature. In one of the passages from Lucretius, cited above, he calls this silence "stern" (*severa*); in another place he emphasises the stillness in his expression "taciturna silentia."[2] Virgil, who so frequently alludes to the silence of night, tells how this very silence may be a source of terror. One of the fullest expressions of this feeling occurs in two lines of Valerius Flaccus: "The very quiet of things, the silence of the world, the stars, and the ether begemmed with its far-spread constellations all fill us with fear."[3]

Among the brief allusions in the *Eclogues* which bring the Virgilian country and its climate before us, the pleasant cool nights are not forgotten. In purple spring, when the ground was carpeted with flowers beside the river, when the poplar was hanging its white foliage over the cave, when the trailing vines were weaving a shady covert, when the surface of river and lake was motionless, and the murmur of the breeze had died away, delightful it was for the poet to outstay the day amidst such a scene, and to

---

[1] *De Rer. Nat.* V. 1204-1210.   [2] *Id.* IV. 460, 583.
[3] *Argon.* II. 41, 42.

P

return home when the stars were up, or still to
stay singing alone under the clear night.[1]

The little vignette of night, which for a
moment relieves the tension of the death-scene
of Dido, forms a pleasing episode in the *Æneid*.

> " 'Twas night when wearied mortals in all lands
> Were sunk in peaceful slumber ; and the woods
> And wrathful sea were still ; it was the hour
> When stars above are mid-way on their course,
> When every field is quiet, and the herds
> And birds of varied hue that haunt the meres,
> Or make their homes among the thorny brakes,
> Are all asleep beneath the silent night." [2]

Possibly Ovid may have had this passage
floating in his memory when he described Medea
stepping out barefoot at midnight to perform the
incantations whereby she restored Jason's father
to youth :

> " The moon was full, and with her radiant orb
> Looked down upon the countries of the earth.
> Deep sleep had fallen on men and birds and beasts ;
> No insect-murmur from the hedgerow comes ;
> Silent and motionless the foliage hangs ;
> Silent the dewy air ; while far above,
> The stars alone are twinkling in the sky." [3]

But apart from the fascination of its beauty
and grandeur, the starry sky came to acquire a
paramount importance in practical life. In the

---

[1] *Eclog.* IX. 40.   [2] *Æn.* IV. 522-527.

[3] *Metam.* VII. 180-188. Ovid expresses tersely another aspect of
night when he describes it as—

" Curarum maxima nutrix nox "—*Id.* VIII. 81.

clear atmosphere of southern and eastern climes, where the nocturnal heavens had long been attentively watched and studied, the planets had been named and distinguished from the fixed stars, among which the brightest had received special designations. Moreover, the apparent movements of the various heavenly bodies across the sky had been carefully observed, the times of the rising and the setting of particular stars had been noted, and thus the year could be divided into seasons, each of which had its beginning and ending defined by the regularly recurring position of some stars or groups of stars. This knowledge, originally acquired by eastern astronomers and astrologers, was gradually diffused among the surrounding peoples to an extent which we now find it difficult to realise. The nightly sky became the time-keeper of the ancient world. A mere reference to the rising or setting of a star was generally understood as an indication of a particular season, or even of a special day. Tables were constructed showing the times of the successive appearances of different stars on the horizon, and this information was engraved on plates that served the purpose of calendars or almanacs. The data contained in them were perhaps seldom strictly accurate, for though they might be so at the places where the observations and calculations were originally made, they became more and more erroneous in proportion to the difference in the geographical

able to assume that the amount of astronomical knowledge which the poet takes for granted in his readers, must have been fairly general among the more intelligent farmers of his time. It is a kind of knowledge, however, which has nearly disappeared from the same class of men in our own day. They have their watches and clocks, their almanacs and calendars, their daily newspapers and all the other multifarious indications of the steady march of time in the modern world. There can be little doubt that, in spite of the progress of science and the spread of education, the average man in civilised countries to-day is much less familiar with the starry sky than were the farmers and shepherds of Republican and Imperial Rome.

In the navigation of the Mediterranean Sea an acquaintance with the starry firmament was obviously of paramount importance, for though much of the sailing was kept near the coast, and vessels in such voyages often anchored for the night in some port or bay, it was constantly necessary to be out of sight of land and to be for many nights together on the open sea. (Chapter xv.)

But it was not only in the agricultural and sea - faring communities that this astronomical knowledge became familiar. An acquaintance with the principal constellations and stars, their relative places in the sky, and the times at which they rise or set or are prominent in the heavens,

seems to have been general among the educated
classes of Rome, if, at least, we may draw an
inference from the frequent allusions in Latin
literature to these matters, as things of everyday familiarity. The poets make abundant reference to them, not only in their more serious
works, but even in their lightest and gayest
lyrics, where recondite allusions would have
been wholly out of place. Ovid is perhaps the
writer in whose verse this kind of knowledge
finds most frequent expression. In his *Fasti*,
or poetical treatment of the Roman calendar, he
naturally had ample scope for making use of it,
and he has availed himself of his opportunity.
He must have been at infinite pains to collect
the large amount of astronomical information
which he there embodies. But he was evidently
unable to judge of the relative value of the
authorities which he consulted. Some of his
dates are quite correct, while others are far
wrong. It would almost seem from his final
and somewhat disparaging reference to a constellation on the last page of his poem, that he
had become tired by the time and trouble which
the collection of all this information had cost
him, and was relieved to have done with it. He
there writes:

" Here is a fellow who comes back not quite
sober from a suburban temple, and utters such
words as these — ' Your belt, Orion, is now
hidden ; perhaps it will still be hidden, to-morrow ;

thereafter it will be visible to me.' But had he not been tipsy, he would have simply said: ' The solstice will be here on that same day.' "[1]

In his other poems Ovid also makes frequent use of astronomical indications of time, as if he were rather proud of his acquaintance with the subject. Even in those written in the dreary years of his exile, he continues this practice; but at Tomi he could refer more pointedly to the constellations which never set in the northern sky, and he seems to have felt that additional poignancy was given to his banishment to so remote a region, in that the stars that never plunge beneath the ocean were so close to his eyes.

The habit of indicating a time or date by allusion to constellations could be carried to a point of absurdity, as where Martial takes two verses to announce that " Now the Tyrian Bull looks back upon the Ram of Phryxus, and winter flees before Castor and his twin brother,"[2] when all that he meant to say was "it is the month of May." As a protest against this kind of affectation Juvenal protests his ignorance of many of the fashionable topics of his day, and among these he takes care to specify that he knows nothing of the movements of the stars.[3]

Besides their use as chronometers, the stars were in ancient times widely believed to have a potent influence on the earth and its inhabitants,

---

[1] *Fast.* VI. 785-790.

[2] *Epig.* X. li.　　　　[3] *Sat.* III. 42.

and many illustrations of this belief are to be
found in the oldest literature. That the seasons
and the weather were immediately affected by
stellar action was a firm conviction, and this
obstinate persuasion has come down to our own
day. Such of the constellations or their more
conspicuous stars as rose or set coincidently with
more or less definitely recurring conditions of
the atmosphere, such as great heat, copious rain,
or violent winds, came to be popularly associated
with these meteorological conditions, and to be
regarded, or at least spoken of, as their actual
cause. Thus from remote antiquity the rising
of the brightest fixed star in the heavens, Sirius
or the Dog-star, in the constellation of Canis or
the Dog, about the middle of July, was looked
upon as in some way the cause of the great heats
of that season, and therefore of all the human
ills which a high temperature and its accompaniments involve. Virgil speaks of the rise of this
brilliant star as bringing thirst and disease to
weak mortals, and saddening heaven with its
maleficent light.[1] Horace, too, repeatedly refers
to the star as a symbol of the exhausting days
of midsummer. In his eyes, as we have seen,
one of the charms of his far-withdrawn valley
was the shelter it afforded him from that trying
season; the fierce hour of the blazing Dog-star
could not reach his cool Bandusian spring. The
evil repute of Sirius has descended to modern

[1] *Æn.* X. 273.

time, for the heats and maladies of the height of
summer are still associated with the " Dog-days."

But the most brilliant of the fixed stars was
not the only luminary in the firmament which
was blamed in old days for the evils that befall
humanity. Orion was held answerable for the
gales and rains that attend his winter setting, about
the middle of November. The epithets applied
to him by Virgil are various, but all uncomplimentary—such as watery, stormy, fierce.[1] Horace
is not less vituperative. He calls the star gloomy
and hostile to sailors, and when he urges his friend
Galatea not to venture on a proposed voyage late
in the season he asks her to note with what stormy
weather Orion is hastening to his setting.[2] The
so-called " equinoctial gales" were laid to the
charge of another constellation, the Kids, of which
the evening rising took place near the end of
September. Virgil alludes to the heavy rains,
storms of hail, and southern gales that attend
the " showery Kids,"[3] while Horace refers to the
fell fury of the setting Arcturus and the rising
Kids. The constellation of the Hyades was
actually so named from its supposed connection
with wet weather. Virgil calls them " rainy,"[4]
and Horace cites, among the terrors which the
first navigator did not fear to meet, the " tristes
Hyades."[5] Lastly Aquarius has acquired an

---

[1] *Æn.* I. 535 ; IV. 52 ; VII. 719.   [2] *Carm.* III. xxvii. 17.
[3] *Æn.* IX. 668.   [4] *Id.* I. 744 ; III. 516.
[5] *Carm.* I. iii. 14.

equally disagreeable reputation which is indicated in his name.   Virgil speaks of the chilly showers wherewith that constellation besprinkles the close of the year, and Horace adds his testimony to the saddening of that season from the same cause.[1]   In all these allusions to the stellar world, so profusely scattered through the writings of the Roman poets, we must assume that they were generally understood and appreciated by readers in those days; but to what proportion of modern readers are they intelligible without some explanation ?

[1] *Geor.* III. 304 ; Horace, *Sat.* I. i. 36.

CHAPTER XI

THE SEASONS

ALTHOUGH the Roman poets loved to boast of
Italy's perpetual spring, the country was not
unacquainted with the other seasons of the year.
The peculiar geographical shape and position of the
peninsula, however, have undoubtedly given it a
more insular climate than is experienced by the
central and eastern parts of Europe. While these
regions in mid-winter lie under a mean temperature
not above the freezing point, the lowlands of Italy,
from the Riviera down to the most southerly
promontory are favoured with a milder air. Frost
and snow, though for months they keep hold of the
uplands all along the chain of the Apennines, make
their appearance only fitfully on the plains, where
for the most part they are neither severe nor of
long continuance. On the other hand, the sea-
breezes on either side of the country and the winds
from the central chain of cool heights temper the
heats of summer. Thus, exempt from the great
extremes of a truly continental climate, Italy in its
meteorological conditions is one of the most
favoured countries of Europe, and well deserves
the enthusiastic appreciation of its poets.

236

The regularity of the succession of the seasons
has impressed mankind from the earliest ages, and
has been the subject of comment in the literature
of every race.

"Spring goes forth," says Lucretius, "and
Venus and the winged herald of Venus steps
before them: close on the wake of Zephyr comes
Mother Flora, strewing all the ways and filling
them with the choicest colours and scents.   Next
follows parching Heat and as its only companion
dust-covered Ceres, and the Etesian breezes of the
Northern winds.   Then Autumn approaches and,
keeping step with him, Euan Bacchus.   Next
other seasons follow and their winds—the loud
thundering Volturnus (south-east) and Auster
(south) with his mighty lightning.   At last the
close of the year brings on the snows, and mid-
winter deals out his benumbing frost and the cold
that sets teeth chattering." [1]

The constancy but fleetingness that marks
the advent of the stages in this invariable succession seemed to Horace emblematic of the
shortness of human life, with no suggestion of
any hereafter beyond the grave.   He impressed
on Torquatus that the lesson to be learnt from
the rapid flight of hours and years is that we
must not hope for immortality—

"the winter chills grow mild under the breath
of the Zephyrs, summer treads closely on spring,
soon herself to perish when apple-bearing autumn
shall have poured forth his fruits, and then immediately sluggish winter returns once more.   Yet

[1] *De Rer. Nat.* V. 737-747.

the swift moons repair such losses as the heavens may suffer. We, when we have descended to where pious Aeneas and wealthy Tullus and Ancus have gone, are no more than mere dust and a shadow." [1]

In the gorgeous picture of the Palace of the Sun where Ovid's imagination and descriptive power reach so high a level, the great luminary is represented as the central figure, with the seasons attending around him, each personified as an individual being, and portrayed with distinctive attributes :

" Arrayed in purple vesture, on a throne
 That sparkled with the gleam of emeralds
 Great Phœbus sat ; on either hand stood round
 The Days, the Months, the Year, the Ages, too,
 And Hours disposed at equal intervals.
 There stood young Spring, with chaplet of fresh flowers,
 And Summer, naked, crowned with ears of corn ;
 There Autumn stood, befouled with trodden grapes,
 And icy Winter, rough with hoary locks." [2]

---

[1] *Carm.* IV. vii. 7-16. Among his earlier Odes (I. iv. ; p. 240), Horace drew the same lesson, with the added Epicurean inference that it is our duty to enjoy this life whilst it is ours. In his somewhat stilted style Edward Young described the same facts and drew another conclusion :—

" Look Nature through, 'tis revolution all ;
 All change ; no death. Day follows night, and night
 The dying day ; stars rise, and set, and rise ;
 Earth takes th' example. See, the summer gay,
 With her green chaplet, and ambrosial flowers,
 Droops into pallid autumn : winter gray,
 Horrid with frost, and turbulent with storm,
 Blows autumn, and his golden fruits away :
 Then melts into the spring : soft spring, with breath
 Favonian, from warm chambers of the South,
 Recalls the first. All to re-flourish, fades ;
 As in a wheel, all sinks, to re-ascend.
 Emblems of man, who passes, not expires."—*Night Thoughts*, VI.

[2] *Metam.* II. 24-30. Ovid's habit of personification set the fashion to our own early poets. Spenser employed it with much effect in his

The return of the time when

> " The Spring shall blow
> Her clarion o'er the dreaming earth,"

has naturally been hailed with special delight among the northern nations who have ample experience of the trials of a long winter. The zest with which the same season has been celebrated by the Latin poets has led to the supposition that the winters in Italy must formerly have been considerably more severe than they are now. The inference may possibly be well - founded, though for its acceptance a sounder basis than the impassioned language of poetry seems to be required. In our own day we are familiar with the popular belief that the seasons have changed much during the last few generations, that the cold was much greater and more prolonged and the summers warmer and more prolific in the times of our great-grandfathers than they have since become. But as far back as meteorological observations have been recorded, no certain proof of such secular change has been found. Severe and prolonged winters and excessively hot and rainless summers have undoubtedly been chronicled during the last few

description of the seasons. Compare, for instance, his amplification of the aspect and attributes of Spring.

> " So forth issew'd the Seasons of the yeare :
>   First, lusty Spring, all dight in leaves of floweres,
>   That freshly budded and new bloosmes did beare,
>   (In which a thousand birds had built their boures
>   That sweetly sung to call forth paramours)
>   And in his hand a javelin he did beare,
>   And on his head (as fit for warlike stoures)
>   A guilt engraven morion he did weare ;
> That as some did him love, so others did him feare."
>   —*Faerie Queene*, C. vii.

centuries, but they were probably as exceptional then as they are now. It may have been much the same in Italy in bygone days. Men are prone to remember and to record the occasional trying winters or summers, while of the ordinary or average seasons no notice is taken.

None of the Roman singers enjoyed and commemorated the pleasures of spring more heartily than Horace. Some of his lyrics were directly inspired by them. Addressing Sextius he wrote :—

" Keen Winter melts beneath the breath of Zephyr and of
        Spring :
    The dried-up ships are dragged again to shore,
  The kine no longer keep their stalls ; the ploughman quits
        his fire ;
    And fields are whitened by the frost no more.

" Now Cytherea leads the dance, the Graces and the Nymphs
    Join hands and beat the ground with rhythmic feet,
  Beneath the full and cloudless moon ; while glowing
        Vulcan toils
    His Cyclopes' forges once again to heat.

" Now is the fitting time anew our perfumed heads to crown
    With myrtle or flowers from the loosened land ;
  Now too in shady groves to Faun we sacrifice a lamb
    Or kidling, as he pleases to command." [1]

To another friend whom he urges to join him in a festive meeting, Horace pleads the invitation which the returning vernal season seems to offer them for joyous intercourse :—

    " Companions of the Spring that calm the sea,
        The Thracian winds are filling now the sails ;
    The frosts no longer stiffen all the lea,
        Nor snow-swollen rivers roar beneath the gales ;

---

[1] *Carm.* I. iv.

" The heart-sick bird that mourns her Itys dead.
Renews her nest ; the shepherds as they fare
With their plump sheep across the fertile mead,
Pipe once again their ditties to the air,
Pleasing the god who ever loves to see
Flocks and the sombre hills of Arcady." [1]

The same Book of the Odes contains another
little picture of spring coupled with the same
moral reflection that this season of the year
especially invites us to enjoy while we may the
pleasures of this brief and uncertain life :—

" The snows have fled ; the fields renew their sward,
    The trees their leaves :
Earth keeps her changes ; falling streams now flow
    Between their banks.
Unclothed, the sister Graces and the Nymphs
    Now dare to dance." [2]

Virgil, to whom the return of spring evidently
brought keen pleasure, has left some brief but
graphic allusions to the vernal changes in the
aspect of Nature, in which his close observation
and happy descriptive power are well shown.
Thus he refers to " early spring when chilly runnels
trickle from the snowy hills, and the crumbling
glebe thaws under the west wind." [3]   Again he
speaks of the time " when first the west winds
ripple the waters, or ever the meadows blush
with fresh tints, before the chattering martin
hangs her nest beneath the rafters." [4]   But his
ample eulogy of the season and the full expression

---

[1] *Carm*. IV. xii. 1-12.   [2] *Id*. IV. vii. 1-6.
[3] *Geor*. I. 43.   [4] *Op. cit.* IV. 305.

of his enthusiasm for this part of the year are to
be found in a passage in the second *Georgic* :—

" In spring the earth yearns for the fruitful seed :
And then the Almighty Father in the sky
Descends in fecund showers upon the lap
Of his glad consort, when his mighty power
Mingling with hers, gives life to all her brood.
Then through the pathless copses, far and near,
The notes of many a warbling bird resound.
The bounteous soil brings quickly into birth ;
The fields disclose their bosom to the breath
Of warm west-winds ; the tender moisture flows
Through all ; the herbage, now secure, can dare
Safely to trust the vernal suns and skies ;
Nor does the vine shrink timorously back,
Through fear of Auster's tempests from the south,
Or northern sleety showers of Aquilo,
But swells its buds, uncurling all its leaves.
        Such was the season, I could well believe,
At the first dawning of the infant world.
Yea, Spring it was ; vast Earth was keeping Spring.
The east winds surely spared their wintry blasts,
When cattle drank their first deep draught of light ;
When, too, the earth-born brood of men upreared
Their head above the hard and stony fields,
When beasts were loosed in woods, and stars in heaven."[1]

The spring songs of the birds suggested a
quaint conceit to Statius :—

" Now every tree is hung all o'er
        With tresses of the spring ;
The birds their new complainings pour
        And untried carols sing,
Which through the silent winter hour
        They have been pondering." [2]

---

[1] *Geor.* II. 324-342.   [2] *Silv.* IV. v. 9-12.

In his Roman calendar Ovid intercalates an occasional picture of the season with which he is dealing. Thus, when he treats of the ceremonies and traditions associated with the month of March, he throws in a few descriptive lines :—

> " Ice-mantled Winter now at last departs ;
> The snows are vanishing beneath the sun ;
> The foliage, shorn away by frost, returns
> To bush and tree ; buds swell on tender shoots ;
> The fertile grass, so long concealed, now finds
> The hidden paths whereby it comes to light.
> Each field with life is teeming, and the birds
> Are building on the boughs their nests and homes." [1]

Still more characteristic of the poet is a passage in the first Book of the *Fasti* where, in his wonted free - and - easy attitude towards the deities of the Italian pantheon, he subjects the god Janus to an examination as to why the year should have been made to begin in January—a rather personal question in this case, which the god might well resent, seeing that the month which stood at the head of the year had actually been named after him. But the poet has no scruples in his interrogatory. He gives to the god a series of reasons for his opinion that the arrangement in the calendar is a mistake :—

> " Come, tell me why the year begins with frosts ;
> Far better had it started with the Spring.
> Then is the fresh time of the year, and all
> Is blooming ; then the vine begins to bud
> And every tree re-clothes itself with leaves,
> While the young blade peeps forth above the soil.

---

[1] *Fast.* III. 236-242.

The birds in concert sooth the tepid air,
And frolic herds disport among the meads,
Then with the pleasant sunshine comes again
The stranger swallow to the lofty eaves,
Where yet once more she piles her clay-built nest,
Then can the plough break up the loosened fields :
Sure such a time might best begin the year." [1]

Ovid adds that while he had put his argumentation into many words, the god courteously, though curtly, gave him in two lines the reason for the present arrangement — that the winter solstice forms the natural end of one year and the beginning of another.

One of the genial influences of spring is recognised by Catullus in the joyous lyric that so well expresses the delight of travel which that season awakens after a trying winter. In his case, there were, indeed, special reasons why he should have been glad to begin his homeward journey from the far Phrygian plains. The winter there is apt to be long and chilly ; when the winds blow down from the snowy mountain ranges. The poet had come to the region on the staff of the praetor Memmius, in the expectation of being able to replenish a fortune which he seems to have impaired by extravagance. But it is clear from several of his poems that this expectation was not realised. The praetor would not allow him to prosecute the too common official habit of enrichment at the cost of the provincials. So he determined to return to Italy as soon as the

---

[1] *Fast.* I. 149-160.

season would permit, leaving some of his companions behind. The lyric in question, like others written at eventful periods of his life, is addressed to himself.

" Now Spring brings back the tepid air ;
   The fury of the equinox
Is stilled before the joyful breath
   Of Zephyr with his golden locks.

" Now let us quit the Phrygian plains,
   Catullus, and the teeming land
Of hot Nicæa ; let us fly
   To the splendid towns on Asia's strand.

" My mind, so fluttered at the thought,
   Longs eagerly to wander on,
My very feet begin to beat
   The ground impatient to be gone.

" Farewell ! dear band of comrades true,
   Who with me left our far-off Rome ;
Other and diverse journeyings
   At last will bring you also home." [1]

Summer has received less unstinted praise than spring from the Roman lovers of Nature. They thoroughly appreciated the joy of the escape from summer heat to the cool retreat of shady woods, and the music of running water. This feature of summer life calls forth frequent reference in Horace's poetry. He seems to have been somewhat sensitive to the " rabies Canis," the " aestus Caniculae," the " atrox hora flagrantis Caniculae,"

---

[1] Catullus, xlvi. His homeward journey as he accomplished and described it, will come before us in chapter xv. in connection with his love of the sea.

the " furor Procyonis," and the " momenta Leonis,"
by which variety of epithets he denotes the season
of mid-summer. How he preferred to spend the
Dog-days may be gathered from various allusions,
such as that in the second *Epode* :—

" 'Tis sweet to lie beneath an old holm-oak,
　Or stretched at length on matted grass,
While birds are singing in the shady woods,
　And steep-banked streamlets softly pass,
With babbling springs whence limpid waters leap—
A scene that much invites to gentle sleep." [1]

The references to summer in Virgil's poetry
stand on a higher plain. He speaks of "the
joyful summer with its zephyrs calling." As was
pointed out in the foregoing chapter, he delights
in the beauty of the early summer morning, ere
the sun has climbed the sky, and again he has a
keen appreciation of the charm of the cool evenings
when the labours of the day are over, and the
stars begin to appear. Even when he describes
the languor of a mid-summer noon, as in the
passages already cited, there is no note of complaint or disparagement of "the heavy summer
lying on the parched crags." He recognises the
beneficence of the provision of the shelter from
heat and glare afforded by trees to man and
beast. Even the sparse shade of the arbutus
shields the cattle from the sun, beside mossy
springs and grass softer than sleep.[2]

But the Italian summer, though tempered by

[1] *Epod.* II. 23-28.　　　　[2] *Eclog.* VII. 45.

breezes from the mountains and from the sea, cannot escape from one of the consequences of the rise of temperature proper to that season, and the consequent disturbance of the atmosphere which results in hail - storms.   These throughout the peninsula are sometimes extremely disastrous to growing vegetation and even to animal life.   They have been noted among the accompaniments of summer by the Latin poets.   Virgil alludes to the rattling of hail on the roofs, and, as one of his similes in the *Æneid*, he describes how

" when the storm-clouds descend in showers of hail every ploughman and farmer flees from the fields and the traveller lies hidden in some safe shelter—the banks of a river or some high over-arching rock—in order that when the sun shines out again they may be able to return to the labours of the day."[1]

Horace complains of the hail beating his vines to pieces, while the heat was devouring his olives.[2]

In respect to such sudden and destructive storms, when vegetation which has been parched in a torrid heat is the next hour beaten down by lumps of ice, the present time fares no better than did the Augustan age.   Thus on 22nd July 1911, when the thermometer had reached 93° Fahr. in the shade, a heavy hail-storm and furious wind fell on Rome and the surrounding country.   Part

---

[1] *Geor.* I. 449 ; *Æn.* X. 803-808.
[2] *Epist.* I. vii. 4, and again of " verberatae grandine vineae" (*Carm* III. i. 29).

of the zinc roof of the railway station was torn
off, the column of Victory in the grounds of the
Exhibition fell, and the wall of the Sardinian
pavilion was much injured. When the storm
passed away, Monte Gennaro, above Tivoli, the
highest summit of the Sabine Hills and so conspicuous a landmark from Rome, presented an
extraordinary appearance, being covered with hail
and as white as in mid-winter.[1]

To the practical Roman mind Autumn would
naturally appeal on account of its harvests of all
kinds. Virgil in depicting this season, writes
thus :—

" Winter is coming : the Sicyonian berry is
crushed in the olive-mill ; the swine return joy-
fully from their acorns ; the woods yield their
arbute-berries ; the autumn drops his varied produce, and high up on the sunny rocks the mellow
vintage is ripened."[2]

In another of the rural similes that diversify
the *Æneid,* the poet introduces " the abundant
leaves that fall in the woods at the first touch
of the chills of autumn."[3] Horace has a more
domestic feeling in his reference to this season :

" When Autumn has raised from the fields his
head adorned with mellow fruit, how joyful is it
to gather the pears of one's own grafting and the
grapes that vie with the purple dye, as an offering
to Priapus and to Father Silvanus, the guardian
of one's bounds ! "[4]

[1] *Morning Post,* 24th July 1911. [2] *Geor.* II. 519-522.
[3] *Æn.* VI. 309.
[4] *Carm.* II. v. 11 ; IV. vii. 11 ; *Epod.* II. 17.

The " season of mists and mellow fruitfulness "
is accompanied in Italy with some of the enervating
and feverish influences which are experienced in
less favoured climes. From the frequency with
which this feature is alluded to by Horace he
would seem to have stood in especial fear of it.
" Through the autumn we dread the south wind
that brings suffering to our bodies," is the language
he uses to Postumus.[1]   One of the great advantages
of his home among the hills was in his eyes that
it saved him from the leaden breath of the south-
wind and the heavy autumn, which were such
sources of profit to the goddess of funerals.[2]

He wrote to Maecenas that he disliked the
season of the year

" when the first fig and the hot weather furnish the
undertaker with his black attendants, when every
father and tender mother grow pale on account of
their sons, and when assiduous courtesies and petty
service at the bar, bring on fevers, and lead to the
breaking of the seals of wills." [3]

Ovid, too, testifies that

" often as autumn comes, when the year is at its
loveliest, and the full grape is getting red with its
purple wine, when we are at one time chilled with
cold and anon melted with heat, the uncertain air
brings on a feebleness of the body." [4]

---

[1] *Carm.* II. xiv. 15.   [2] *Sat.* II. vi. 18.
[3] *Epist.* I. vii. 5, and also xvi. 16 (" Septembribus horis "), already
cited, p. 80.
[4] *Ars Amat.* II. 315-318. These autumnal returns of great heat
are referred to in one of Cicero's letters to his brother Quintus, written
towards the end of September :—" After very hot weather, I do not

With regard to winter it may be frankly admitted that the Romans had little or no appreciation of what we now regard as some of the characteristic charms of that season. The keen clear frosty air that braces us to exercise, the firmly frozen roads and pathways that ring under our feet and often surprise us with the beauty of the fern-like crystallisations on their surface, the leafless trees with their purple skeletons standing out against the sky in all their manifold variety of form and colour; the snow-storm in its various stages of progress, as it fills the air with flakes, and ends by wrapping the whole landscape in one vast pall of dazzling white; the fairy-like scene after this transformation, and the way in which the gentlest inequalities and unevennesses of the ground are revealed by a thousand delicate blue-shaded dimples that disclose features never otherwise noticed; the marvellous grace of the trees when every branch and twig bears its cornice of snow, or has been silvered by hoar-frost with a crystalline crust that sparkles gem-like in the sun ere it melts away; the lakes and rivers lying smooth and still under their cake of ice on which we can walk or skate—these and other delights which far more than compensate in our eyes for the discomfort and gloom of many days in our northern winter seem to have awakened no

remember greater heat, I have come to Arpinum, where, while the games were going on, I have been refreshing myself with the extreme charm of the river" (*Epist. Quint. Frat.* III. i.).

admiration among the Roman poets when now
and then the winters happened to be severe
enough to let such landscapes be seen in Italy.
This absence of appreciation is doubtless mainly
attributable to the fact that, as a whole, winter at
Rome and in the surrounding Campagna, then
as now, was seldom long enough or severe enough
to give the people an opportunity of becoming
familiar with the varied characteristics which are
so well-known to us. To this day it is common
to find in the houses of that part of Italy no
adequate provision for heating in cold weather.
The winters are for the most part so short and
comparatively so mild that the abundant fire-
places and hot pipes of more northern countries
are not thought either necessary or desirable.

Yet now and then, in ancient as in modern
times, winter has descended with great rigour upon
the lowlands of Italy. We learn, for instance,
from one of Cicero's letters that in the month of
February B.C. 54, the cold in Rome was so great
that the assembled Senate raised a clamour about
it, and forced the Consul to dismiss them.[1] Horace
tells how one winter Mount Soracte, the conspicuous conical hill that rises out of the plain
some five-and-twenty miles to the north of the
city, was covered with deep snow, "when the
straining woods were no longer able to bear their
wintry burden, and the rivers were motionless
under the keen frost."[2] When the cold was

[1] *Epist. Quint. Frat.* II. x.   [2] *Carm.* I. ix.

continued under a clear sky the new-fallen snow
might be frozen hard.[1]

Virgil's allusions to winter are mainly connected
with the labours of agriculture.   He refers, indeed,
to times " when the snow lies deep, and rivers push
along their blocks of ice," " when the vine has shed
its latest leaves, and the icy north-wind has shaken
down the glory of the woods."[2]   But he does not
dwell on those features and their accompaniments
in a severe winter, as if they gave him pleasure.
From the point of view of the husbandman,
winter was the idle time of the year, when work
of various kinds fell to be undertaken indoors, but
not much outside.   Looked at from this agricultural point of view, the poet could speak of
" genial winter " when the farmer could afford to
take a holiday and to enjoy merrymakings with his
friends and neighbours.[3]   Winter, too, was the
time for sport, the proper season " to set gins for
the cranes and nets for the stags, to hunt the long-
eared hares, to transfix the fallow-deer with the
whirling sling."[4]   Horace also, among the occupations of a country gentleman cultivating his own
acres, mentions the sports of winter, when, as
Jupiter tonans gathers his rains and his snows, it
is the time with many a dog to drive the fierce
wild - boars into the hunting - nets, to spread nets
for the voracious thrushes, or to snare the timid
hare and the immigrant crane.[5]

[1] Horace, *Carm.* III. x. 7.   [2] *Geor.* I. 310; II. 403.
[3] *Id.* I. 299-304.   [4] *Id.* 307.   [5] *Epod.* II. 29.

Among the characteristic features of woodlands
in winter there is one which did not escape Virgil's
observant eye, and of which he makes use as a
simile in the *Æneid*—the conspicuous visibility of
the mistletoe when every leaf has fallen from the
trees.

> " In winter's chill, among the leafless woods,
>   The mistletoe, not sown by its own tree,
>   Is wont to bloom, and with its saffron shoots
>   To clasp in firm embrace the tapering stems." [1]

The general impression conveyed by Latin
literature is that on the whole, except by those who
were strongly addicted to field-sports, dwellers in
the city, as well as in the country, disliked winter.
It was with them apt to be a chilly, cloudy, and
wet season, when no doubt the streets were muddy
and the air full of smoke.[2]   There was a general
sigh of relief when the warm west-winds returned
as harbingers of spring. The prevalent feeling was
probably expressed by Horace when in an epistle
to Maecenas he wrote that

"if winter shall smear snow on the Alban fields,
your poet will come down to the sea, and take
care of himself and read his books in narrower
quarters. If you will let him, he will revisit you
with the Zephyrs and the first swallow." [3]

His choice of the expression "smear" (*illinet*)
would hardly have been made had the sight of
a snowy landscape appealed to him as a thing

---

[1] *Æn.* VI. 205-207.
[2] Martial alludes to " fumosus Decembris" (V. xxx.).
[3] *Epist.* I. vii. 10.

of beauty, worthy of a poet's admiration. He
probably used the word to convey his repugnance.
In another poem he asks when he is to be free
from the cold weather, and he exaggerates its
severity by calling it Pelignian,[1] as if he were
living on the very highest and coldest part of the
Apennine chain. And in his dislike of wintry
weather he even goes so far as to reproach his
own beloved valley by calling its village of
Mandela "wrinkled with cold."[2]

Not improbably the popular judgment of winter
was strengthened by the reports that came to Rome
from the northern and eastern parts of the empire.
Virgil has embodied some of this information
from abroad in his longest and most detailed
reference to this season of the year, where he
describes the exaggerated horrors of the Scythian
winter. But his description, being from hearsay,
lacks the vivid simplicity and picturesque terseness
and truth which are so characteristic of what he
narrates from his own observation.

The fullest accounts of these north - eastern
winters to be found in any of the poets are those
which are scattered through the poems written by
Ovid in his exile at Tomi. Coming to that distant
spot with the national prejudice against the cold
season of the year, and finding there that the
discomforts and trials of an Italian winter were
aggravated tenfold, he was easily led to exaggerate
them. His narratives contain statements which

---

[1] *Carm.* III. xix. 8.   [2] *Epist.* I. xviii. 105.

we know to be erroneous, such, for instance, as the assertion that at Tomi the snow in many places lasts for two years. Yet where he describes what he has seen with his own eyes, his great descriptive power does not forsake him even in that cold region. He makes us realise the intensity of the effects of frost not only in hardening the fields but in covering the rivers with ice, so that where ships had once sailed men could walk dry-shod, and Sarmatian oxen could drag the barbarian waggons. And not the rivers only but the very sea was frozen.

" I shall hardly be believed," he says, " but where there is no gain from falsehood the word of an eye-witness should be accepted. I have seen the wide sea lie stiff with ice, while a slippery crust pressed upon the motionless waters. Nor is it enough to have merely seen this : I have myself trodden on the hard surface of the deep which lay beneath my unwetted feet. Although Boreas may howl with tossing wings, there will be not a wave upon the blocked up gulf, and the ships will stand enclosed in the ice, as if in marble, nor could an oar cleave the rigid waters." [1]

It was a relief to the misery of his banishment to send home these pictures of his surroundings, and we can read them still with interest and sympathy.

" Should any one ask," he says, " why I tell these things and describe them in verse, I will confess

[1] *Trist.* III. x. 35-48. *See also* V. x. ; *Pont.* III. i. 7-16 ; IV. ix. 85 ; x. 32 ; xiv. 61 ; xv. 35.

that I have thereby whiled away the time and beguiled my sorrows. Such is the fruit which the present hour has brought me. While writing, I have been away from my grief, and have not felt that I was still in the midst of the savage Getae." [1]

[1] *Pont.* IV. x. 65.

CHAPTER XII

IF mankind are prone, as Lucretius complained, to let familiarity with the firmament by day and night dull their perception of its glories, even more are they wont to leave unnoticed the manifold evidence of that ordered system of phenomena upon the surface of the earth on the due sequence of which their very lives depend. How seldom, for instance, is it intelligently appreciated that the presence of life upon this planet, whether plant or animal, is bound up with the circulation of water. Not only do we owe our continued existence to this circulation, but we derive from it, in a thousand ways, the pleasures of that existence. It is not necessary to journey through a waterless and lifeless desert to have this dependence brought vividly home to our minds. A little reflection should impress it alike on our reason and our imagination. When we think of the clouds that gather in the sky; of the showers that fall from them to refresh the earth; of the springs that gush forth from underneath the land and feed the brooks and rivulets; of

R

the thousands of ample rivers which all over the globe are ceaselessly carrying the drainage of the continents and islands to the sea, which nevertheless receives it all without overflowing; of the ceaseless evaporation from the surface of the ocean, from all terrestrial waters and from all lands; of the diffusion of this unseen vapour through the air, there to be condensed into clouds and thence to descend once more upon land and sea—when all this complex but exquisitely adjusted machinery is reflectively contemplated, it should fill the mind with wonder and admiration. But how seldom do these familiar things awaken any such feelings?

The general features of the circulation of water over land and sea were understood by Lucretius, and are clearly portrayed by him in the sixth Book of his poem, though he imperfectly conceived some parts of the system. His scientific insight served to increase his delight as a poet in the contemplation of the regulated economy of Nature, and in the ever-renewed beauty and harmonious activity of Nature's processes. The movement of water upon the land was happily expressed in Latin by the phrase "aqua viva," living water, as especially displayed in springs and rivers. In his impressive account of primitive man and the gradual evolution of human knowledge and habits, Lucretius alludes to the way in which he supposed that running water was discovered and utilised by the earliest race of mankind.

After stating that these primitive men must have betaken themselves to springs and streams in the same way that the thirsty tribes of wild beasts do still, he tells how they sought the woodland retreats of the nymphs where waters issued with copious overflow, washing the wet and slippery stones and dripping on the green moss, and in places gushing forth upon the level plain.[1] In coupling the nymphs with the doings of the first human beings, the poet sees no anachronism in the association, nor does he allow his own antipathy to the national divinities to withhold him from a seeming acceptance of the popular and picturesque belief in the sanctity of springs and the guardianship of this sanctity by appropriate local *numina*.

While springs in general were regarded as sacred spots, a special sanctity was attached to those which served as the immediate sources of large streams, and particularly of important rivers. When Seneca enumerated various natural scenes that strongly appeal to the religious instincts of man, he included the fountain-heads of great rivers.[2] Virgil, in referring to the departure of the shepherd Aristaeus from the Vale of Tempe, tells how he sadly stood at the sacred source of the Peneus, and called to his divine mother in her chamber beneath the deep river.[3] Of all

---

[1] *De Rer. Nat.* V. 945.
[2] " Magnorum fluminum capita veneramur."— *Epist.* XLI. 3.
[3] *Geor.* V. 319.

the fountain-heads in Italy the most famous for
the picturesqueness of its scenery, and the most
deserving of its reputation, was that of the river
Clitumnus, in Umbria. The Apennine limestone
has there been tunnelled by underground waters
that issue to the surface in such volume as almost
at once to become a navigable stream, which is
further augmented by other lesser springs from
the rocks around. This sudden appearance of
an ample river was one of the natural wonders
of the country, to which visitors repaired from
all quarters. The younger Pliny has left an
excellent and accurate account of the place in
a letter, in which he blames himself for never
having seen it before, and urges his friend Romanus
to pay it a visit as soon as he can. The broad
basin in which the various outpourings of water
unite is described by him as being as cold as
snow, and so clear that the pebbles and the
pieces of money thrown in by pious pilgrims
could be seen lying at the bottom. This basin
lay in a shady ravine covered with some old
cypresses and with many ash-trees and poplars
which were mirrored on the tranquil surface of
the water. An ancient and sacred temple of
the river-god and other shrines around showed
the place to have been long venerated. Pliny
remarks that beside the statue of Clitumnus,
clothed in his robe, the actual presence of the
divinity was further indicated by the prophetic
responses which visitors could there obtain, and

he adds that the popularity of the locality was made evident by the vast number of inscriptions in praise of the place and its tutelary god, which had been scribbled all over the pillars and the wall. The sanctity of the portion of the stream immediately below the well-head was protected by a bridge above which no swimming was permitted.[1]

While the sacred character of such places was respected, they were often in themselves so attractive as to draw people to them for the purpose of social reunions. Reference has already been made (p. 152) to the pleasure which the Romans found in refreshing themselves under trees by the side of running water. And no form of this pleasure could be greater than to enjoy it at the very fountain head of a river. Horace, who has celebrated these *al fresco* meals with such fervour, was fortunate in possessing in his Bandusian spring, the source of the stream Digentia which watered his land and all the valley below. So that he had not to go far to find the delight of being

"Stratus nunc ad aquae lene caput sacrae."[2]

One of the blessings for which the neighbours of Tityrus envied him was that, while they would have to seek other homes, he would be left undisturbed "to enjoy the cool shade among the familiar streams and by the sacred springs."[3]

---

[1] Pliny, *Epist.* VII. viii.   [2] Horace, *Carm.* I. i. 22.
[3] Virgil, *Eclog.* I. 51.

When Propertius sought to convince Tullus that, in spite of all his foreign travel, he would find no land to equal the charm of Italy, the poet enumerated among the attractions of that country some of the varied streams and lakes of which it could boast — the Anio of Tibur, the Clitumnus of Umbria, the Marcian aqueduct, built for eternity, the Alban Lake with its neighbour in the Nemus, and that healthful spring whereat Pollux's steed drank.[1] His selection of waters was excellent.   The Anio was almost as dear to the citizens of Rome as the Tiber itself.   The attractions of the Clitumnus have just been alluded to, and they would be especially dear to the heart of an Umbrian like Propertius.   The Marcian conduit might well be cited by the poet as a work meant to endure for ever ; restored in modern times, it still brings into Rome the coolest and purest water from the Sabine hills.   The Alban and Nemi lakes continue to attract every year thousands of admiring visitors.   And the fountain of Juturna, whether healthful now or not, still rises in the Forum of Rome, where the Twin Brethren watered their horses at it, when announcing the Roman victory at Lake Regillus.

The brooks and rivers of Italy are, as a whole, distinguished by two characters. Owing to the configuration of the country—a central backbone of mountains with flatter tracts on either side—the earlier portion of the courses of the larger streams

[1] *Eleg.* IV. xxii. 23-26.

is more or less rapid. Their little tributaries are
indeed often impetuous torrents. Where the
streams quit the hills and debouch upon the plains,
their rate of motion speedily lessens, and they are
then prone to meander in serpentine curves. The
nearness to the mountains and the heavier rainfall
over these heights lead to a rapid swelling of the
rivers in their lower course, and hence serious floods
have been chronicled from the earliest times down
to the present day.

These varied features, materially affecting, as
they did, the prosperity and comfort of the population, necessarily attracted much attention on the
part of the governing powers in Rome. While
they engaged the practical energies of the skilled
Roman engineers, they also appealed to the
imagination of the poets. Thus Catullus, grateful
for all the helpful kindnesses that had been shown
to him by Mallius, compares the beneficence of his
friend to the bounteous service rendered by a stream
to the land through which it flows, from its source
to the populous plains :

> " As from the mossy rocks on some high mountain-crest,
>   A limpid stream leaps out into the day,
> And pours in headlong course adown its sloping vale,
>   But through the plain more gently takes its way;

> " Winding by thorpe and farm, where the fierce summer sun
>   Has burnt and cracked the soil on holm and lea,
> And bringing solace sweet to weary wayfarers—
>   Such help has Mallius bestowed on me." [1]

---

[1] Catullus, LXVIII. 57-62.

It is, however, the destructive aspect of running water that finds most frequent treatment by the Roman poets. Such a form of terrestrial energy would naturally appeal to the scientific interest and poetic imagination of Lucretius. He has sketched a flood in a few vigorous lines :—

"When after heavy rains a vast body of water rushes down from the high mountains, sweeping along broken branches and whole trunks of trees ; the strongest bridges cannot withstand the sudden energy of the rising flood, which, made muddy by the great rainfall, assails the piles with all its force, and with mighty roar spreads ruin in its course engulfing under its waters huge rocks and whatever opposes its onset." [1]

Virgil has left some vivid pictures of swollen rivers, of which he doubtless had experience both in his early home and afterwards in more southern parts of Italy. Even in his youth he had learnt that rivers have no regard for their banks.[2] Again and again in the *Æneid* he makes use of the irresistible force of river-floods as an image to illustrate the unbridled fury of onsets in battle. On each occasion, however, he varies the description of the flood. In one scene he pictures a mountain-torrent, rushing across the fields, destroying the smiling crops, tearing up and carrying away headlong the forests, while the shepherd, hearing the uproar, stands dumfoundered on the crest of a high rock.[3] In another fight the simile is that of a foaming river

[1] *De Rer. Nat.* I. 280-289. [2] *Eclog.* VII. 52.
[3] *Æn.* II. 305-308.

which has burst its barriers and, escaping in furious
mass, sweeps herds and their stalls all over the
fields.[1]   In a third comparison it is the sight of
froth-laden torrents which resound in their rapid
rush from lofty mountains, and speed over the
plains, each on its own path of devastation.[2]

Some of the aspects of a mountain-stream are
sketched in a whimsical elegy of Ovid's, in which
he represents himself as stopped on a journey to
his lady-love by the unexpectedly swollen condition
of a brook.   Whether or not the incident ever
really occurred as depicted, and whether the lady
was or was not a mere creation of his own lively
imagination, there can be little doubt that his
description of the stream is a faithful representation
of what he must have been familiar with among the
rivulets around his early home at Sulmo, in the
heart of the high Pelignian hills.   He tells how he
had previously been easily able to ford the brook
which would scarcely reach to his ankles.   But in
that mountainous region where snow lingers on
into summer and may be rapidly melted on a
warm day, the rivulets which, in many cases, may
be mere dry channels in the morning, will sometimes fill their beds and continue to swell rapidly
as the day advances.   The brook in question, on
the day of Ovid's visit, had undergone this change.
It could boast neither of bridges nor of ferry-boats,
and as the poet could not cross its torrent, his love
of legend led him to conjure up visions of some of

[1] *Æn.* II. 496.   [2] *Æn.* XII. 523.

the means of transport celebrated in ancient myths.
He wished that he could borrow the winged shoes
of Mercury or the dragon-drawn chariot of Ceres ;
but he consoled himself with the reflection that,
after all, these tales were only the marvellous
inventions of poets, as such things had never really
existed and never would exist.   The thought then
came into his head that rivers, instead of opposing,
ought to assist lovers in their adventures, and he
thereupon indulged in a retrospect of cases in
Greek and Roman legend where famous rivers
had experienced the pleasures and pains of love.
But while he was engaged in his rhapsody, the
remorseless water had been continuing its rise.
On recognising its indifference to his plight he
reproached and reviled the stream as a nameless
thing, fed by no constant spring (that is, without
a *caput sacrum*), but by rain or melted snow, so
as to be either muddy in winter or filled with
dust in the hot weather.   His tirade ends with
the expression of a hope that the brook which
has so shamefully used him may be fitly recom-
pensed with summers always fiercely hot and
winters always dry.[1]

As each Italian river had its own tutelary
deity, it possessed a certain kind of individuality
by which it was more or less marked off from the
rest of its brethren, and which was recognised
as embodying its own distinctive features.   By
general consent, the Po was allowed to stand at

[1] *Amor.* III. vi.

the head of all the rivers of the country,[1] although the Tiber came first in the affections of Roman citizens. Among the sights with which, according to Virgil, Aeneas was favoured in his subterranean journey to the Seats of the Blest, he was permitted to behold the fountain head or sacred source of Italy's greatest river. We are told that "in a scented grove of laurel the mighty Eridanus issues from below and rolls his waters through the forest."[2] Elsewhere the poet pictures this stream "with its golden horns and bull-like countenance, than which no more impetuous river flows through the fertile plains to the purple sea."[3] And among the direful omens that accompanied the assassination of Julius Cæsar, we learn that "Eridanus, King of rivers, seizing the woods in his mad whirl, swept away whole fields, and carried off the cattle and their stalls."[4] The poet's own Mincius, one of the tributaries which help to swell the Po in its course across the Lombardy plains, is called by him the "Son of Benacus" from its flowing out of the lake of that name (Lago di Garda). He loved to remember its ample volume as it slowly wanders in wide curves across the plains, between its banks fringed with tender reeds.[5]

Of all the Italian rivers the Tiber naturally receives most notice in the literature of ancient Rome. Though inferior to the Po in the length

---

[1] "Pater ipse superbus aquarum
Ausonidum Eridanus."—*Sil. Ital. Pun.* IX. 187.

[2] *Æn.* VI. 658.   [3] *Geor.* IV. 372.
[4] *Id.* I. 481.   [5] *Id.* III. 14 ; *Æn.* X. 205.

of its course and the volume of its waters, it far
surpassed that river in the number and interest
of its historical associations. The Romans were
with good reason proud of their river, which
had been so intimately associated with their
history since before the first settlement of the
state and the building of the city. " Horn-bearing
river, sovereign of the western waters,"[1] is the
title given to the stream by Virgil, who, in his
patriotic devotion to Rome, loses no opportunity
of celebrating its natural features. Rising among
the Etruscan Apennines, and making a long
journey through successive ridges of that central
chain of heights, the Tiber, for the greater part
of its course, has many of the aspects of a
mountain-stream. Only after it quits the limestone hills and enters upon the volcanic district
does it assume the full character of a river of
the plains. But, even there, its nearness to the
flanks of the hill - country and its reception of
several tributaries, notably the Anio, that come
directly from the uplands, continue to impart
to the Tiber a more variable disposition than a
longer journey on low ground at a progressively
greater distance from the hills would have
produced.

Flowing through the city of Rome and liable
to the usual changes of mood in rivers of such
a type, the Tiber was always a source of lively
interest to the inhabitants. Pater Tiberinus had

[1] *Æn.* VIII. 77.

been one of their early *numina*, to whom they offered worship. He seemed to be almost a fellow-citizen. They loved his characteristic tawny hue derived from the yellow sand and clay so abundantly suspended in the water, which was consequently so different from the clearer tributaries among the hard limestone hills. They called him "amoenus," charming in his quieter moods, but apt to become violent, overflowing his banks, and bearing along, under the bridges and past the streets of the city, the wreck of fields and farms over which he had swept in his furious career.

In the scene depicted by Virgil when Aeneas first catches sight of the Tiber, the poet displays his consummate art, and at the same time his proud appreciation of the river so dear to every Roman. He takes care to place the incident in early morning, and in spring or opening summer, when the landscape would be at its loveliest, and when the first impression of the scene would be such as might well delight the hearts of the Trojans as they entered on their promised land :—

> " Now from her rosy car the golden Dawn
>   Was reddening with her rays the tranquil sea.
>   The winds sank down, and still was every breath,
>   While through the sluggish tide the oarsmen toiled.
>   Aeneas from the deep beholds a grove,
>   In midst whereof the Tiber's pleasant stream,
>   With rapid swirls and freight of yellow sand,
>   Impetuous sweeps into the open sea.

All round and overhead were flocks of birds
Of many varied hues, that haunted then
The banks and channel of the ample stream,
Soothing the air with diverse melody,
And flitting through the umbrage of the grove.
Aeneas bids his men to change their course :
Turning their prows towards the verdant land,
He gladly steers into the river's shade." [1]

In a later part of the epic the poet introduces the river-god himself into the scene. Aeneas, weary and anxious, is represented as having stretched his limbs for rest by the banks of the river, whereupon "the god himself, Tiberinus of the pleasant stream" appears to the hero, raising his venerable head from among the poplar leaves, draped in thin flaxen mantle of silver-grey, with his hair wrapped round with shady reeds. After speaking some comfortable words of advice and prophecy to the Trojan leader, and promising his assistance, he concludes his address thus : " I am he whom thou beholdest, gently touching my banks with my brimming stream and winding through the teeming fields, caerulean Tiber, river dearest of all to heaven." [2] The adjective " caerulean" which he here applies to himself was in common use among the poets as an epithet for river - gods, but there was probably no river in the country the waters of which less deserved it. Yet every one who has wandered by its banks will remember times when the sky overhead wore its deepest Italian blue,

when the air was still, and when the smooth
unrippled surface of the river in its wider reaches,
seen at the proper angle, reflected in perfection
the colour of the heavens above, though when
looked into from the bank, the water was seen
to be as yellow and turbid as ever.

In continuation of the passage just cited,
Virgil, proceeding to recount how Father Tiber
fulfilled his promise of aid to Aeneas, takes
another opportunity of dwelling on the varied
beauties of the Roman river :—

> " That livelong night the Tiber calmed his stream,
> And stilled its brimming current till it lay
> Silent and smooth, like to a placid lake
> Whereon no hindrance would retard the oar.
> So now, the warriors, raising shouts of joy,
> Speed fast upon their way.   The well-caulked pine
> Glides o'er the depths.   The water and the grove,
> Unused to such array, are sore amazed
> As flashing shields and painted galleys pass.
> All night and day the men toil at the oar,
> Sweeping around the long bends of the stream,
> Beneath the shade of many varied trees,
> And cutting through the sylvan greenery
> Mirrored upon the glassy flood below.
> The fiery sun had scaled the vault of heaven
> Ere they descry walls, tower, and scattered roofs—
> Where mighty Rome has now built to the skies,
> But in those days Evander's poor domain—
> They steer to shore, and soon draw near the town." [1]

Disastrous floods of the Tiber have been
recorded in history, some of them within the
decades with which we are dealing in these

----

[1] *Æn.* VIII. 86-101.

chapters. Thus Cicero, writing to his brother in
November B.C. 54, refers to a great inundation
which extended on the Via Appia, as far as the
temple of Mars, washing away promenades,
pleasure - grounds, and a great many shops, and
accumulating as a wide sheet of water that
stretched up to the public fish-ponds.[1] To most
readers of the classics, however, the most familiar
of these floods is that so vividly described by
Horace in his first Ode to Augustus, when the
waters penetrated into the very heart of the city, as
if to destroy the Regia and the Temple of Vesta in
the Forum. The poet draws a doleful picture of
what might be expected. The city and the country
had been terrified by storms of snow, hail, and
lightning. Men feared lest Pyrrha's deluge was
coming back, when seals and fishes would swim
about the high hills, and among the tops of the
elms which had hitherto been the haunt of wood-
pigeons.[2] Horace gives another graphic picture of
the Tiber in flood in the Ode wherein he compares
the vicissitudes of human life to those of the
familiar river of Rome, which at one time glides
peacefully along in the midst of its channel down
to the Etruscan Sea, but at another time sweeps
along huge boulders, tree-trunks, cattle and houses,
in one vortex of destruction, not without clamour
re-echoing from the hills and neighbouring woods,
when the fierce deluge chafes the quiet streams.[3]

[1] *Epist. Quint. Frat.* III. vii.
[2] *Carm.* I. ii.   [3] *Id.* III. xxix. 33-41.

About three miles above Rome, the Tiber receives the Anio, which, after its course among the Apennine valleys, plunges over the falls at Tivoli, and winds for a direct distance of some sixteen miles across the volcanic plain of the Campagna. Where it quits the hills it well deserves the epithet "headlong" (*praeceps*) which Horace applies to it. But from that picturesque spot onward its speed slackens, and its course on the plain is, on a smaller scale, not unlike that of the Tiber itself in the Campagna. In the first century of our era the banks of the Anio vied with those of the Tiber in the number of their villas and the beauty of their surroundings. Pliny the Younger called it "the most delightful of rivers," and he thought that it looked as if it were invited and detained by the attractions of the villas and gardens through which it flowed. He was referring, of course, to its route below the falls. In the higher part of its course it is rather a mountain stream. Though it may remain for some time with little change of volume, it is liable to be rapidly swollen by heavy rains among the hills or by the melting of snow, and it then sweeps an enormous body of water into the main river. Pliny describes one of these disastrous floods on this stream which broke down and carried away a great part of the shady woods along its banks, undermined hills, blocked up its channel, and in the effort to force a passage pushed down houses and spread itself over their

S

ruins, while on the raging torrent, the movables
and heavy furniture of wealthy families, agricultural implements, oxen, ploughs, herdsmen,
scattered herds of cattle, tree-trunks, beams, and
roofs of villas floated far and wide. [1]

The frequent and appreciative allusions made
by Horace to the great Aufidus of his native
Apulia have already been referred to (p. 73).
While he liked to recall the impetuosity of that
river, he had also a regard for gentle streams, and he
especially singles out for remark the Liris, once so
dear to Cicero (p. 51). He calls it a quiet and silent
stream,[2] and Silius Italicus repeats these epithets
when he describes the river as concealing its current
by its quiet flow, and, unaffected by rain-storms,
kissing the silent banks with its sparkling stream.[3]
The Sabine bard, however, seems to have noticed
that not only did the rushing Aufidus sweep away
its banks, but that even the gently gliding Liris
was no exception to the rule that moving water
tends to corrode and remove the surfaces over
which it flows; for he speaks of the Liris eating
away the fields through which it traced its way.
Elsewhere he alludes to the smoothed rocks of his
low-lying Ustica, and the worn blocks of stone
swept along by a river-flood, and he may perhaps
have connected these signs of tear and wear with

---

[1] *Epist.* VIII. xvii. Silius Italicus gives a vivid picture of the
turbulent Durance, in its descent from the Alps, and its changing
course across the plains below (*Pun.* III. 468-476).

[2] *Carm.* I. xxxi. 7.　　　　　　　　　[3] *Pun.* IV. 348.

the abrading action of running water, which is so obvious to observant eyes.[1]

That hard stone may be worn away by the long continued fall of water had long been familiar, and the fact had often been made use of by the poets. None of these writers, however, nor any of the philosophers of Rome realised it so vividly as Lucretius, whose observant and poetic eye perceived

"Where wasteful Time debateth with Decay."

He recognised with singular clearness the striking evidence that all over the surface of the earth a continual process of disintegration is at work, whereby minute particles of matter are separated from solid bodies and diffused through the world.[2] His observations are forcibly expressed in the following passage:—

"Do you not see that stones are vanquished by age; that high towers tumble to the ground; that rocks crumble away; that the monuments of men fall down; that the temples of the gods and their images, worn out with time, come to pieces; and that not even the holy deity can protract the bounds of fate or strive against the laws of Nature?"[3]

The effect of the water-drop and the corroding influence of the atmosphere even on hard stone were often alluded to by the successors of Lucretius.

[1] "Levia saxa" and "lapides adesos" (*Carm.* I. xvii. 12; III. xxix. 36).

[2] *De Rer. Nat.* I. 313.   [3] *Id.* V. 306-310.

Ovid, for instance, is fond of quoting it for widely different purposes. Thus, in the hey-day of his prosperity, he makes use of it as an argument in favour of his recommendation that a lover should persist in his addresses, despite all obstacles.[1] In his exile, however, it served him in a sadder way, for he made it the ground of a complaint that while even the hard stone is hollowed by the water-drop, and gnawing time consumes everything, the poet himself is left unregarded to endure his misery.[2]

Martial, amid all his clever trifling, was observant enough to note the sad reality of this universal disintegration which spares no human monument, not even those that have been erected at vast cost and with loving care in the hope that they will last for ever. He read this lesson along the public highways with their flanking rows of tombs. Such structures, often ample in size and elaborate in ornamentation, enjoy no immunity from the universal progress of decay, but require to be kept in repair. When the generation that erected them has, however, passed away, the needful care of them is apt to be neglected by the dwindling circle of surviving relatives and friends. Even the monuments of men who were great personages in their day at Rome were allowed to fall into ruin. Martial was impressed by some instances of this neglect. He saw the marble tomb of the illustrious Messala to have been split open by the

[1] *Ars. Amat.* I. 475.   [2] *Pont.* IV. x. 5.

growth of a wild fig-tree. He noticed too that the horses on the costly monument of the rich Crispus, half gone to decay, were a source of merriment to the passing muleteer. But he consoled himself with the reflection that a poet's immortality does not depend upon a tombstone, how large and costly soever. He looked forward to a time when the stones of Messala's tomb would be disrupted from their place and lie scattered about, and when the lofty marbles of the splendid monument of Licinus, the wealthy freedman of Augustus, would be dust.[1] He could wish for a friend's last resting-place no nodding pile of Parian stone, which was a vain and perishable offering to the dead. He would rather have easily-trimmed box-trees and shady palms and flowers from the dewy meadows, which he could water with his tears. As for himself, he felt sure that he would live to future ages: "for literary work cannot be injured by thieves and gains by the lapse of time; such are the only monuments that know not death."[2]

Propertius, as we have seen (p. 94), averred that he had made a provision, with the knowledge and sanction of Apollo, whereby his tomb was to be protected from desecration or destruction. The

[1] This tomb on the Salarian Way gave rise to the following epigram:—

"Marmoreo Licinus tumulo jacet; at Cato parvo,
     Pompeius nullo; quis putet esse deos?"

[2] *Epig.* I. lxxxviii.; VIII. iii. 5; X. ii. 9-12. Ovid had already made the same reflection (*Pont.* IV. viii. 49-52), and Pliny the Younger also expressed it (*Epist.* I. iii.).

suggestion has been made that he may perhaps
have referred to the admission of his poems into
the Palatine library. Certainly if he imagined
that any means could be devised, other than
perennial human care, for the upkeep of his actual
tomb, he could have read no such lesson as Martial
did from the sepulchral monuments along the
public highways, where he would have learnt
that even the benevolent interposition of Apollo,
whose aid he thought he had secured, would be
of no avail to ward off the attacks of "Tempus
edax rerum." But, like Martial, though his grave
is unknown, he still lives in his poems, and wil
continue to be read as long as Latin literature
has readers.

The Lakes of Italy take a less conspicuous
place than the rivers in the poetry of ancient
Rome. Those in the northern part of the country
include the largest and noblest sheets of water
in the southern half of Europe, while those in
the central and southern districts, lying as they
do at the bottoms of extinct volcanic craters, are
often wonderfully picturesque. Reference has
already been made to the latter series of lakes, and
to the impressive features which led to some
of them being considered as sacred places and
dedicated to special divinities, like the Lake of Nemi
consecrated to Diana. To what extent the crater
lakes of Central Italy were chosen as localities
for the erection of country-houses has not been
definitely ascertained. Professor Lanciani, indeed,

has expressed the opinion that the Romans did
not care for lakes, and he states by way of illustration that the remains of only one villa have been
found along the shores of the Lake Bracciano.[1]
But the lakes of Albano and Ariccia had villas on
their slopes, and from the language of Seneca,
already cited (p. 46), it might be inferred that such
places were rather sought after as country retreats.
In the north, too, the Lake of Como had villas on
its shores, and the Lago di Garda was similarly
furnished.

Of the great northern lakes the two just
mentioned are more particularly referred to by
the poets of Rome and by other writers in
prose. The Lacus Larius, or Lake of Como, finds
pleasant mention in the letters of the younger
Pliny. Himself a native of Comum on the banks
of that sheet of water, he possessed several villas
there. In writing to his friends in this home
of his youth he affectionately called the lake
" Larius noster." His love of the place and
appreciation of its attractions are manifest in
the letter to Caninius Rufus which has been
already quoted (p. 33). In another letter to the
same correspondent he expatiates on the numerous
advantages of that locality. If a man loved sport
the lake would furnish him with fishing, and the
woods with game; while if he were disposed to
study he would find his taste abundantly provided
for in that deepest seclusion (*altissimus secessus*).[2]

---

[1] " Wanderings in the Roman Campagna," p. 45.   [2] *Epist.* II. viii.

To another friend who was erecting a house on
the sea-coast, he gave a pleasant account of
building operations which he too was at the same
time carrying on upon the banks of the Lake of
Como. In his letter he enlarges upon the attractions of two of his villas there, each of which had
its own special charm. He remarks upon the
amusement and gratification that he found in
adding to each of them other beauties in which
it might be deficient.[1] The district, besides its
charm for him as his native place, had many
attractions for a studious and observant man, who
loved the country and country life, and took his
daily walks with his eyes open to every change
in the aspects of Nature. When Pliny chose to
record what he had observed he showed an un-
common descriptive power, of which an excellent
instance occurs in one of his letters from Comum,
wherein he gives a detailed account of an oscillating
spring which he had come upon in one of his
walks, and which he found to rise and fall regularly
three times a day.[2]

In his enumeration of the glories of Italy
Virgil includes its great lakes, of which he invokes
two by name, those of Como and Garda.[3] The
former he merely mentions, giving it the name
of "Larius maximus," as if he believed it to be

[1] *Epist.* IX. vii.

[2] *Id.* IV. xxx. There is said to be still a spring of this kind at
Torno on the side of the lake ; not improbably the same as that
described by Pliny.

[3] *Geor.* II. 159.

the largest of the northern group of lakes. But
he adds no words which might indicate that he
had himself seen the place. In the case of the
Lacus Benacus,[1] or Lago di Garda, however, he
accompanies the mention of its name with a few
words that suggest personal acquaintance. He
had not improbably seen this lake in stormy
weather, when the winds from the mountains
were sweeping down upon the water, for he
speaks of the lake as "surging with the billows
and tumult of the sea." Elsewhere, in the midst
of his narrative of the warfare of Aeneas with his
Italian foes, he introduces an allusion which again
brings up his own personal recollections. He calls
the lake Father Benacus, as the parent of his
beloved Mincius, on whose reed-fringed stream
the five hundred warriors of Mezentius were borne
down into the main.[2] But the chief claim of this
lake to the affectionate regard of all lovers of
Latin literature arises from the association of the
scene with the muse of Catullus. To these restful
shores this poet returned, weary with travel and
saddened by the death of his brother, to find
there the quiet and repose of which his ardent
spirit stood so much in need. The little promontory of Sirmio which he has immortalised in

---

[1] This name has a curiously Celtic look. Its first syllable is the
same as the familiar Gaelic term for a mountain, and the last two may
be the Latinised equivalent of some Celtic designation of a particular
height near the lake. It may be compared with Benachran, the name
of a lake in Ross-shire.

[2] Æn. X. 205.

one of the most exquisite odes in the Latin or
any language, has become a place of pilgrimage,
and among the varied beauties and interests of
the Lago di Garda there mingles in the mind
the recollection that it was the home of Catullus
and has been consecrated by his genius.

> " Paeninsularum, Sirmio, insularumque
> Ocelle, quascumque in liquentibus stagnis
> Marique vasto fert uterque Neptunus,
> Quam te libenter quamque laetus inviso,
> Vix mi ipse credens Thyniam atque Bithynos
> Liquisse campos et videre te in tuto !
> O quid solutis est beatius curis,
> Cum mens onus reponit, ac peregrino
> Labore fessi, venimus larem ad nostrum
> Desideratoque acquiescimus lecto !
> Hoc est, quod unum est pro laboribus tantis,
> Salve, o venusta Sirmio, atque hero gaude :
> Gaudete vosque, o Lydiae lacus undae :
> Ridete, quicquid est domi cachinnorum ! " [1]

---

[1] *Carm.* XXXI. The original language is here given, for no
translation can reproduce its music. But the following version is
perhaps as nearly literal as English octosyllabic verse, even without
rhyme, will allow.

> " Sirmio, thou dearest little eye
> Of all peninsulas and isles
> Which Neptune rules in liquid lakes
> And on his mighty realm of sea !
> How willingly, how glad at heart,
> Do I revisit thee once more,
> Scarce crediting that I have left
> Bithynia and Bithynians,
> And safely gaze on thee again !
> O what more blest than cares dispelled,
> When the tired mind has dropped its load,
> And, worn out with our foreign toil
> We come at last to our own home,
> And rest upon the longed-for bed !
> This, this alone is recompense
> For all the toils that we have borne.
> Hail to thee, lovely Sirmio !
> Rejoice to have thy master here !
> Rejoice, O wavelets on the lake,
> And laugh in merriest mood with me ! "

CHAPTER XIII

MOUNTAINS

WORDSWORTH, contemplating the subjugation of Switzerland, wrote:

> "Two voices are there; one is of the Sea,
> One of the Mountains; each a mighty voice."

And he thought with grief of the possibility that their appeals to the spirit of Liberty might be in vain,

> "That Mountain-floods should thunder as before,
> And Ocean bellow from his rocky shore,
> And neither awful voice be heard."

Appreciation of the solemn majesty of the mountains and of the infinite beauty and grandeur of the ocean is of comparatively recent growth. The Romans as a people were insensible to it, though by some of their finer spirits its early stirrings were felt. Until hardly more than a century and a half ago, as is well-known, mountains all the world over were commonly looked upon with more or less abhorrence, as barren, repulsive, and dangerous parts of the earth's surface, haunted by wild beasts, and in some places by still wilder men. They were therefore places to be

283

avoided, or only to be traversed when necessity compelled, and then not until every precaution had been taken against possible disaster. When we remember the conspicuous place which mountains hold in Italian landscape, it may seem strange that they should have received such scant and unappreciative treatment in Latin literature. On the northern frontier of the country, the chain of the Alps, which Hannibal had proved to be no insuperable barrier to invasion, had to be crossed in later years by the Roman armies before the Transalpine territories could be conquered and incorporated into the empire. After the conquest came the crowd of traders who, following the standards, established commercial communications with all parts of the subject lands. The various passes through the mountains, especially after good roads had been constructed in them, must have been frequently traversed, and had become fairly well-known by the beginning of the Christian era. Again, the range of the Apennines brought mountain-scenery of a lesser type within reach or sight from one end of the peninsula to the other. Yet to our modern eyes it may seem astonishing that not only is little notice taken of these conspicuous features in the scenery of the country by the writers either of verse or prose, but that such brief references as are made to them not unusually include some accompanying epithet of disparagement.

It is deserving of remark that the Romans

employed their word "mons" in reference to
any eminence, altogether irrespective of its size
or height.[1] The most trifling elevations and the
loftiest chain of mountains were all "montes."
Thus the Mons Sacer to which the plebeian
legionaries seceded from Rome is a hardly noticeable prominence on the volcanic plain through
which the Anio winds. The hills on which the
city of Rome was built are of no great altitude,
yet they also were "montes," and their appella-
tion and number were perpetuated in the name
of the festival of the Septimontium. As there
was no other word in use that could distinguish
the lofty mountain-chains of the Alps and the
Apennines, they too were "montes," and unless
they were mentioned by name, some qualifying
epithet was needed to denote their greater height
and importance. But in the application of such
epithets Latin writers were no more precise than
in the use of the word "mons." Thus when
they speak of the " Alpes aeriae " or of " aetherius
Olympus," we recognise at once the appropriate-
ness of the adjectives as expressive of portions of
the earth's surface that tower far up into higher
regions of the air. But our satisfaction is damped

---

[1] The word is even occasionally applied to loose masses of stone
which can be moved from one place to another. Thus Virgil, in
referring to river-floods, speaks of them as whirling in their waters the
blocks of rock which they have swept together

("Flumina correptosque unda torquentia montes," *Geor.* III. 254),

and Juvenal alludes to the collapse of a wagon laden with Ligurian
stone and the fall of the "mons" upon the crowd in the street
(*Id.* III. 257).

when we find the same epithets given to mere low prominences on the plains. The most frequent adjective applied to mountains is "altus," which, if translated "lofty," would be a fitting designation for any mountain chain. But the word is affixed also to quite minor eminences on the low grounds.[1]

Interesting proofs of how real among the Romans was the dread of wild mountain scenery have been found in some of the higher Alpine passes in the form of offerings to the local divinities to propitiate their favourable notice or to express gratitude when the dangers had been surmounted. Pious travellers in recognition of the protection thus afforded would leave money or votive tablets on which they recorded their thanks and their names. A number of such bronze tablets have been found at the passes of the Great and Little St Bernard. One from the latter locality in the British Museum bears an inscription in dotted letters which may have been punched with some sharp-pointed instrument by the dedicator himself — "POENINO SACRUM. P. BLATTIUS CRETICUS." This grateful traveller

---

[1] Virgil applies "aerius" not only to the Alps, but to the Aventine Hill of Rome and to the headland of Misenum on the Bay of Naples (*Æn.* VI. 234 ; VIII. 221), and he speaks of peasants with straining neck dragging their creaking wains "montes per altos" (*Geor.* III. 535). The same wide acceptation of the word "mons" has been transmitted to the languages directly derived from the Latin. Thus in French the highest mountain in Europe has been named Mont Blanc, but the same word is shared all over France by thousands of eminences of all dimensions down to scarcely perceptible mounds upon the plains.

recognised that he owed his safety to the favour
of Jupiter Poeninus, the local deity whose name
is still perpetuated in that of the Pennine Alps.

On the other hand, there were callous spirits
who cared neither for the grandeur nor the dangers
of the mountains, with their storms of snow and
their thundering avalanches. The mercantile men
who braved the dangers of the deep were not
likely to quail before those of the Alps. How
completely some men of commanding genius could
detach themselves from even the most imposing
aspects of Nature is indicated in the remark of
Suetonius that Julius Cæsar, in traversing the
Alps from Cisalpine Gaul to rejoin his troops on
the other further side of the mountains, employed
himself in composing his treatise on the Latin
language.[1]

Of all the poets of the golden age of Latin
literature, Lucretius is the only one who appears
to have himself climbed mountains and to have
taken pleasure in their ascent. His keen interest
in the grand elemental forces of Nature would
induce him to venture into those rugged, lofty,
and solitary regions, where cloud and storm have
the noblest theatre for their display. He complains, indeed, that half of the surface of the
earth has been greedily seized on by mountains,
forests of wild beasts, rocks, desolate swamps,

---

[1] *Julius Cæsar*, cap. 56. This may well have been after the passes of
the mountains had become familiar to him from frequent journeys
through them.

and the sea.[1] He alludes to some of his own
experience in the ascent of mountains, and in
watching the movements of clouds above their
summits (*antea* p. 211).   After a picturesque
account of a review of great legions on the
plains, with their marches and charges of infantry
and cavalry, he adds that, seen from a place
among the high mountains, this tumultuous
mass of men appears to be at rest.   In another
passage he alludes to forest fires among the
mighty mountains, when, as the fierce south-
winds blow, the tops of the tall trees are rubbed
together, until at last they burst into flame.   His
excursions with friends into the sombre recesses
of the mountains gave him experience of the
reverberation of echoes, six or seven times repeated, till these rocky places seemed full of
voices, and he could easily understand how such
solitary retreats had come to be regarded by
the country - folk as the haunt of goat - footed
satyrs, fauns and nymphs, that keep up their
revels through the night, while " Pan, tossing the
pine wreaths on his half-bestial head, often with
curved lip runs over the open reeds and pours
forth unceasingly a woodland music."[2]

Although Virgil was born and spent his youth
with the Alps at no great distance on one side
and the Apennines on the other, neither range
draws from him any description or encomium.

[1] *De Rer. Nat.* V. 200.
[2] *Id.* I. 897 ; II. 323 ; IV. 572-589.

He several times merely mentions the Alps.
Among the weird prodigies that preceded or
accompanied the assassination of Julius Cæsar
he enumerates the sympathy of Ætna which
boiled up among the Cyclopean fields, surging
and bursting through its furnaces, and hurling
forth balls of flame and molten rocks, while
the Alps shook with unwonted tremors. He
speaks of the northern lofty (*aerias*) Alps and
alludes to their snows. In one passage Jupiter
is represented as prophesying Hannibal's invasion
of Italy, "when through the opened Alps fierce
Carthage shall hurl vast ruin against the towers
of Rome."[1] The poet once singles out a special
Alpine peak, that of the pine-clad Vesulus
(Monte Viso)—the loftiest and most conspicuous
height to the west of the basin of the Po.
The *Eclogues* contain allusions to "montes"
that are not named, and it is uncertain, even
when they are coupled with the adjective
"altus," whether they belonged to the higher
ranges of Northern Italy or to minor elevations on the plains, or were not rather part of
the imaginary half-Sicilian, half-Greek landscapes that figure in these poems. Virgil's most
detailed reference to an Italian mountain is, if
I mistake not, that in which he alludes to "great
Father Apenninus as he soars through his quivering ilexes, and joys to raise his snowy crest into

---

[1] *Æn.* X. 12. Juvenal wrote that against Hannibal
"Opposuit Natura Alpemque nivemque."—*Sat.* X. 152.

prevent his visits to it from being frequent. In one of his rapturous odes in which he recounts the favours received by him from Calliope and her sisters he speaks of being borne up into the steep Sabine hills ("in arduos tollor Sabinos").[1] But this figurative journey in the company of the Muses belonged to the "amabilis insania" which makes the ode so delightful. It may not impossibly have been the only visit which he ever paid to the remoter and wilder fastnesses of his surrounding mountains. The epithets which he applies to mountains are usually more or less depreciatory, such as cold, wintry, snowy, remote, inhospitable, frightful; and they are unaccompanied by any appreciation of the beauty or grandeur of the scenery.

Even Catullus, with a home on the Lago di Garda, in view of the encircling mountain-ridges and the snowy Alps at no great distance beyond, makes no mention of these features which to modern taste are the noblest in his landscape, save in one passage wherein he speaks of "marching across the lofty Alps." His sonnet on Sirmio contains no allusion to the mountainous girdle that encircles the lake (p. 282).

The prevailing impression among the Romans in regard to mountain scenery is well expressed by Silius Italicus in the following passage which occurs in his description of the passage of the Alps by Hannibal.

[1] *Carm.* III. iv. 21.

"As the soldiers drew near to the mountains the recollection of their previous toils was forgotten in face of the far more serious trials that now confronted them. Here everything is wrapped in eternal frost, white with snow, and held in the grip of primeval ice. The mountain steeps are so stiff with cold that although they tower up into the sky, the warmth of the sunshine cannot soften their hardened rime. Deep as the Tartarean abyss of the underworld lies beneath the ground, even so far does the earth here mount into the air, shutting out with its shade the light of heaven. No Spring comes to this region, nor the charms of Summer. Misshapen Winter dwells alone on these dread crests, and guards them as her perpetual abode. Thither from all sides she gathers the sombre mists and the thunder-clouds mingled with hail. Here, too, in this Alpine home, have the winds and the tempests fixed their furious dominion. Men grow dizzy amidst the lofty crags, and the mountains disappear in the clouds. Were Athos piled on Taurus, Rhodope on Mimas, Ossa on Pelion, and Othrys on Haemus, they would all yield to the Alps.

"Hercules was the first to scale these yet-un-attempted citadels. The gods above gazed at him as, cleaving the clouds, he conquered the steeps of the mountain, and with mighty force overcame the rocks which from the beginning of time no footsteps had ever violated."[1]

Prose-writers were not more appreciative than poets of the grander elements in Italian scenery.

---

[1] *Punic.* III. 477-499. The narrative of Polybius, descriptive of Hannibal's passage of the Alps, and the later account by Livy, based on that narrative, must have helped to strengthen the popular dislike of mountain-scenery. Livy alludes to the Alps as the "prope inexsuperabilem finem" between Italy and Gaul.

Cicero, for example, when discussing the force of habit which reconciles us to what we may naturally dislike, remarks that we may come to find pleasure even in mountainous and wooded places, if we have lived long enough in them.[1] The younger Pliny, while, in letters to a friend, he praises the view of the Lake of Como as seen from one or other of his villas there, has nothing to say of the mountains on which, to our modern eyes, the charm of the scenery there so greatly depends. Again, when he describes in some detail the views to be seen from his Tuscan villa in the vale of the Tiber, he makes no further reference to the adjacent Apennines than that their summits bear tall and ancient woods.

Little can be learnt from the extant ancient frescoes as to the conception which Roman artists had of mountain forms. An attentive examination of the Pompeian pictures has led me to recognise among them three different types in the delineation of hilly or rocky landscape, and to form the opinion that some at least of the subjects depicted were taken from scenes in Campania.[2]

1. Among the backgrounds of the larger Pompeian pictures, and also of the little landscapes inserted amidst the mural decorations, there are some which include conical hills that remind one

---

[1] *De Amic.* XIX.

[2] Wolfgang Helbig was of opinion in 1873 that only one landscape yet discovered could certainly be referred to a Campanian origin, namely the riot between the Pompeians and Nucerians in the amphitheatre of Pompeii ("Untersuchungen über die Campanische Wandmalerei," p. 95). But this, though Pompeian, can hardly be called a landscape.

of Vesuvius or some of the abundant volcanic cones of the Campi Phlegraei. In the House of the Centenario one such hill was depicted with wooded sides, like Astroni or Gauro. In another picture, showing part of the garden of a villa with its impluvium, there rises beyond the boundary-wall a group of pine-clad conical hills. The perspective is peculiar, but the scene would recall to the dweller in Pompeii the aspect of the heights to the west of Naples. In a dainty little picture representing a chariot-race of winged cupids with stags yoked to the cars, the grassy foreground is bounded in the middle distance by a group of conical hills beyond which a blue mountain range rises against the sky—a combination of Campanian scenery which could hardly fail to please those who dwelt among the narrow streets within the walls of the little city.

2. In a number of the Pompeian mural paintings the rocky foregrounds may have been taken from studies among the flanks of the limestone hills between Rome and Naples. The two sets of divisional planes caused by bedding and jointing, whereby the rocks split up into rudely quadrangular blocks have been more or less truthfully rendered. In one picture of a leopard attacking a bull in the midst of rocks, the bedded structure of the limestone is well-expressed. In another painting, where Europa is represented as being bound to the bull, an effective back-ground of vertical limestone beds rises into peaks, from

which flat slabs have been detached by the weather.
One of these blocks lies horizontally on the tops of
some of the lower peaks, while another is inclined
against the cliff behind. The artist has evidently
been impressed by the ruinous aspect of the scene,
as any modern observer will be who enters one of
the narrow, rugged valleys on the flanks of the
Apennine chain. In another picture of Europa
and the Bull, the scene is laid among mountains
which rise into forest-clothed crests in the distance,
while craggy rocks protrude among trees in the foreground. Elsewhere a glimpse is obtained beyond
the broken rocks in front into a mountainous
country which is accessible by a path frequented
by shepherds with their flocks. Or we meet with
a rock-bounded valley traversed by a stream or
clothed with flowery meadows. In these and
similar subjects it is only the outer fringe of the
mountain-world which is depicted. Care is usually
taken by the insertion of a rustic temple with its
overshadowing sacred tree, to give a human touch
to the scene, and this impression is sometimes
heightened by a sacrificial procession approaching
the little shrine.

3. In some respects the third type of delineations of rocky scenery is the most interesting,
though least artistic. To modern eyes the landscapes look like gross and clumsy caricatures of
what they are intended to represent. Thus, in a
picture of Diana, surprised by Actaeon, found in
the House of Sallust, a group of perilously over-

hanging rocks has been placed in the background. In another painting which depicts a bull-baiting, the rocks are represented as branching out into huge fantastic arms from a narrow base on the ground. It would seem that in these and other delineations of scenery where the rocks are placed in impossible positions, impending in such evident instability as to convey the impression of serious danger in approaching them, the artists endeavoured, out of their own imagination, to embody in visible form the widespread popular conception of the mountain-world, where crags and cliffs, in all varieties of strange and threatening shapes, forbade the approach of man.

CHAPTER XIV

THE SEA-SHORES

A STRIKING contrast is to be remarked between the Greeks and Romans in their relation to the sea. Subdivided by the waters of the Ægean into innumerable islands and peninsulas, where the scattered communities could only keep in touch with each other by boat or ship, Greece naturally became a nursery of seamen. Her more adventurous spirits sailed westward, and founded colonies on the most distant shores of the Mediterranean. This national familiarity with the sea is abundantly reflected in the literature of the country. From the time of

> " That blind bard who on the Chian strand,
> By those deep sounds possessed with inward light,
> Beheld the Iliad and the Odyssee
> Rise to the swelling of the voiceful sea,"

the descriptive and musical epithets applied to the deep in Greek poetry show how much its endless variety of surface and of colour, its beauty and majesty appealed to the Hellenic imagination.

Italy, with its peninsular form and its coast-

line on two seas, might have been supposed to be
likely to foster a strong body of sailors. But as
the country was almost one continuous mass of
land, and as communication between its different
parts could be maintained by roads or tracks, there
was much less occasion in Italy than in Greece for
transport by water. Moreover, the Latin race and
the surrounding tribes which it gradually absorbed
into the growing Republic, were mainly farmers
and shepherds. When they came into conflict
with Carthage, they realised for the first time the
necessity of being strong at sea as well as on land.
Having, however, as yet, no fleet of war-galleys,
they had to borrow vessels from the more important Greek colonies in Southern Italy.[1] Not
until the year 260 B.C., during the first Punic War,
were they able to build a navy of their own. Yet
it was not commanded by Romans, but by Italian
Greeks, while its crews were made up of men
from the subject states, and even of slaves and
outcasts.[2] The naval service, indeed, was never
held in high esteem among the Romans. After
the destruction of Carthage, the fleet was allowed
to fall into such neglect that piracy became ram-
pant in the Mediterranean. In the year B.C. 67,
Pompey cleared the seas of the corsairs, but not
until Augustus had established fleets at Ravenna,
Misenum, and Frejus could sea-borne commerce
pass freely to the Atlantic ports on the one side

[1] Polybius, *Hist.* I. xx.
[2] Mommsen, "History of Rome," Books III., V.

and to the shores of India on the other, and the Romans could justly be regarded as

"Lords of the wide world, and wild watery seas." [1]

Yet although a considerable sea-faring element may have grown up in the population from the early years of the Empire onward, the changes and excitements of sea-voyages do not seem to have had much attraction for civilians. Here and there a philosopher journeyed for the purpose of making acquaintance with far countries, or a tourist travelled to scenes of historic, picturesque, or scientific interest, and youths went in numbers to Greece for the prosecution of their education; but for the most part, only men who had some official or other duty abroad or an overmastering curiosity to visit foreign scenes chose to run the risks of the open sea. [2]

As already pointed out, however (p. 40), in one respect the sea had great attractions for the Romans. While they were chary of venturing on

[1] My friend Mr J. W. Mackail has pointed out to me that the difference between the Greeks and Romans in their respective relations to the sea must have been largely due to the question of the food supply, as determined by the physical characters of the two countries. Greece, from its comparative sterility and poverty in water, was ill fitted for raising crops and rearing herds, and was thus in great measure dependent on the supply of fish, which, owing to the lack of abundant rivers and lakes, could only be obtained from the sea. The Romans on the other hand had wide, fertile, well-watered plains, where they could obtain all the necessaries of life, and hence for generations they were under no imperative necessity to venture on the sea.

[2] The Italian farmer was at all times distrustful of the sea. One of the three things in his life which Cato regretted was, that he had travelled by sea, when he might have gone by land (Mommsen, "History of Rome," Book III. chap. ii.).

its surface far from the shore, they were in the
habit of flocking in large numbers every summer
to the coast, where they could look out upon the
wide Mediterranean and enjoy the freshness of the
sea-breezes.   From the mouth of the Tiber southward to Naples, somewhere about a dozen of little
towns were disposed at irregular intervals along
the coast, while in the spaces between them many
villas with their surrounding gardens and pleasure-
grounds were to be found.   Some of these towns
were doubtless pleasant watering-places, at least
for the wealthier citizens who owned houses in
them.   A special interest is attached to those of
them, already enumerated (p. 42), where Cicero had
his seaside residences, and from which he wrote so
many of his delightful letters—Antium, Astura,
Formiae, Cumae, Puteoli, Pompeii.[1]   So long as
he possessed his house at Antium he was much
attached to it.   Writing thence he assured Atticus
that nothing could be quieter, cooler, or prettier
than his own dear home at that place, that he was
even thinking of spending the rest of his life there,
and that during his stay he had fallen so completely
into the arms of idleness that he could not extricate
himself, but was enjoying his books, of which he
had a delightful supply, all arranged in the cases
wherewith the kindness of Atticus had furnished
him.   In the intervals of reading he betook himself
to the shore and counted the waves, when the

[1] Besides these places there were others much frequented, such as
Tarracina (Anxur) of which Martial wrote so appreciatively (*Epig.* X. 8).

weather prevented him from indulging in the sport
of catching lizards.[1] At a later date it was at the
little islet of Astura that he sought the solitude in
which he could indulge his overmastering grief
at the loss of his daughter. In his own words,
this was

"indeed a charming spot, standing right in the sea,
and within sight of Antium on the one side and
Circeii on the other. . . . Nothing is pleasanter than
this seclusion. I cannot think that anything can
be more delightful than my villa here, the shore, the
sea-view, the hills and all the rest."

There in the midst of his deep sorrow he spent
whole days in literary composition, finishing the
long treatises of the *Academicae Quaestiones* and
De Finibus.[2] Next year in reply to a question
put to him by Atticus, Cicero wrote :—

"You have asked me, and you even think I
can't answer, whether I would choose hills and a
view, or a walk on a flat shore. By Hercules, as
you say, the charm of either is so great that I am
in doubt which is to be preferred."[3]

When Cicero visited his villas in the Bay of
Naples, as he seems to have done once each summer,
he found the journey from his residence at Puteoli
to that at Pompeii to be shorter and, unless in

---

[1] *Epist. Att.* II. vi. ; IV. viii. Strabo describes Antium as the resort
of statesmen for leisure and refreshment after their political duties,
and it was thus covered with sumptuous mansions appropriate for such
rustication (*Geog.* V. iii. 5).

[2] *Op. cit.* XII. ix., xiv., xix., xx.

[3] *Id.* XIV. xiii.

rough weather, more agreeable, by pinnace across
the bay, than by the circuitous coast road, which
was probably uneven enough to make a journey
on it somewhat fatiguing. Even at Puteoli, when
the statesman was going to dine with his friend
Vestorius, the Puteoli banker, he sometimes preferred to make the little trip by boat. Much as
he shrank from voyages on the open sea, he could
enjoy boating on the smooth waters of the bay.
There is a pathetic sadness in the last letter which
he wrote from Pompeii.[1] He had reluctantly
made up his mind to leave Italy for a time, where
the clouds of civil war were gathering so ominously,
and go to Greece. He wrote to Atticus that he
was about to spend in foreign travel the time that
might have been passed at his little country-places,
which were so well constructed and so charming.
These words were penned just as he was about to
embark from the harbour of Pompeii, with his
household in three ten-oared barges, his intention
being to make for Sicily and thence to secure a
passage to Greece. But he was a bad sailor, and
the prospect of the voyage distressed him. In the
end he turned his face once more towards Rome,
plunged into the seething political vortex there,
and fulminated his *Philippics* against Antony.

At these towns and elsewhere along the coast

---

[1] Before the coast was so much altered by the eruption of Vesuvius
in A.D. 79 this little town, with its harbour and the river Sarnus winding
to the sea, must have been an agreeable spot. Statius speaks of the
"Pompeiani otia Sarni" (*Silv.* I. ii. 265), and Silius Italicus alludes to
the "mitis Sarnus" (*Pun.* VIII. 537).

a favourite amusement of the wealthier proprietors
was to construct artificial fish-preserves (*piscinae*)
into which the weak Mediterranean tide entered
freely. These were stocked with fish caught in
the open sea, which were prevented from escaping
by a grating across the entrance. The old fish
became tame, and it was one of the attractions
to visitors to see these creatures come when
called and when food was offered. Martial has
left an account of one of these fish-ponds at
Formiae. He describes the sea there as being
stirred only by a gentle wind that bore along
the painted yacht, and was pleasant and cool,
like the air wafted by the purple fan of a
maiden who disliked the heat. Nor had the
fishing - line to seek its catch in the open sea,
for from one's bedroom, and even from bed, the
fish in the *piscina* might be seen taking the
bait that was thrown to it. Should foul weather
come, the table, sure of its supply, could laugh
at the storm, for the enclosed pool fed the
turbot and the bass; the delicious sea-eel would
swim up to its master; the sea-mullet came at
the call of the keeper, and the old mullets made
their appearance when summoned.[1]

---

[1] *Epig.* X. xxx. There were likewise extensive *piscinae* at Baiae;
Martial gives a less pleasing description of those of Domitian at that
place. Cicero refers sarcastically to certain rich and stupid fish-breeders
(*piscinarii*) who cared not whether the Republic were destroyed, so
long as their *piscinae* were safe (*Ad Att.* I. xviii. 6). Varro makes a rather
depreciatory allusion to the fish-ponds, which he thinks were meant
more for the eye than the purse; they were expensive to make,
to stock, and to keep up (*Re Rust.* III. xvii. 2).

How far the little coast - towns provided accommodation for visitors who had no villas of their own is a matter on which further information would be welcome. It was possible in some of them to purchase a mere " deversorium " or house-of-call, where one could break a journey to a more distant residence. This was desirable in the case of the journeys which involved more than a day on the road, unless the traveller could claim the hospitality of a friend on the way. But a frequent repetition of this claim would in many cases be inconvenient.

Owing to the state of some of the roads, travelling to the sea - side resorts might be neither expeditious nor comfortable. Admirably devised as was the system of highways through Italy, and excellently as these main roads were generally constructed, they were not everywhere smooth enough for easy travelling in the carriages then in use. While the chief lines of route were usually kept in good repair, the cross-roads and less frequented tracks might become uncomfortably rough. Even the Via Appia, the " queen of highways," does not appear to have been everywhere as smooth as its reputation required, for Horace in his famous journey to Brundisium, found that great road to be uneven enough to make the travellers glad to lessen the fatigue of driving on it by going slowly, and taking two days to traverse

U

a distance which more active tourists would
have accomplished in a single day.[1]

The roads in some parts of Southern Italy
left much to be desired. Statius gives a lively
picture of one to the north of Cumae, travelling
on which was like sailing on a tempestuous sea.
The improvement of this road was undertaken
by Domitian, and after his operations were completed, a journey which had previously taken a
whole day could then be accomplished in less
than two hours. As a result of this repair of
the line of through communication, it became
possible to leave the Tiber at daybreak and sail
on the Lucrine Lake by the evening.[2] There
are still to be seen at Pompeii examples of the
roads of that region as they existed in the time
of Statius. Those within the walls of the town,
being under the control of a municipality, would
probably have a greater share of attention than
those across the adjoining open country. Yet
nobody can walk along the ancient streets of
Pompeii to-day without vividly realising that a
few hours of jolting on such pavements in a
biga, or even in a modern vehicle with springs of

[1] "Nimis est gravis Appia tardis" (*Sat.* I. v. 6). In Ovid's time
the Appian Way must have been sensibly uneven in some places, for
he alludes to its being worn away by the curved wheels (*Pont.* II. vii.
44). Statius, who, as a resident in Campania, must have had constant
occasion to make use of the road bestows several complimentary epithets
upon it. He calls it "longarum regina viarum" and speaks of it as
"nobilis," "annosa," and "ingens," but he admits that it is also
"saxosa."

[2] *Silv.* IV. iii.

the utmost strength, would be an experience in travel which he would never forget, and would be careful not to repeat.

To enjoy a wide view of the sea was evidently a prime object with the citizens of Rome in their choice of residences on the coast. By the wealthier portion of the community the pursuit of this object was often carried to an extravagant length. At a vast expense huge moles were piled up on the beach and pushed out into the sea. On these substructures palatial mansions were erected.[1] The owners had thus nothing to interrupt their outlook on the open sea, whose surface rippled against the base of their walls. So common had this practice become in Horace's time that he again and again alludes to it, going even so far as, with pardonable poetical exaggeration, to declare that the luxury of his time was covering the seas on both sides of Italy with these amphibious structures.[2]

It may readily be believed that as regards a large proportion of the visitors to the seaside their cup of pleasure would not be filled by merely gazing at the blue Mediterranean or

---

[1] The way in which huge blocks of stone were brought in barges and discharged into the sea to form such moles is described by the younger Pliny (*Epist.* VI. xxxi.), as having been witnessed by him at the construction of Trajan's harbour at Centumcellae (Civita Vecchia). The operation must have been seen and heard by Virgil at Baiae (*see postea* p. 315).

[2] *Carm.* II. xviii. 20 ; III. i. 33 ; xxiv. 3.   Ovid also notices the practice (*Ars Amat.* III. 126).

serenading each other in gaily decorated boats
upon its surface. Each of the populous seaside
resorts presented other attractions more akin to
those of the city. At some of these places, such
as Baiae, there were luxurious thermae ; at others,
like Puteoli and Pompeii, there were theatres
and amphitheatres, where the performances were
modelled on those of the capital. And there was
always the perennial and predominant pleasure,
so tersely expressed by Ovid :—

"Spectatum veniunt; veniunt, spectentur ut ipsae."

Besides the local establishments for amusement
the wealthier visitors no doubt brought with
them their portable luxuries and pastimes from
Rome. The lower orders, besides the public
shows and the itinerant jugglers, had their
savoury cook - shops and wine - taverns. Thus
places which in themselves were fraught with
natural beauty, tended to become more and
more vulgarised, and less agreeable to those
who sought rest in the quiet enjoyment of
Nature. Baiae, with its glorious bay, its unrivalled
distant view, its inland lakes, its hot springs and
baths, was the favourite Roman watering-place,
and its praises were sung by successive generations of poets :—

"Nullus in orbe sinus Baiis praelucet amoenis."

But it shared the fate of other choice spots, and
in the end acquired such a reputation for vice

and extravagance that respectable people preferred not to stay there.[1]

The kind of coast that was popular among
the Romans in the first century of the Empire
may probably be fairly judged from the Pompeiian
frescoes. Among these paintings, inserted here
and there in the mural decorations, a number of
the little landscapes include representations of
various shore-scenes. These are characterised by
a pervading feeling of brightness and repose. The
sun seems to be ever shining, while the blue sea
is uniformly calm or, at most, only ruffled by a
gentle ripple. Nothing wild or solitary is depicted.
No storm-clouds, nor angry seas, nor surf-beaten
cliffs are to be seen. Everywhere buildings of
some kind betoken the presence of man. Little
shrines or sanctuaries look out, each from under
its sacred tree, with perhaps groups of peasants
coming with their offerings to the divinity of
the place. In other examples some of the
palatial mansions are shown built on their massive
submarine foundations, or harbour scenes are

[1] From a reference to Baiae in one of Cicero's letters to Atticus it
would appear that to have been seen at Baiae might be made a reproach
(*Att.* I. xvi. 10). Propertius gave the place his malediction (I. xi. 30).
Seneca tells how he had to leave Baiae the day after his arrival, on
account of the drunken revellers on shore and afloat in every kind of
variously painted boats, the lake strewn with floating roses, and the air
loud with the clamour of the singers. The place had become in his eyes
the abode of iniquity, and was not a fit residence for a wise man
(*Epist.* LI). Statius refers to it as a place where " Romanus honos et
Graia licentia miscent." (*Silv.* III. v. 94). The crowded state of the
seaside resorts in summer is referred to by Cicero, who writing to
Atticus from Astura, says that he was unable to stay at his little places
on that coast because of the throng of visitors (*Att.* XII. xl.).

represented with ships and vistas of open sea beyond. Where the space of placid sea is large enough, it may bear one or more vessels in full sail or manned with oars, and sometimes a ship appears drawn up on the beach. In these pictures the topographical facts are portrayed clear and hard, under the brilliance of an Italian sun, but with no attempt to give the effect of atmosphere, and with only a feeble appreciation of the elements of perspective. Yet though poor as works of art, these old frescoes possess much interest, inasmuch as they bring vividly before our eyes those aspects of sea-shore scenery which seem to have specially appealed to Roman taste.

For the seaside visitors who wished to be thoroughly but innocently idle, there was the time - honoured pastime of gathering shells and pebbles on the beach.[1] They might remember the example of such great men as Scipio and Laelius, who, when they could escape from town, as if from prison, were wont to rusticate together, playing as boys again on the shore at Caieta and Laurentum, gathering shells, and happy in descending to all kinds of relaxation and frolic.[2] Corinna was counselled by Ovid not to venture on the

[1] To Lucretius the gathering of shells was not a mere idle amusement. He speaks with evident appreciation of the beauty of form and colour in the shells which lie on the beach, where the sea with its gentle waves beats on the thirsty sand of an embayed shore (II. 374).

[2] Cicero, De Orat. II. 22. Scipio and Laelius are said to have been as sportive indoors, with the poet Lucilius as their playmate, chasing each other round the table while supper was cooking (Horace, Sat. II. i. 72).

open sea, but to remain on the bibulous sands of the shore, where she might enjoy a protracted pleasure in collecting the delicate shells and variegated pebbles.[1] Cicero, as we have seen, found solace from the fatigue of literary work in merely counting the waves.

But to lovers of Nature and men of an observant turn of mind, there was much on the less frequented parts of the coast to engage their attention, in the movements of the sea and sky and the life of the shores. Of one striking coast-feature of the outer ocean they could have no real experience on the nearly tideless beaches of the Mediterranean—the alternate tidal retreat and advance of the sea, whereby such wide spaces of sand are elsewhere laid bare at low-water, and such remarkable changes in the scenery of a coast-line are brought about twice a day. Natives of the Mediterranean lands were astonished when for the first time they beheld these tidal effects on the margin of the outer ocean. Silius Italicus, for example, contrasts the astonishment of Hannibal and his Carthaginians, when they saw the tides at Cadiz, with the indifference of the native sailors who sat on their benches quietly waiting till the rising tide would set their boats afloat once more.[2]

To Virgil in his Campanian home, the margin

---

[1] *Amor.* II. xi. 13. The sandy beaches furnished Juvenal with a telling simile descriptive of the Grub Street writers of his day,

"Litus sterili versamus aratro."—*Sat.* VII. 49.

[2] *Pun.* III. 45-60.

of the sea seems to have been a favourite place
for observation and meditation, and he has put
into words some memorable records of his musings
there. Although his youth was passed in an
inland district, he may, as already remarked,
have beheld with his own eyes the mirror-like
surface of the neighbouring Adriatic, and listened
to the murmur of its waves breaking along the
flat shores. But it was only after he had made
his home on the Bay of Naples that he became
fully familiar with all the varying moods of the
deep.

The aspect of the sea depicted in the *Eclogues*,
and undoubtedly imitated from Theocritus, har-
monises with the air of slumberous quiet and
bucolic peace that reigns over the inland scenes
in these poems. In one passage we catch sight
of the wide surface of the deep, stilled into silence,
while the lightest breathings of the air have sunk
to sleep. On such a glassy surface the shepherd
sees his own reflection and feels sure that, unless
that mirror is speaking falsely, he is not less
handsome than his rival. Yet even towards its
head the Adriatic is not always motionless, and
its agitation likewise finds expression in these
poems, but in association with images of gentle
movement. When Mopsus wishes to thank
Menalcas for his lay, he can find no fitter com-
pliment than to aver that the song has given
him more pleasure than the rustle of the coming
south wind, or the breaking of the swell upon the

shores, or the murmur of the streams down their rocky valleys.[1]

Virgil's enlarged acquaintance with the sea after he had made his home on the Campanian coast is traceable all through the *Georgics* and the *Æneid*. No one can read these poems attentively, with recollections of one's own sojournings on a coast, and fail to feel that the poet must have been in the habit of musing by the shore, watching the various aspects of the deep, now in calm, now in storm, at one time on the flatter selvage of the curving Bay of Naples, at another on the western cliffs where the full swell of the open sea breaks against the land. His marvellous acuteness of observation, his sympathy with Nature in all her moods, and his gift of concise and melodiously onomatopœic expression are nowhere more conspicuous than in the similes connected with the sea in his two great poems. We can imagine that the line—

" Qua vada non spirant nec fracta remurmurat unda "[2]

was inspired by the remembrance of a day or days when, on the flat shore, he stood watching the little broken Mediterranean waves rolling across the shallows with a continuous melancholy cadence.

In the neighbourhood of Naples there are ranges of cliff which command wide views of the

---

[1] *Eclog.* II. 25 ; IX. 57.
" Nec percussa juvant fluctu tam litora."—V. 83.
[2] *Æn.* X. 291.

open sea, and furnish excellent opportunities of
witnessing the bursting of the waves against
precipitous faces of rock.   Immediately to the
west of the town the ridge of Posilipo is readily
accessible, while further west the island of Nisida,
the headlands of Miseno and Monte di Procida,
and the islands of Procida and Ischia are all
within easy reach. That Virgil often availed himself of the facilities for observation thus afforded
cannot be doubted. The graphic details of his
sea-pictures are evidently the result of long and
frequent study. We can imagine him seated on
one of these eminences after a south-west gale
has subsided, but when the long swell is still
rolling to the shore, and penning the lines which
may be thus translated :—

> "The wave that speeds from out the midmost deep
>   Begins afar to whiten as it comes :
>   Bearing an ample breast it rolls to land,
>   Falls like a mountain-mass with thund'rous din
>   Upon the rocks, and stirs up from the depths
>   A surge that whirls the black sand high aloft." [1]

The application of the term "black" to sand
in this passage deserves remark, for ordinary shore
sand is familiarly known to be pale yellow or even
white. Virgil was well aware of its common
colour. The "flavus Tiberis" had printed itself
deeply on his mind. In this same book of the
Georgics he mentions the "fulvas arenas" of the
Circus, and the "flaventes arenas" of the eddying

[1] *Geor.* III. 237-241.

Danube.¹ There can be little doubt, however, that the epithet (*nigram*) in the passage quoted was deliberately chosen, and accurately describes what the poet himself had actually seen somewhere. My own belief is that the storm which furnished the simile was witnessed by Virgil on a part of the Bay of Naples where the shore sand is black from the trituration of the dark lavas of the district. This peculiarity is now more especially visible along that portion of the coast-line where the lava-streams from Vesuvius have flowed down to the sea, and where south-west gales break with great violence upon the rocks. That the black sand was seen by the poet in the Bay of Naples is made certain by a simile in the *Æneid*, in which he describes the disturbance of the water caused by the building of the moles for the construction of the shore villas at Baiae. The huge masses of stone that were there cast into the deep, raised such a tumult of waves as to stir up the black sands from the bottom, while lofty Procida trembled at the commotion, and Ischia too, where lay the hard subterranean couch to which Typhoeus was hurled by the commands of Jove.²

In his numerous allusions to the breaking of rough seas upon the land Virgil varies his descriptions, and introduces into each of them some fresh aspect of the scene. Thus Mezentius, assailed by

---

¹ *Geor.* III. 110, 350. In the underworld, too, he represents the Blest as sporting on the "fulva arena" (*Æn.* VI. 648).

² *Æn.* IX. 710-716. This simile is used to illustrate the thunderous fall of men and armour pierced by the weapons of Turnus.

a swarm of Trojans and resisting their attacks
alone, is said to be—

> " Like to a cliff that rises from the midst
>   Of the vast ocean, fronting winds and waves,
>   Bearing the force, the fury, and the threats
>   Of sky and sea ; itself unmoved the while." [1]

Along the varied coast-line of this region there
are little exposed recesses and longer stretches
of gravelly beach, which receive the full rush of
the breakers during a south - westerly gale and
the swell of the rollers which for a time come to
shore after the storm has spent its force. It was
doubtless while watching the movements of the
sea on one of these exposed beaches that Virgil
received the vivid impression which furnished him
with perhaps the most original, and certainly one
of the most picturesque and accurately depicted
similes in any part of his poetry. The passage
occurs in the eleventh Book of the *Æneid*, where
the alternate advance and retreat of the embattled
armies of the Latins and Trojans are described.

> " Qualis ubi alterno procurrens gurgite pontus
>   Nunc ruit ad terram, scopulosque superiacit unda
>   Spumeus, extremamque sinu perfundit arenam ;
>   Nunc rapidus retro atque aestu revoluta resorbens
>   Saxa fugit, litusque vado labente relinquit." [2]

In these verses there is no weakening of the
majestic roll of the Virgilian hexameter. The
feeling of the forward and backward tumult of
the wave is conveyed with a simplicity and energy

---

[1] *Æn.* X. 693.   [2] *Id.* XI. 624-628.

that bring the scene clearly before the eye. But it is not until, with recollections of personal observation of such a shore scene, we examine the passage in detail that we realise with what extraordinary fidelity and conciseness the poet has reproduced in words a picture, the details of which he must have studied with the closest attention on the spot. His description has the breadth and colour of a skilfully executed painting, and at the same time the faithful detail of a photograph. Thus, he takes separately the two courses of the wave, as it advances and retreats (*alterno gurgite*). In the first part the water rushes ashore (*ruit ad terram*), surmounts the rocky ledges (*scopulos superiacit unda*), and, breaking into foam (*spumeus*), sweeps onward to the sandy beach at the upper end of the cove which it drenches (*perfundit arenam*). In the second or downward journey, the wave flees swiftly back (*rapidus retro fugit*), dragging along with it the stones and pebbles of the beach which are kept spinning round in its boiling current (*aestu revoluta resorbens saxa*), and it finally recedes from the shore in the thin stream of water that glides down the beach in the wake of the retreating wave (*litusque vado labente relinquit*). It may well fill us with astonishment to find that Virgil should have observed and pictured in four pregnant words one of the great dynamical processes of the sea—the rotation of shingle in the course of abrasion, and that he should have noticed that, after the main mass of water has retreated, a portion, detained by friction on the higher part of the beach and augmented by what oozes out of the saturated sand, flows more slowly down the slope. He, of course, knew nothing of the scientific meaning of the facts which he noted, but no man of science could have observed them more accurately or described them with more concise precision. At the same time we can recognise how graphic and appropriate for poetic use is the comparison of the surging of the two armies in battle to the alternate advance and retreat of the successive waves, and all the noise and fury with which they assail the shore.

But there is still another feature in the passage which deserves to be noticed. One of the most imposing elements in a storm at such a shingly beach is the noise made by the harsh grating of the stones against each other as they are sucked back by the retreating wave—a noise which on exposed Atlantic coasts may sometimes be heard at a distance of eight or ten miles. Virgil could not fail to be impressed by this characteristic sound. In his singularly condensed description, where every word is full of meaning and no single word could be spared, there was no room for additional epithets, but the poet's musical ear led him to indicate the grinding noise of the shingle by the choice and disposition of the words in his simile. He has selected a series of epithets in which the recurrent sound of the letter "r" is evidently meant to convey his impression of the peculiar rasping sound—"nunc rapidus retro atque aestu

revoluta resorbens saxa." Again, in the last line
of the simile, the contrast between the grating
sound of the retreating gravel and the almost
noiseless flow of the sheet of water that follows
down the beach seems to be marked by the assonant
repetition of the liquid "l"—"litusque vado labente
relinquit." [1]

Other similes in the *Æneid* might be cited in
further illustration of the keen eye wherewith
Virgil looked on the varying aspects of the sea,
more especially on its turmoil. He evidently loved
to watch the gradual whitening of the face of the
deep under the breath of a rising storm, the shore-
ward race of the rollers before the gathering fury
of the gale, the wild rush of the breakers as they
burst with thunderous clamour against a cliff
which stands unshaken and immovable, while the
barking waves that vainly chafe its sides hurl forward the sea-weed that sinks back into the foam.[2]

---

[1] It is interesting to compare the picture drawn here by Virgil with
some of those of the same aspect of the shore depicted in modern poetry.
Crabbe, so faithful a delineator of Nature, describes, as one of the
features of a storm on the east coast of England, how the billows,
chasing each other from the outer sea, hurry to their utmost stretch ;—

> " Curled as they come, they strike with furious force,
> And then, re-flowing, take their grating course,
> Raking the rounded flints, which ages past
> Rolled by their rage, and shall to ages last."
> *The Borough*, Letter i.

Readers of Tennyson will remember his allusion to a shingle-beach
in *Maud* (I. iii. 11).

> " Listening now to the tide in its broad-flung, ship-wrecking roar,
> Now to the scream of a maddened beach, dragged down by the wave."

In his note on this passage the poet remarks ;—" In the Isle of
Wight the roar can be heard nine miles away from the beach '
(Annotated edition (1908), vol. iv. p. 274).

[2] *Æn.* VII. 528, 586 ; XII. 365.

One further quotation may be given as proof that Virgil's marine studies were not confined to the shores of the mainland. The charming picture which he has drawn of the gull-haunted rock, chosen by Aeneas as the goal for his boat-race, was probably a reminiscence of some boating excursion made by the poet himself along a rocky part of the Italian coast :—

" Far out at sea, fronting the spray-lashed shore
There stands a solitary rock, at times submerged,
And swept by swelling waves, when all the stars
Are hidden from sight by wintry north-west gales ;
But when the heavens are clear, the ocean calm,
It lifts its silent, level summit to the air,—
A place where sea-fowl love to sun themselves." [1]

In both the *Georgics* and in the *Æneid* Virgil has introduced coast-scenes which are not perhaps referable to any special localities, but must be regarded as fanciful generalisations. Much ingenuity has been shown by commentators in tracing among the Greek poets passages from which Virgil may have borrowed some of the features of his pictures. Even if the debt be acknowledged, we may contend that he generally expands and improves his materials. But it is also permissible to believe that the vividness of his descriptions may sometimes have been inspired by recollections of scenes which he had himself visited in the course of his travels. As examples of these pictures may be cited the cavern of

[1] *Æn.* V. 124.

Proteus on the side of a sea-girt mountain, with its
sheltered anchorage for storm - stayed mariners,[1]
and the lively sketch of the Libyan bay, walled
round with cliffs and a background of forest, and
screened from wind and waves, where Aeneas and
his battered fleet found refuge after Juno's storm.[2]

The poems of Catullus contain some charming allusions to sea-shores. But as most of his
sea-pieces are taken rather from the open sea
than from the land, the whole will be considered
in the following chapter.

[1] *Geor.* IV. 418.   [2] *Æn.* V. 159-169.

CHAPTER XV

THE OPEN SEA

GREAT as was the attraction of a wide view of the sea to all classes of Roman citizens, to be far out on the surface of the open Mediterranean was a situation which few enjoyed. In calm summer weather and in sheltered bays like that of Baiae,[1] boating and yachting were doubtless favourite pastimes. But there was nevertheless a prevalent conviction that the sea, on the whole, was most safely and pleasantly viewed from the land. And this belief is amply expressed in Latin literature. We look there in vain for anything akin to the enthusiastic admiration of the grandeur and beauty of the open ocean, now so fully recognised by the modern world. We can hardly conceive how a Roman audience would have received one of our joyous sea-songs, which awaken a responsive chord in the heart of every average Englishman, or what would have been thought in the Augustan age of the sanity of a poet who could have penned the stanzas on the Ocean in *Childe Harold*.

The general burden of Roman writers in their

[1] The Baiana cymba, or skiff of Baiae, was a well-known object at that place. It was only adapted for smooth water.

allusions to the sea is one of disparagement and
complaint, sometimes even of passionate invective.
The fickleness and treachery, the fury and destructiveness of the deep are continually dwelt upon,
and the risks of venturing on its surface are painted
with wearisome iteration.   Even Lucretius, whose
imagination was so alive to the mightier forms of
physical energy in the world, could see in disastrous
storms, which strew the shores with wreckage, only
a "warning to mortals to shun the wiles of the
sea, its force and its snares, nor ever to trust it,
even when it treacherously smiles with an alluring
calm."[1]   The same caution is repeated again and
again by later poets.   Thus Propertius, in his
touching lament over the death of Paetus, bitterly
complains that by taking to the sea men have
introduced another opening for their own destruction; as if the land had not been fateful enough,
we have added the waves; and the risks of chance
we have increased by art.   Whatsoever we may
gain belongs to the winds; no ship ever grows
old; the very harbour is deceitful.[2]

Ovid in his earlier poems, before the sad experiences of his exile, is loud in his warnings against
venturing on the sea.   He asserts that there is no
safety further than the beach, all that lies beyond
that terraqueous limit being a blind path.[3]   In his
version of the legend of Ceyx and Alcyone, he puts
into the mouth of the heroine sentiments which

---

[1] *De Rer. Nat.* II. 552.   [2] *Eleg.* IV. vii. 29-36.
[3] *Amor.* II. xi. 16.

were also frankly his own—"the waves affright
me, and the sad thought of the deep; lately have
I seen broken planks upon the shore, and often
have I read the names on tombs wherein no
body lay."[1] In his later poetry written at Tomi
after the rough experiences of his voyage thither,
references to the sea become more frequent and
more melancholy, for they are used in illustration
of his own shipwrecked life. Thus in the last
Book of the *Tristia*, he speaks in one elegy
of his ship having been broken, not sunk nor
overwhelmed, and though without a harbour
yet still standing above the waters. In another
place he says that his friends looked on at his
shipwreck from their safe hill, and never held
out a hand to him as he swam in the cruel
deep. Again he complains that whereas formerly,
when a prosperous breeze filled his sails, he
was borne along by the splendour of reputation,
now he cares not for glory and would fain be
unknown to any one; his enfeebled poetic vigour
leads him to compare himself to a skiff that has
been long out of water and is now gaping with
cracks and turning to mere crumbling tinder. He
is full of fears and forebodings, as one who has
been shipwrecked shudders at the sight even of
calm waters.[2]

Nowhere does the general Roman dislike or even

[1] *Metam.* XI. 427.
[2] *Trist.* V. ix. 17, 18; XI. 13, 14; XII. 27, 39, 50; *Pont.* II.
vii. 8. The Pontic Epistles contain many similar marine allusions, *e.g.*,
II. iii. 25; vi. 9; ix. 9.

abhorrence of the open sea find such repeated and characteristic expression as in Horace's poems. This writer makes no attempt to disguise or apologise for the intensity of his feeling on the subject. In the course of his life he had several times occasion to cross the Adriatic Sea, and his experiences on those voyages left an indelibly unpleasant impression on his memory. He hardly ever mentions the name of that sea, without the addition of some uncomplimentary epithet, such as unquiet, black, hoarse, wicked.[1] Like Lucretius, he preferred to behold the fury of the deep from a firm and safe platform on land.[2] It was his conviction that a man who sailed three or four times a year into the Atlantic and came back each time safe and sound, must certainly be under the protection of the very gods themselves.[3] He evidently found a difficulty in believing that anything but the lust of gain or the dread of poverty could induce a man voluntarily to make a sea-voyage. And he seems to have had a conviction that when they went to sea neither the sailor nor the trader could possibly divest himself of the terror which the poet thought should be the uppermost sentiment in all seafaring minds. He speaks with commiseration of the

---

[1] Horace's vituperative vocabulary when he has occasion to allude to the sea is remarkably varied. I have noted the following epithets and doubtless the list is not exhaustive — curvans, raucus, inquietus, improbus, ater, turgidus, ventosus, belluosus, dissociabilis, avarus, hibernus, iratus, inversus, furens.

[2] *Epist.* I. xi. 10.
[3] *Carm.* I. xxxi. 13.

"pavidus nauta" and of the "mercator metuens Africum."[1]

If we try to account for this general national dislike of the sea, we may, I think, recognise two chief causes to which it may be assigned. In spite of all the prognostics, physical and biological, which observation and tradition had handed down (in large part, however, only useful on land) it was impossible to guard against the sudden and unexpected rise of a storm, and the vessels, often deckless and leaky, were not always well-fitted to cope with a rough sea. In those days there were no Admiralty charts, nor any organised service of local pilots. Sunken reefs and shoals were doubtless often only detected by vessels actually grounding on them even in clear daylight. Hence shipwrecks were of common occurrence, and as we know of no life-saving apparatus carried on ship-board, the average proportion of survivors from wrecks was probably much smaller than it is now. The Romans were certainly not adventurous sailors. They laid up their ships and boats in winter, and the close time for navigation on the open sea seems to have lasted from the middle of November to the middle of March. When spring returned, the vessels were hauled down again on rollers into the sea, often

---

[1] *Carm.* I. i. In another poem he refers to the trader who only through fear of poverty is driven to brave the perils of the sea, of rocks, and of fires (*Epist.* I. i. 46). Cato's opinion of the merchant's calling has already been referred to (p. 27).

with their dried-up timbers for a time leaky and unseaworthy.[1]

In the second place, I have little doubt that another powerful influence which contributed to the wide-spread Roman dislike of the open sea was to be found in a general constitutional temperament that made the population specially liable to sea-sickness. Then, as now, no rank of society was exempt from the complaint; the wealthy owner in his own luxurious trireme being, as Horace remarks, as liable to be prostrated as the man who had to content himself with a hired boat.[2] Poets who had once undergone the miseries of this malady revenged themselves and their fellow-sufferers by heaping opprobrious epithets on the cause of their distress. And the Sabine bard leaves us in no doubt as to what his sufferings had been on the Adriatic Sea.[3]

It became a habit of the poets to utter maledictions even on the invention of ships. Lucretius dwells on the safety of primitive man, for whom the sea would rage in vain, and who could not be lured to his destruction by the wiles of the laughing waves, because the wicked art of shipbuilding lay still unborn.[4] The theme was congenial to the exuberant imagination of Ovid. In the golden age, he wrote, the pine had not yet come down from the mountains to the waves, and men knew

---

[1] See the Ode of Horace cited *ante* p. 240; also Ovid, *Fast.* IV. 131-132.
[2] *Epist.* I. i. 92.   [3] *Carm.* III. xxvii. 18.
[4] *De. Rer. Nat.* V. 1002.

no coasts but their own. The sea was disturbed for
the first time by the oarsmen of Jason ; and would
that the *Argo* had foundered, so that there might
then have been no navigation.[1] Horace held that
the first sailor must have had a heart cased in the
strength of triple brass.[2] Propertius cursed the same
daring navigator, but as the imprecation was drawn
forth in the midst of a storm off the Greek coast,
the poet's strong language was perhaps excusable.[3]
Statius carried the idea to a still higher flight of
exaggeration when he said that before there were
vessels of any kind, the ocean lay in sluggish
slumber, and dared not foam and sprinkle the
clouds with its spray ; but that at the first sight of
ships the waves began to swell and the tempest
arose against men.[4]

A vivid perception of how seafaring was looked
upon by an accomplished Roman is obtained from
a perusal of Cicero's letters. This great man, as
was remarked in the last chapter, had a full complement of the national dislike of the sea. In the
course of his life he was under the necessity of
making a voyage to take up his duties as pro-consul
of Cicilia. The letters written by him to his friend

[1] *Metam.* I. 94 ; *Pont.* III. i. 1 ; *Amor.* II. xi. 5. Lucan repeats the
charge that by the *Argo* another mode of death had been added to the
fate of mankind (*Phars.* III. 193).

[2] *Carm.* I. iii. 9.

[3] *Eleg.* I. xvii. 13. His deliberate judgment is expressed in his
Elegy IV. ix. 35.

> " Non ego velifera tumidum mare findo carina :
>   Tuta sub exiguo flumine nostra morast."

[4] *Silv.* III. ii. 71.

Atticus during the journey allow us, as it were, to accompany him in his crossing of the Adriatic and as he threaded his way among the Greek islands. It will be understood that he was seldom or never out of sight of land, and he appears to have usually spent the night in some sheltered anchorage.

He left Brundisium early in June B.C. 51. His crossing of the Adriatic is described by him as "most disagreeable," so that on reaching Actium he determined not to face the seas that might await him in rounding the headlands of Leucadia, but, quitting the vessel, to cross by land to Athens. He arrived there on the 24th of the month, and after a stay of about a fortnight, set sail from the Piraeus on 6th July. On that day, however, he only got as far as Zoster at the foot of Hymettus, a few miles down the coast, where, as the wind proved unfavourable, he remained for a day. On the 8th the crossing to Ceos was agreeable, but from that island a strong wind carried him to Gyaros and thence by Syros to Delos, more rapidly (and we may suppose on a rougher sea) than was pleasant to him. He thus took six days from Athens to Delos, a distance of somewhere about 100 English miles. Well might he begin a letter to Atticus—"travelling by sea is a mighty business, especially in the month of July." [1]

---

[1] If the aphract Rhodian vessel which carried Cicero had its full complement of rowers as well as sails, so that when the wind fell, it was "juvenum sudantibus acta lacertis," we can imagine how trying to his landsman's susceptibilities must have been the odours of the ship on a hot July day.

He adds that Atticus knew the kind of vessel he was sailing in — one of the deckless Rhodian craft, than which nothing was less able to stand the sea. So he will not be in a hurry, nor stir from Delos till he sees all the headlands of Gyræ clear. It was a fortnight from the time of his leaving Athens before he landed at Ephesus. He wrote again from that city to Atticus, telling quite frankly that he had accomplished the voyage from Delos "without fear and without sea-sickness, but rather slowly because of the feebleness of these open vessels of the Rhodians." The rest of the journey was made by land, and he reached Laodicea on 31st July.[1] Thus from the time he left Rome he must have been altogether some two months on the way.

Next year on his journey back to Italy Cicero again encountered contrary winds as well as fair weather, and he found a deckless Rhodian vessel to be no faster nor more comfortable than in the previous year. He complained of being much hindered by the Etesian winds, of the slowness of the ship which had taken twenty whole days to reach Ephesus, and of having had to wait at that port for the calm weather which these Rhodian barks required. The passage from Ephesus to Athens again took up a fortnight, and is described by him as "slow and disagreeable." Contrary winds and rough weather caused various irksome detentions between Athens and Corcyra, but he

[1] *Ad Att.* V. ix., xii., xiii.

was at least fortunate in having a pleasant traverse of the Adriatic Sea, and on 24th November B.C. 50 he had the happiness of landing once more at Brundisium.

Cicero had left his faithful amanuensis, Tiro, ill at Patrae, and after making all arrangements for his being taken care of there, wrote some affectionate letters to him from halting places on the journey, showing at once his regard for his devoted secretary and his anxiety for any one who had to make a sea-voyage. His first care on setting foot again upon Italian soil was to send Tiro a solicitous letter which contained the following injunctions :—

"Let me beg and beseech you not to set sail rashly (seamen are apt to hurry for the sake of their own profit): be cautious, my dear Tiro; there remains for you a wide and difficult sea to cross. If you can, come with Mescinius, for he is wont to sail with prudence; if not, come with some person of consideration, by whose authority the shipowner may be influenced."[1]

From his repugnance to sea-faring, Cicero's sympathy was at once enlisted for any relative or friend who had to make a voyage, and at times it rose to keen anxiety. This kindly feeling is well shown in his correspondence with his brother Quintus. When the latter was about to return from his official duties in Sardinia, Cicero wrote begging him to act cautiously and carefully

---

[1] *Ad Att.* VI. viii. ; VII. ii.; *Ad Fam.* XIV. v. ; XVI. ix.

in regard to sailing in December. While he longed to see his brother again, he hoped Quintus would not think of starting unless in settled weather. Again, when his brother was with Julius Cæsar in Gaul and Britain, Cicero's anxieties increased in proportion to the distance between them, and to his own ignorance of the character of those far distant regions. He wrote: "How delightful to me was your letter from Britain. I was afraid of the ocean: I was afraid of the shore of the island." And when no tidings had come from the north for a space of more than fifty days he wrote again that "both land and sea out there make me anxious, nor can I help thinking of what I least wish to happen."[1]

When during those weary months of hesitation whether or not to join Pompey in Epirus, Cicero had at last planned to cast in his fortunes with that leader, he wrote to Atticus from Formiae that he had arranged for everything save a concealed and safe journey across the Adriatic Sea, for at that season of the year (March) he could not venture on the Tyrrhenian sea in front of him. And five years later, when, amidst the political convulsions of his country, he seriously attempted to quit Italy for a time, the thought of the inevitable sea-voyage distressed him. Atticus had told him that the Adriatic might be crossed in five hours from Hydruntum, to the south of Brundisium, and at one time he had thought of

[1] *Ad Quint. Frat.* II. i., xv. ; III. iii.

starting from there, as he shrank from the long voyage from the west coast of Italy. Eventually he sailed and got as far as Syracuse. Starting from that port he was compelled by the south wind to put into Rhegium, where, hearing news from Rome that led him to hope that he might still be of use to the Republic, he abandoned the voyage, hurried back to the city and plunged once more into the political arena. But the end was now near. When he heard that his name was included in the proscription he tried to escape by sea. Finding a vessel at Astura, he sailed as far as Circeii. Plutarch states that the pilots wished at once to put out to sea from that place; but whether or not from dread of another voyage, Cicero quitted the ship and returned to Astura. He was persuaded by his servants to sail to Caieta, near which was his villa at Formiae, and thus for the last time he ventured upon the surface of the deep. But the assassins had tracked him to his villa. As they were approaching, his attendants attempted once more to carry him down to the sea; but they were overtaken, and he boldly met the death that awaited him.

That even a Stoic philosopher, who could pen admirable precepts of fortitude in all the ills of life, and who showed his own courage in calmly committing the suicide which the cruelty of Nero assigned to him, yet quailed before the discomforts of sea-sickness, has been revealed by himself. Seneca, in one of the letters with which

he amused and instructed his friend Lucilius
Junior, gives an account of his experience in a
boating expedition of some nine miles from Naples
to Puteoli.   The day was overcast, but there was
no storm; the sea, however, was unquiet enough
to make him sick, and in the end he imperatively
insisted on being put ashore anywhere.   When
the reluctant skipper, who said he was more
afraid of the land than of the sea, brought the
boat near the beach, so eager was the philosopher
to escape from the discomforts of the deep that,
donning a garment of thick frieze, he jumped into
the water and scrambled up the rough shore.
The details of this adventure were thought by
him to be of such moment as to deserve ample
recital, since they fill nearly half of the letter,
and, after the writer's characteristic manner, are
made the text for a moral exhortation.[1]

The impressions of sea - voyages from the
landsman's point of view, recorded in Latin
literature, are not, however, invariably clouded
with reminiscences of bodily discomfort.   Lucretius
has expressed the pleasure of scudding before a
breeze, when

" the ship in which we are carried, though it seems
to be at rest, is yet borne along, while another
which is at anchor looks as if it were actually
passing us.   The hills and fields seem to be
fleeing astern, as we drive past them, and fly
along under sail."[2]

----

[1] *Epist.* LIII.   [2] *De Rer. Nat.* IV. 386.

That Catullus, too, enjoyed cruising in his yacht in Eastern waters will be more particularly noticed later in this chapter, p. 342.

In his narrative of the journey of Aeneas with his fleet from Troy to the Tiber, Virgil has succeeded in presenting a vivid impression of the variety of incident, of scene, and of weather in a long sea voyage. Though he was undoubtedly indebted to the *Odyssey*, even borrowing whole descriptive lines from that poem, it is yet difficult to avoid at least the suspicion that he also drew on personal reminiscences of some early wanderings of his own in the same delightful region. There is some ground of probability for the opinion that he had been to Greece long before the visit which he paid to that country in the last year of his life. Horace's early ode, addressed to the vessel that was to carry Virgil to Attica, shows at least that the journey was planned, and on the eve of being actually undertaken.[1] The earlier part of Aeneas's seafaring is somewhat vaguely described, but after the Trojans quitted Crete and entered scenes which the poet may himself have beheld, the narrative becomes more detailed and lively. The voyage from the Strophad Isles up the west coast of Greece, reads like the account of a writer to whom the localities were not unfamiliar, and who remembered the succession of islands, hills and towns that came, one after another, into

[1] *Carm.* I. iii. *See* Sellar's *Roman Poets of the Augustan Age—Virgil*, p. 118.

sight to right and left, as his vessel threaded its way northward to Actium.

" The southerly breezes filled our sails; we sped over the foaming waves whither the wind and our steersman willed. And now in mid-ocean came into sight the grove-clad Zacynthus, and Dulichium and Same, and the steep crags of Mount Neritos. We shunned the rocks of Ithaca, the kingdom of Laertes, and cursed the land that bred the fierce Ulysses. Then the cloud-capped crests of Mount Leucata opened out to view, and the Apollo so feared by sailors. Wearied we make for the little town (Actium), the anchor is thrown out from the prow and the sterns are ranged upon the shore." [1]

When the poet brings the fleet to his own more familiar Italian coast, his narrative becomes increasingly detailed and spirited. In the rosy dawn, as the low hills of Italy rise into view on the far horizon, the excitement of the crews finds vent in shouts of "Italy." The shores of Magna Graecia are skirted, each little town or temple being noted as the ships pass along, till the Sicilian strait is entered. There the terrors of Scylla and Charybdis are duly encountered and surmounted, and at last, within hearing of the thunders of Etna and in a night of darkness and gloom, anchors are cast at the Æolian Isles. [2] The rest of the voyage up to the Tiber is lightly sketched, but room is found for one or two effective touches. After Aeneas has had his

---

[1] _Æn._ III. 268-277.   [2] _Id._ III. 568-586.

journey into the nether world and has rejoined the ships that were drawn up on the Cumaean shore, the fleet is represented as renewing its voyage to Caieta. In the evening they sailed thence when the deep was still and the breeze was freshening as the night came on, while the pale light of the moon gleamed over the tremulous sea.[1] They came near to the famous hold of Circe and her sorceries. But lest the good Trojans should run the risk of falling under her foul spells, Neptune filled their sails with a favouring wind that carried them past the fateful headland, and brought them to the mouth of the Tiber just as the rosy dawn was reddening the sea. The end of their long wanderings being thus over, they entered the promised land amidst all the glories and happy auguries of sunrise.[2]

Since the treachery and blind fury of the sea were so vividly realised by the Latin poets, descriptions of storms and allusions to shipwrecks are not infrequent in their writings. For the most part, however, these descriptions are pictures taken from safe shelter on land. Lucretius makes several references to the subject, besides the famous Epicurean passage already referred to (pp. 212, 222, 223). Virgil has portrayed various storms, chief among which is his account of that invoked by Juno for the destruction of the Trojan fleet (p. 218).

---

[1] *Æn.* VII. 6-9.

[2] The description of this dawn has been already cited (p. 269).

Y

Another tempest described from his own experience has also been quoted (p. 220).

Probably, however, the fullest and most vivid descriptions from actual participation in storms at sea are those of the facile Ovid. The picture which he has drawn of the tempest wherein Ceyx, the husband of Alcyone was lost, is a brilliant example of his power in word-painting.[1] Its details may have been partly supplied by some experience of the poet's own in his youthful travels to the East. The account of the rise of the storm, and of the various actions of the captain and crew, is forcible enough to have been derived from personal recollection of rough weather at sea. But certainly in later years, during that miserable journey into life-long banishment, of which the poet has left such a melancholy record, he had ample opportunity of knowing what it was to be in a storm at sea. His narratives of the tempests through which he came on the Adriatic and Ægean seas, while less detailed, are more impressive than his description of the Ceyx storm. They bring us more directly into the fury of the wind and sea, and make us realise more vividly the despair of those on board. Ovid assures us that the verses in which he describes these storms were not composed, as of old, in his gardens, but under wintry skies on the boisterous deep, which was dashing its blue waters over the very paper on which he was writing.[2]

It is deserving of remark, however, that though

[1] *Metam.* XI. 461-572.   [2] *Trist.* I. ii., iv., x., xi.

he was not shipwrecked, but arrived at his dreary destination and could look back in safety upon the perils from which he had escaped, he found no words of admiration for the grandeur of the storms. He could remember only their horrors—the groaning ship, battered by the waves, alternately sinking into deep Tartarean abysses and mounting towards the stars; the deluges of salt spray that swept over him; the brilliance of the lightning and the instantaneous rattle of the thunder; but, above all, his own sore bodily discomfort, his sense of imminent danger, and the dread of being drowned. He declares that he did not fear death; that he would, indeed, have counted it a boon to die a natural death ashore, or to perish by the sword, so as at least to be buried on firm ground and to hope for a tomb. But to be shipwrecked, "et aequoreis piscibus esse cibus," was a thought that added tenfold to the misery of the storm.[1]

In voyages upon the Mediterranean Sea, vessels whether with sail or oars were often necessarily for days together out of sight of land—

> "Nec amplius ulla
> Occurrit tellus, maria undique et undique caelum."

There was, however, at least among boatmen and the owners of small craft, a natural and pardonable reluctance to be on the open sea after dark. Lucan no doubt expresses the prevalent feeling

---

[1] Juvenal, perhaps in allusion more especially to Ovid, makes sarcastic reference to "poetical tempests," where everything happens so violently (*Sat.* XII. 22).

when he makes the peasant boatman reply to
Cæsar who had roused him out of bed and
demanded to be ferried across the Ægean Sea to
the shores of Italy, "there is much to keep us
from trusting the sea by night."[1] But unless for
mere coasting voyages, when, under the most
favourable conditions, it might be practicable to
anchor each night in some harbour or sheltered
bay, it was impossible to avoid being on the sea
night after night for days together. The navigator
had therefore to learn how to steer by the sun
during the day and by the stars at night. Hence
to him, when

> "Nocte sublustri nihil astra praeter
> Vidit et undas,"

an acquaintance with the chief stars in the nightly
sky and their varying positions was essential.
Before Palinurus gave the signal for the sailing of
the Trojan fleet, we are told that " he first noted all
the stars that were gliding through the silent
heavens—Arcturus and the rainy Hyades, and the
twin Bears; he marked likewise Orion clad in
armour of gold."[2] And when at a later time the
treacherous God of Sleep tried to tempt him from
his post, the heroic pilot kept his hand firm on
the rudder and his eye on the stars.[3]

---

[1] *Phars.* V. 540. The forebodings of the poor fisherman proved to
be true. Lucan gives a graphic account of the storm through which
Cæsar was carried back to rouse his tardy followers. The poet says of
that great warrior that he was
> " In omnia praeceps,
> Nil actum credens quum quid superesset agendum."—*Id.* ii. 656.

[2] *Æn.* III. 515.   [3] *Id.* V. 852.

The contemplation of the starry heavens at sea awakened thoughts which have here and there found expression among the Latin poets. Amid all the incessant changes of earth and sea and sky, the stars retain their places seemingly unchanged and their lustre undimmed as the centuries roll on, so that they have served to mankind as emblems of steadfastness. Horace speaks of the "certa sidera." Tibullus, in a single pregnant line, has drawn a contrast between the unsteady ships and the sure fixedness of the stars by which they are steered.

"Ducunt instabiles sidera certa rates." [1]

Virgil in lamenting the dead Daphnis, pictures the mother clasping the lifeless body of her son, and appealing to the gods and the " astra crudelia " which in their cold, silent apathy remain unmoved. [2]

Among the natural phenomena to be seen at sea there is none more weird and impressive than what is known as St Elmo's Fire—a silent form of electric discharge, which in certain states of the weather appears as a ball of pale light on the tops of masts of vessels and the ends of yard-arms. Such an appearance could not fail to excite the imagination of the ancients. Unlike lightning, it is noiseless, harmless, and persistent for some time on the same spot. As it did no injury, it was naturally enough looked upon as a good sign, and by the Greeks and Romans was associated with the great

[1] *Eleg.* I. ix. 10.   [2] *Eclog.* V. 23.

twin-brethren, Castor and Pollux, who, as legend
told, had taken part in the famous voyage of the
Argonauts, during which stars were said to have
appeared on their heads. These mythical heroes
became the protectors of travellers, especially by
sea, and the luminous orbs of St Elmo's Fire,
settling on the projecting spars and masts of ships
at sea, were looked upon as visible manifestations
of the active and benign interposition of these
divinities. Thus Horace calls Helen's two brothers
"lucida sidera," when he invokes their protection
for Virgil in his voyage to Greece. Elsewhere the
poet speaks of them as a bright star (*clarum sidus*)
that rescues shattered barks from the depths of the
waves, and still more fully he says that "no sooner
has this white star beamed upon sailors than the
foaming water streams off the rocks, the winds fall,
the clouds flee away, and the threatening billow
sinks down upon the deep."[1] Statius expresses
still more precisely the popular conception when
he invokes "the Spartan brethren to bring out
their benign stars, and settle upon the twin horns
of the sail-yard," in order that Maecius Celer may
have a prosperous voyage.[2]

Of all the Latin poets none has so fully fore-
shadowed as Catullus has done the modern love
of the sea, and none has clothed his appreciation
in such joyously expressive language. We hear

[1] *Carm.* I. iii. 2 ; xii. 27 ; IV. viii. 31.
[2] *Silv.* III. ii. 8. Seneca, as a philosopher, treated the appearance
as a natural phenomenon, but he had no conception of its nature and
origin (*Quaest. Nat.* I. i., ii.)

from him no complaints of the discomforts and
perils of sea-faring.   On the contrary, he conveys
to us something of his own pleasure in being upon
the water, and watching there the ever-changing
aspects of sea and sky.   Although he died when
he was no more than thirty years of age, he had
already travelled far both by land and sea, and in
the precious little volume of poems which is all
that has descended to us as his memorial, many
reminiscences of his journeys are preserved.

When he determined to end his sojourn in
Bithynia, whither, as above referred to (p. 244), he
had gone on the staff of the praetor Memmius,
he purchased and manned a yacht, with which to
make the long voyage home.   In the charming
sonnet, already quoted, wherein he bids farewell
to his companions, he gives words to his exuberant
delight that the coming of spring allows him to
escape from the Phrygian plains.   During the
many weeks in which the yacht was his home,
he came to look on the vessel almost as a living
friend that shared with him the daily pleasures
and risks of the voyage.   The pride and affection
with which he regarded his "phaselus" found
vent in another exquisite little poem, written on
his return, in which he bids his friends listen to
the tale which the ship has to tell them of her
adventures:—how no craft afloat could ever out-
strip her, whether with sails or oars; how she
had braved the threatening Adriatic, had threaded
her way among the Cyclad Isles and past famous

Rhodes, had sailed over the Ægean, had coasted Thrace and the Propontis, and had made acquaintance with the wild Euxine. It was from the Pontic shores that the timbers had been brought of which her frame was built. He was evidently gratified to have visited the birthplace of his favourite yacht, to have seen her native forest, and even perhaps to have heard the wind whistling through the surviving pines. He appealed to Pontic Amastris and box-clad Cytorus as witnesses that her timbers had once waved green on their mountains, and that her oars had first been dipped in their waters. From that far-distant clime the vessel had borne her master through many stormy seas, and through all kinds of weather, until at last, quitting the salt main, she was steered up the broad rivers Po and Mincio into the placid Lake of Garda, where in peaceful old age she was dedicated to the sailor's friends Castor and Pollux.[1]

Recollections of this voyage, or of others made by the poet, seem to be sprinkled all through his poetry. There can be little doubt, for instance, that the beautiful description of the dawn at sea, in the *Peleus and Thetis*, represents a scene which he himself witnessed from the deck, when

---

[1] Catullus, IV. The vessel into which Ovid was transhipped at Cenchreae, and which bore him through various perils in the Ægean Sea to Samothrace, elicited from the poet a grateful eulogy. But though she was praised by him as the faithful leader and companion of his anxious voyage, she was, at the same time, the prison in which he was being carried into distant exile, and his language naturally lacks the joyful tone with which Catullus celebrates the bringing of his yacht to the smooth waters of his beloved lake (*Trist.* I. x.).

the first breath of morning was roughening the placid deep, and the wavelets, rippling gently with a sound of laughter against the sides of the vessel, broadened more and more as the breeze freshened and as they glided far away from the brilliant reflection of the rising sun.

The same masterpiece among his poems begins with a striking exordium wherein the thought of the voyage of the Argonauts at once calls up with characteristic enthusiasm a vision of the pine-clad Mount Pelion, whence, according to tradition, the timbers of their vessel were brought. Pallas herself had built the frame, joining the ribs to the curved keel, and completing a sea-chariot that would fly before the lightest breath of wind. The memory of the deeds of his own yacht may well have risen in the poet's remembrance as he pictures the *Argo*, the first vessel that ever dared to scour the blue deep, now under sail and scudding across a windy sea, and now speeding along under oars that lashed the water into white foam. As in imagination he watches her progress, he thinks how in that heroic age (*nimis optato saeclorum tempore*) when gods and men were young, the faces of the Nereids would peer above the waves to gaze with wonder on this new monster of the Ocean.[1]

Although he makes little account of them in his verse, Catullus did not wholly escape the storms that sometimes beset the Adriatic and

[1] Catullus, LXIV. 12-15.

Ægean waters. He speaks of having sailed through many furious seas (*tot impotentia freta*), but he avers that never did he make any vows for safety to the gods of the shores by which he sailed,[1] whence we may perhaps infer that he rather enjoyed rough weather at sea. But his crew were probably less self-possessed, and he may have been thinking of them when, in an ode to Mallius, he alludes to the prayers to Castor and Pollux for a calm and prosperous voyage offered up by sailors who have been tossed about in a dark tempest.[2]

In his cruises the poet would learn the seaman's habit of scanning the changes of the winds and other aspects of the sky and the weather. The fickleness of atmospheric conditions, together with their independence and disregard of all human wishes and efforts, had doubtless impressed him in his musings on ship-board. He puts his own experience into the mouth of Ariadne when he makes her exclaim, "Why do I vainly complain to the regardless and senseless winds, which can neither hear the words addressed to them, nor return any reply."[3] And when she is forsaken by Theseus, the faithless memory of the hero is likened by the poet to the clouds which, driven by the breath of the winds, leave the lofty crest

---

[1] Catullus, IV. 18, 22. In the touching poem on his brother's tomb he speaks of himself as

"multas per gentes, et multa per aequora vectus."—*Id.* CI. i.

[2] *Id.* LXVIII. 63.   [3] *Id.* LXIV. 164.

of a snowy mountain [1]—a simile which may be a recollection of what he had seen when coasting past the ranges of Thrace, or perhaps a reminiscence of the Alps beyond the far recesses of the Lago di Garda.

The epithets applied by Catullus to the sea and its shores are always happily descriptive, and such as would naturally be selected by a man to whom the objects were familiar and pleasant to recall. The frequency of these marine allusions is especially noticeable in his longest poem, the *Peleus and Thetis*. He there more than once picturesquely varies the word for " shore " (*litus*) by using in its stead the word for " sea-weed " (*alga*) in allusion to a characteristic feature of the strand.[2]   His sea-faring experience suggested the figurative language in which he often alludes to human grief, as where he compares his sorrowing friend Mallius to a " shipwrecked man who has been cast ashore by the foaming waves of the deep," and speaks of himself mourning the loss of a beloved brother, as " plunged in the billows of misfortune." [3]   His eye had been continually fixed with delight on the waves breaking along lines of beach, and he refers again and again to a whitening shore (*albicans litus*), foaming shores and frothy waves (*spumosa litora, mare spumantibus expuit undis*). [4]   The vast expanse of the open sea and its ceaseless motion greatly impressed his imagination; he speaks of the "pelagi

[1] Catullus, LXIV. 239.   [2] *Id.* LXIV. 60, 168.
[3] *Id.* LXVIII. 3, 13.   [4] *Id.* LXIII. 87 ; LXIV. 121, 155.

vastos aestus," the "tremuli salis adversas undas,"
the "ponti truculentum aequor," and the "rapidum
salum truculentaque pelagi." [1] The cadence of
his verse seems at times to be charged with the
life and movement of the waves, as where in two
lines he brings before eye and ear the plunge of
the breakers on a long stretch of sandy beach :—

> " Litus ut longe resonante Eoa
> Tunditur unda." [2]

---

[1] Catullus, LXIV. 127, 128, 179 ; LXIII. 16.
[2] *Id.* XI. 3. It would even seem that the common language of
his day was sometimes unequal to express the wave-music that dwelt
in his memory, so that he had to coin new epithets for his purpose, as
where he represents Ariadne gazing from the "*fluentisono* litore Diæ"
(LXIV. 52).

CHAPTER XVI

THE UNDERWORLD

IN no country of Europe does the underground heat of the earth show itself in such abundant and varied forms as in Italy. From one end of the peninsula to the other hot springs are numerous. There are many mysterious-looking places from which steam and other vapours and gases escape to the surface. And, above all, the great active volcanic centre of Europe lies entirely within the Italian borders.

Prominent as these features are to-day they were not improbably even more conspicuous in the infancy of Rome. During upwards of twenty-six centuries, which have elapsed since the foundation of the city, there has been time for some of at least the feebler manifestations to grow weaker or to become extinct. The whole of the region around Rome has once been the theatre of vigorous volcanic activity. Although the full energy of the volcanoes had spent itself long before either City or State had come into existence, it is possible that some of the later waning eruptions may have been witnessed by the earliest human inhabitants of the

349

country, although the evidence that has been adduced to prove that they came within what may be regarded as historic time is not wholly satisfactory. Among the records that have been preserved of the early centuries of Roman history showers of stones are chronicled. The Alban Mount is said by Livy to have been visited in the hundredth year of the city by one of these portents, which was accompanied by loud noises from the wood on the top of the mountain. More than four hundred years later a fall of stones at the same place is recorded to have lasted continuously for two days amidst alarming storms. And in subsequent years, it is reported, there was a rain of stones at Aricia, Lanuvium, and on the Aventine. Such incidents have been set aside as part of the mythical marvels with which legendary history is so apt to be crowded. But there does not seem to be any inherent improbability that some of these tales may have had a foundation in fact. The phenomena may have been of a nature similar to that of a remarkable case which occurred so recently as the year 1831, when at the site of a dried-up fetid lake near Mount Soracte, a series of loud reports, like the thundering of cannon, issued from the ground, accompanied with an outrush of mephitic gases, white dust, and large blocks of erupted earth. From time to time during the Republic, and afterwards under the Empire, occurrences of this kind may have taken place near Rome, which have not found mention in the chronicles of history.

As the Roman sway was extended over the rest of the country, the conquerors met with other and more striking manifestations of subterranean energy than they were familiar with in their own territory. By contact with the Greek colonists to the south of them they doubtless heard of the marvels of Etna long before a single legionary had set foot on Sicily. From the same source they would learn that not only Sicily but some of the islands between that island and Naples had been devastated by terrific eruptions from which the inhabitants had to flee elsewhere. They would be told, too, that one of the chief portals of the infernal regions lay close to the sea in the Bay of Naples. When they had made themselves masters of Magna Graecia, and had wrested Sicily from the Carthaginians, they came immediately face to face with all these places and would gain a more vivid appreciation of the Greek legends that had gathered round them. What impression these various indications of the underworld of Greek imagination made on the minds of the early Romans must be matter of conjecture. The literature of later times, however, indicates how the phenomena were looked upon by subsequent generations. The quieter displays of underground heat, such as the uprise of the abundant hot springs of Italy, would no doubt be regarded as part of the ordinary economy of Nature, evoking little or no surprise at their occurrence. Like springs in general, these thermal waters would be held to be sacred and under the care of local or national divinities. When their beneficial therapeutic properties were found out, they in many places became the centres of extensive and much frequented bath-establishments.[1]

The displays of subterranean energy in the form of volcanic eruptions could not fail to impress the Roman mind as they had impressed the Grecian. Etna, the greatest of the volcanoes of Europe, had been at various times seen in vigorous activity by the Greek colonists before it was included within the conquered territories of Rome. Its characteristic features had been vividly portrayed by Aeschylus and Pindar, and through their poems had been made familiar to cultivated Romans. The lively Greek imagination had likewise created a legend that connected Etna with the primæval conflict between Zeus and the Titans. One of these monsters was fabled to have been hurled to earth and buried beneath the vast mass of the volcano. The tremors, rumblings, and fiery

---

[1] Within a few miles of Rome, the warm sulphur springs of the Aquae Albulae between the city and Tibur and the hot sulphur waters of the Aquae Apollinares near Bracciano were much in request for medical treatment among the Romans, and their reputation is still maintained in modern days. At the latter place large numbers of coins, bronze vessels, goblets and cups of silver and gold, rings and other objects have been found which the patients in old days left as memorials of their gratitude to the divinity of the place for the benefit they had derived from the waters. Such establishments were created by the Romans all over their vast empire where suitable hot springs were met with. On the utmost limit of the Roman dominions the hot waters of Bath were thus utilised, and the buildings erected there by the Romans still form part of the modern and popular establishment.

blasts of the mountain were said to mark the efforts of the imprisoned Titan to turn his body for ease as he lay on his burning pallet.

The Greek philosophers, too, had considered the problems presented by Etna. Regarding them, of course, as entirely arising from natural causes, these writers had come to the conclusion that, as air in tempestuous motion was the mightiest form of physical energy of which they had experience, nothing short of this motive force could be conceived to account for volcanic eruptions. They accordingly framed a theory that inside the earth there must be vast cavernous spaces wherein wind is imprisoned, which from time to time works itself up into furious tempests, as it does above the ground. The violent efforts of these caged subterranean hurricanes to find some escape to the surface, were looked upon as the cause of the tremblings and earthquakes that precede or accompany volcanic eruptions; and as in the atmosphere, the clouds were seen to evolve lightning, apparently by their violent concussions when the wind drove them together, so it could be believed that the underground tempests in their whirling fury would strike out fire which would catch and inflame the sulphur, bitumen, and other combustible materials within the earth. When the over-arching roof of the great subterranean caverns, shaken and riven by the mighty energy of the wind, at last gave way, the pent-up tempest with its accompanying steam,

z

smoke, flames, and molten rock would rush out into the upper air and devastate the surrounding country.

By the time that these questions found their way into Latin literature, Greek philosophy and Greek myths had to a large extent become acclimatised in the Roman Republic. As the chief old Italian divinities had been one after another identified with gods in the Hellenic pantheon, so the Greek materialistic explanations of natural phenomena were in like manner adopted by those who studied philosophy at Rome. Hence when the Latin poets came to touch on the volcanoes of the Mediterranean it was natural that both their ideas and their modes of expressing them should bear strong evidence of Greek influence.

The eruptions of Etna might be separated from each other by long intervals of quiescence, during which the traces of devastation were well nigh effaced by the progress of renewed cultivation. To younger generations the realities of eruption might thus become little more than a mere tradition. In so fruitful a soil and in so genial a climate as that of Sicily, it is marvellous how soon the healing hand of Nature, combined with the busy hand of man, can efface the superficial marks of even the most disastrous calamities. There was a severe eruption of the volcano in the year B.C. 121. As this event happened only about a quarter of a century before Lucretius was born, he may have had accounts of it from eye-witnesses. In his allusion to the wonders of Sicily, the birthplace of Empedocles, he naturally gives a leading place to the great volcano. He says that

"the Etnean rumblings are threatening again to wake the flaming wrath of the mountain, and it may yet once more belch fires from its throat, and cast again to the heavens the flashing of its lightnings."

In another passage he refers to the

"Etnean fires that are breathed forth with so mighty a whirl from the throat of the mountain. With no common destruction did the flaming tempest overwhelm the Sicilian fields, and draw to itself the eyes of the neighbouring peoples, who saw all the circuit of heaven smoking and gleaming, and whose dismayed hearts were filled with dread of what new design Nature might be planning." [1]

Lucretius accepts and expounds the Greek wind-theory as the explanation of volcanic outbursts.

Virgil, also, may have heard in his youth from old men, accounts of the havoc which they had seen to have been wrought by the eruption of Etna in B.C. 121. During the years 49 and 44, when less destructive outpourings of the mountain occurred, he was probably living at home on the plains of the Mincio. He alludes to the eruption of the latter year as one of the portents that heralded or accompanied the assassination of Julius

[1] *De Rer. Nat.* I. 722.; VI. 639.

Cæsar.[1] During his occasional residences in Sicily
he may himself have seen the mountain in one
of its minor phases of activity.   It is in his latest
poem that he makes the fullest references to Etna
and volcanic matters.   He there tells, as already
mentioned, how Aeneas and his fleet, after their
long and trying journeyings, cast anchor among
the Æolian Isles, and heard the ominous growlings
of Etna not many miles distant.   As the scene
which he describes, shaped itself in his imagination,
all that he had read and all that he had ever heard
or seen of the stupendous mountain would crowd
into his mind.   The graphic pictures drawn by
the Greek poets, the legend of the buried Titan
and all the human associations of the volcano
were present before him, heightened perhaps and
defined by what with his own eyes he may have
witnessed.   The well-known passage in the *Æneid*,
wherein he briefly sketches an eruption, has a
special interest from the way in which he has
seized upon the leading features in the phenomena,
and has grouped them, on the whole, in the order
of sequence which they usually follow—the uprise
of the dark cloud that marks the earliest phase
of explosion when the imprisoned vapours are
clearing the throat of the volcano, then the
whirling masses of black detritus, the rain of

[1] *Geor.* I. 471.   Ovid recounts a doleful list of portents on that
occasion (*Metam.* XV. 780-798. Compare the account of prodigies given
by Lucan, *Phars.* I. 522 *seq.*; VII. 151 *seq.*).   There were eruptions of
Etna in the years B.C. 38 and 32, of one or other of which Virgil may
possibly have been an eye-witness.

white ashes, the uprise of red - hot stones like
globes of fire, the huge blocks torn from the
very heart of the mountain, and at last the ascent
and outflow of molten lava :—

> " With startling uproar Etna thunders near,
>   Now launching to the sky a darksome cloud,
>   With whirls of pitchy smoke and white-hot ash,
>   And balls of flame that mount even to the stars :
>   Now belching from its heart huge crags of rock,
>   And rolling to the air the molten stone,
>   It groans and surges from its lowest depths.
>   'Tis said the body of Enceladus,
>   Half-burnt up by the thunder-bolt of Jove,
>   Lies pressed beneath the mighty mountain-pile
>   Of Etna, breathing flame from every vent ;
>   And often as he turns his weary side,
>   Through Sicily a rumbling tremor runs,
>   And all the heavens above are veil'd with smoke." [1]

In the Greek myth as recounted by Aeschylus
and Pindar, the Titan buried under Etna bore
the name of Typhoeus. In the passage just cited
Virgil calls him Enceladus, and in another part
of the poem he says that Typhoeus was entombed
beneath the volcanic piles of the islands of Procida
and Ischia, on the north-west side of the Bay
of Naples.[2] He would thus seem to indicate
that two different monsters were plunged below
the volcanoes of Southern Italy, for he would
hardly be likely to regard the two names as
designations of the same being, who in that

---

[1] *Æn.* III. 571-582.
[2] *Id.* IX. 715. The statement is repeated by Lucan who speaks of
Enceladus as lying below Etna (*Phars.* V. 100 ; VI. 293).

case would have been well entitled to rank
among the giants and Jove's most formidable
opponents, for his frame must have been some
sixty English miles in length.[1]

Ovid, who in his version of the legend
restores Typhoeus to his place under Etna,
relates in characteristic detail under which tracts
of Sicily the various parts of the Titan's body
lay. He makes Typhoeus a more vigorous
prisoner than Virgil represents him, for he
describes him as fiercely belching sand and flame,
struggling to throw off his load and to roll
aside the huge hills and the cities that rested
upon him, till the earth trembles and Pluto
himself becomes nervous lest the ground be
rent open and daylight be let in to affright the
trembling shades that people his underworld.[2]
Ovid had himself spent the greater part of a
year in Sicily with his friend Macer, and had
visited all that was thought to be worth seeing
in the island. In one of his Pontic Epistles
he reminds Macer that they had together watched
the heavens aglow with the fires of Etna. But
he neither gives any description of what he
saw nor states the impression which all this
varied and interesting scenery had left on his

---

[1] Strabo, who has the credit of being the first traveller to recognise
the probable volcanic origin of Mount Vesuvius (he died long before
the great eruption of A.D. 79), was of opinion that the whole region
from Cumae to Sicily must be regarded as one continuous volcanic
tract, and he pointed out that Pindar has pictured Typhon as lying
underneath the whole of it (*Geog.* V. iv. 9).

[2] *Metam.* V. 346-358.

mind. His epistle to his friend was sent from Tomi, when the reminiscences of their journeyings in company awakened all the horror of the contrast to his former life presented by his exile far away "under the north pole of the world."[1] The legend of the Titan beneath Etna is alluded to by Horace, who remarks with regard to it that fire, which usually does its work swiftly, has not yet eaten through the overlying mass of mountain, so that the load which presses upon the entombed giant has not yet been sensibly reduced in bulk.[2]

Etna was made the subject of a poem called *Ætna* consisting of 646 hexameter verses, the authorship of which is not certainly known. As a contribution to science it has little or no value, and from the literary side is intolerably dull. Latin literature, indeed, can hardly furnish a more striking contrast than that between this ambitious but jejune performance and the two famous letters of the younger Pliny on the Vesuvian eruption of A.D. 79, to which reference will be made later in this chapter.

In the group of the Æolian Isles, lying not far to the north of Sicily, volcanic outbreaks began before the earliest times of human history. They were on a smaller scale than at Etna, but on the other hand, they were much more frequent than in the great volcano. In one case, indeed, that of Stromboli, they appear to have been

[1] *Pont.* II. x.   [2] *Carm.* III. iv. 7.

continuous till now all through the centuries
that have passed since the earliest Greek colonists
reported their eruptions to the mother country.
These islands were represented by the Alexandrian
poets as the workshop of the fire-god Hephaistus.
The Roman poets in this case also adopted the
legend as told by the Greeks. The island which in
their time was most remarkable for the activity of
its vent was named by the Greeks Hiera, being
regarded as sacred to Hephaistus, and where he had
his abode. The Romans who identified their fire-
god Vulcanus with the corresponding Greek divinity,
knew the island as Vulcan's Isle, and it still goes
by the name of Volcano and still from time to
time breaks out in eruption.

Virgil makes several allusions to this remarkable centre of volcanic activity, the most detailed
of these being that in which he represents Vulcan,
at the urgent request of Venus, leaving his
couch in heaven, to repair to his Æolian furnaces
in order to arrange with his Cyclopes for the
fabrication of arms for Aeneas. The various
subterranean noises, sometimes alarming enough
to the population above ground, are described by
the poet as resounding from a vast workshop
down in the depths, where amidst the ruddy glow
from their furnaces, these legendary workmen
are busy smiting with mighty blows the hissing
bars of white-hot steel on their anvils. Out of
these bars, combined with shafts of hail, and
watery cloud, and fire, and the winged south wind,

mingled with appalling flashes, and sound and fear and anger, they are fashioning the thunderbolts which the Father of gods and men hurls forth from the wide heaven.[1]

The widespread acceptation of the explanation given by the philosophers that volcanic energy is primarily due to the movements of wind imprisoned in vast subterranean chasms led to the establishment of another popular belief in connection with the Æolian Isles. As some of the vents in that group were so frequently in eruption as to give rise to the belief that they marked the fire-god's favourite abode, so they came to be associated also with Æolus, the god of the winds, from whom they actually received the name by which they are known. This divinity was reputed to have his dwelling under these islands, where he kept watch and ward over the various winds, letting them out or restraining them within their prison as seemed good to him, or as might be required by the powers above.

It is to these head-quarters of tempest that Virgil brings Juno in quest of the storm wherewith she sought to overwhelm Aeneas and his fleet. The poet describes Æolia as the home of rain-clouds and furious gales. He pictures Æolus as seated there on his lofty citadel, sceptre in hand, ruling over the struggling winds and the resounding tempests, and bridling them with chains and prison. As they impatiently growl round

[1] *Æn.* VIII. 416-432 ; *Geor.* IV. 170-175.

their dungeon, the mountain overhead murmurs
loudly. But he moderates their impulse and
curbs their wrath, else would they assuredly, in
their swift flight, bear away sea and land and
even the high heavens. In fear of such a catastrophe, the almighty Father has hidden them in
dark caverns, has piled a huge mass of high
hills above them, and has given them a king
who by a settled compact knows, when commanded, both to tighten and to loosen the
reins.[1]

Allusion may be made here to another belief
connected with the Æolian Isles which has survived
down to our own time. Polybius has recorded
that the weather could be foretold from the
behaviour of the volcanic vents. Before the
coming of the south wind, the little island
(probably Stromboli) was shrouded in mist, but
if the wind was to be northerly the summit was
clear and emitted flames that rose high into the
air with increased rumbling noises.[2] The Italian
fishermen still regard Stromboli as a weather-
glass whereby they are guided as to the kind of
weather that may be expected. There is probably
a foundation of truth in this long-established belief.
High atmospheric pressure, which generally brings
good weather, must tend to repress the eruptive
vapours in the chimney of the volcano, while low

[1] *Æn.* I. 50-63. The storm resulting from Juno's visit has
been referred to on p. 218.
[2] *Hist.* XXXIV. xi. The observations are repeated by Strabo and
Pliny.

pressure will increase their facility of escape. The greater activity of the vent therefore would be an indication of stormy weather. It is perhaps to this popular belief that Horace alludes when in the ode already cited (p. 240) he speaks of Vulcan kindling the forges of the Cyclopes. He may allude to the return of spring as heralded by storms that are succeeded by the balmy west winds of that season.

The most interesting and important narrative of a great volcanic eruption which has come down to us from antiquity is that by the younger Pliny in the two famous letters already alluded to. As an actual eye-witness he there describes the memorable outbreak of Vesuvius in A.D. 79, whereby the Campanian cities were overwhelmed. Tacitus, desirous of handing down to posterity an accurate account of the circumstances in which Pliny's uncle, the illustrious author of the *Historia Naturalis*, met his death, asked the nephew to furnish it. This request was complied with in the two letters in question. The first of them describes the keen interest of the naturalist in the wonderful scene presented by the commencement of the outbreak of Vesuvius, and goes on to narrate how from Misenum, where he was in command of the fleet, he sailed across the bay to get a nearer view of the mountain, how he landed on the further coast and courageously advanced on foot along the shore in the direction of the volcano, how a hot and sulphurous blast, perhaps somewhat like the *nuée ardente* which proved fatal to so many thousand people at the isle of Martinique in 1902, suffocated him, and how, when daylight returned after the eruption, his body was found lying where he fell, uninjured, and looking more like one asleep than dead.

The second letter records the writer's own experience at Misenum, with that of his mother, who was his only companion at this trying time. They endeavoured to escape together, but in the dense darkness and amidst the rain of ashes and stones, they withdrew from the public road to escape being crushed by the crowd of terrified fugitives, and sat down to await what he thought was the end of the world, only rising now and then to shake off the accumulating mass of *débris* under which they might have been crushed. At last the fall of volcanic material slackened, dim daylight began to reappear, and by degrees the sun could be seen faintly through the lurid atmosphere. When the air had cleared the whole country appeared under a deep covering of ashes like snow.

This relation, so clearly and tersely composed, is a document of high scientific interest, for it gives a vivid picture of the successive phases of one of the greatest and most disastrous volcanic eruptions within the times of history. The writer was not a scientific man and drew no conclusions from what he witnessed. But he observed with intelligence and tells his story in the simplest

language. We obtain from his narrative a clear
conception of the wonderful scene as it appeared
to the eyes of a cultivated and observant Roman
gentleman.

But beyond their scientific importance these
two letters possess no little literary value. Even
if their stoical calm may seem a little forced, they
must be admitted to present a memorable example
of the Roman qualities of "firmitas et constantia,"
calm courage and self-possession in the presence
of danger, and quiet restraint and dignity in
describing one of the most dreadful catastrophes
that man can behold. The appalling scene is
depicted with no floweriness of language, but with
a simplicity and directness which make the narrative
not unworthy to have been incorporated in Tacitus's
own pages. We have to remember, moreover,
that the writer was at the time of the eruption
only a lad of eighteen. The proof of his devotion
to his mother and of hers to him, so lightly
indicated in his description, adds another charm
to the letters.

Among the later poets of the first century of
the Empire various references occur to this great
Vesuvian catastrophe and to the aspect of the
region after its devastation. Martial makes the
subject the theme of one of his epigrams:—

"This is Vesuvius, only lately so verdant with
umbrageous vines. Here the noble grape pressed
the moist vats ; these ridges were dearer to Bacchus
than even his Nysan hills. Here was the dwelling

of Venus, pleasanter to her than Lacedaemon.
Here, too, stood a place illustrious from bearing
the name of Hercules—the whole now lies buried
in flames and melancholy ashes.   The gods must
surely wish that they had not been allowed to
inflict such evil." [1]

Statius, though he lived within sight of
Vesuvius, gives no description of the eruption in
his *Silvae*, but makes several allusions to it.
Writing at Cumae soon after the catastrophe,
he mentions that the volcano was still active,
though with lessened energy,

" pouring out his fires in emulation of the flames
of Sicily. How wonderful, yet true! Will the
coming generations of men believe, when the
crops shall have returned, and when these deserts
will once more be green, that towns and people
lie pressed below, and that the fields of their
grandfathers disappeared in a boiling sea? Nor
has the summit of the mountain yet ceased to
threaten death."

In another passage he refers to " the Vesuvian
fires, when the Father sent the mountain from
the earth to the skies, and hurled it far and wide
over the wretched towns." Again, alluding to
the revival of cheerfulness and life in the region
after the eruption, he rejoiced that the Vesuvian
peak and the fiery tempest of that dread mountain
had not yet drained the anxious cities of all
their men. There were still left Puteoli, with
its busy harbour, Baiæ that welcomed all the

[1] *Epig.* IV. xliv.

world to its shores, and, above all, "our own Naples, neither weak in her own population nor scantily supplied with country-folk."[1]

With the volcanic history of central and southern Italy the popular Roman conception of the under-world and of the future state of human beings after death is curiously and closely linked. All over that region, as has already been mentioned, among the manifestations of decaying volcanic energy, there are places where hot vapours and ill-smelling or suffocating gases rise into the air. These localities are not infrequently extinct volcanic vents whence eruptions of ashes and stones once came, but which, on the cessation of the explosions, gradually had their crater-bottoms filled with rain and surface water. In some cases where the water has mostly disappeared, it has left on its site an expanse of fetid mud from which the malodorous vapours continue to rise, sometimes with little explosions whereby the mud is spirted up into the air. Such weird spots were called by the Romans "spiracles" or "Charon's ditches," from the opinion that they were outlets from the lower regions where Charon and Pluto were believed to dwell.[2] The Vadimonian lake, so well described by the younger Pliny (*antea* p. 148), was one of these outlets. The

[1] *Silv.* III. v. 72 ; IV. iv. 78 ; V. iii. 205.

[2] Pliny, *Hist. Nat.* IV. xcv., "spiracula, Charoneae scrobes, mortiferum spiritum exhalantes." Pliny thought the only explanation of them was to be found in the supposition that the whole of Nature is pervaded by a spirit (*numen*) which is continually breaking forth, now in one form, now in another.

small circular lake or tarn of greenish-blue water,
lying in the cup of an ancient crater, which in
his day gave off sulphureous vapours, is now dried
up and is known as the Laghetto di Bassano.
Virgil mentions another example, the valley of
Amsanctus, which still retains much of the aspect
which it had in his day.   He describes it as a place
lying in the middle of Italy, beneath high hills,
and renowned in legend on many shores.   Pent
between wooded cliffs and under gloomy over-
arching foliage, it shows in the midst a roaring
torrent that dashes in whirling eddies over the
rocks; likewise a horrible cavern, "the breathing
vent of cruel Dis," and a vast pestilential abyss
that leads down to Acheron.   Into this ghastly
hollow Virgil represents the Fury Allecto plunging
on her return to the lower world after the
accomplishment of her fateful errand on earth.[1]
The noisome gases which still continue to rise from
the pool that fills the bottom of the hollow, escape
in bubbles that burst with some little noise, and
infect the air to such a degree as to suffocate birds
and other animals that venture near.

To the west of Naples lay a district full of
hot springs, sulphurous emanations, and mouths
that emitted steam, sometimes with loud noises.
Certain of these orifices still remain active, but
probably a number of them which were so in Virgil's
time are now quiescent.   By far the most famous
of them all was the Lake Avernus—a sheet of

[1] *Æn.* VII. 563-571.

water filling the bottom of an extinct volcanic
crater, close to Baiæ on the shores of the Bay.
Long before the dawn of history this mysterious
hollow had so impressed the minds of the Greek
colonists of the neighbourhood that they carried
the report of its marvels back to the mother-
country, where its fame became widely spread.
The poet of the *Odyssey* brings Odysseus to the
spot as the portal from which he could come
into touch with the nether world.   Even now
when the progress of time and the interference of
man have shorn the place of much of the weird
aspect which it must have worn more that two
thousand years ago, it is still an impressive spot.[1]
But in the olden time, when the steep slopes of the
crater in which the lake was embosomed were
clothed with dense forest, when beneath the gloom
of the trees deadly vapours escaped from many
rifts into the air, which became so pestilential as to
give rise to the general belief that no bird could
fly across the expanse without being suffocated,
and when the lake was thought to have no bottom,[2]
it requires little imagination to understand the

[1] Strabo says that in his time, the woods having been cut down by
Agrippa, the hills about Avernus were well cultivated, but that in the
olden time they had been covered with wild, vast, and impenetrable
forest, which overshadowed the lake, and gave the place the feeling
of superstitious awe for which it was so famous.   He adds that it was
a " Plutonium," where people make sacrifices and offerings to the
infernal deities (V. iv. 5).

[2] The belief that Avernus was fathomless lasted long.   Lucan relates
that if the neighbouring mountain Gaurus, the largest among the
volcanic cones of the Campi Phlegraei, were to fall into the stagnant
Avernus, it would be swallowed up in the lake (*Phars.* II. 667).

deep impression which it made on the minds of
men long ago. Its fame as the main gateway of
Orcus or the infernal regions was widely diffused
all over the Mediterranean shores. Reports of its
marvels had no doubt reached the Romans before
they had begun to annex the Greek colonies to
their dominions. And as the Greek legends gained
increasing acceptance among them, the high importance of Avernus was sure to be recognised. The
conception of the underworld and of the future
state there, which Hellenic imagination had evolved,
having been assimilated by the Romans, together
with the rest of the mythology, the river Styx, with
its unkempt ferryman Charon, probably became
to the populace of Rome much more familiar
than Olympus and the doings of the higher deities.
For the belief had become general that the Styx
must sooner or later be crossed by every mortal. A
family would have been miserably poor that could
not afford to place in the mouth of their dead the
small coin that would pay for the passage of the
fatal stream.[1]

How prevalent this belief had grown in Italy
long before the end of the Republic is apparent
from many allusions in contemporary literature.
It was denounced and ridiculed by the philosophers.
Lucretius in his earnest crusade against the religious
creed of his day, declared that " the fear of Acheron
must be driven headlong out of doors, for it
disturbs human life from its very foundations

[1] Juvenal, III. 267.

suffusing everything with the blackness of death, and leaving no pleasure pure and unsullied." In another passage he takes pains to point out the real nature of Avernus, showing that there is nothing supernatural or specially wonderful about the spot, but that it is only one of many places in the country whence poisonous vapours rise into the air.[1] The very vehemence of his denunciation affords evidence of the wide popularity of the belief which he opposed. Cicero, too, asked mockingly whether any silly old woman could be found in his day who still believed in these monstrosities of the nether regions.[2] A century later Seneca affirmed that nobody was then so childish as to give credence to the tales about Cerberus and the shades below,[3] while Juvenal declared that the boys of his day did not believe in departed spirits, the underground realm, and the black frogs in the Stygian gulf, or that a single skiff carries so many thousand ghosts across the deep.[4]

It is evident, however, that a belief which had been so firmly and widely established was not likely to be easily discredited by the sarcasms and sneers of either philosophers or satirists. And in actual fact, though its hold on the popular mind was gradually relaxing, it lasted as long as paganism itself. Avernus, too, retained its place as the gateway to the other world; for so late as the end of the fourth century of our era, as a Neapolitan

---

[1] *De Rer. Nat.* III. 37 ; VI. 737. [2] *De Nat. Deor.* II. ii.
[3] *Epist.* XXIV. 18. [4] *Sat.* II. 149-152.

inscription records, a procession of pious pilgrims
went from Capua on 27th July to visit that famous
spot.[1]

There can hardly be any doubt that the prevalent conception of the underworld received fresh
and powerful support from the publication of
Virgil's *Æneid*. Of that poem, which attained
so wide a popularity,[2] no portion, we may be sure,
would appeal more forcibly to the feelings of the
average Roman than the sixth Book. While it
would warm his patriotism to learn in the other
Books, from what early struggles the mighty
Roman Empire had been evolved; and while he
could read with enjoyment of the travels and
toils, the pious endurance and courage of Aeneas,
of the battles in Latium, and of the interest
which the gods and goddesses above took in the
foundation of Rome, it touched him far more
nearly to be told something authentic about the
next world. When, moreover, the intelligence
was communicated by a gifted poet who had
solemnly invoked the gods in charge of souls,
the silent Shades, Chaos and Phlegethon, to
permit him to tell to mortals what he had
heard, and to reveal the secrets of the world
below,[3] we can well believe that Virgil's verse
went far to impart fresh strength to the belief

---

[1] Boissier, " La Religion Romaine," tome. I. p. 286.
[2] An indication of this popularity is furnished by the graffiti on the
walls of the houses in Pompeii, where the first words of several of the
Books of *Æneid* are found (Mau, " Pompeii," 2nd ed. p. 514).
[3] *Æn.* VI. 264-267.

against which the philosophers had uttered their protests or had thrown their scorn.

In this famous sixth Book, where the poet's imaginative energy reaches its highest level, Aeneas meets the Cumaean Sibyl at the dread Avernus. Entering a yawning cavern with its poisonous breath the two companions plunge into the darkness of Orcus. They then pass, one after another, the features so firmly impressed on the popular imagination as landmarks in that gloomy region [1] —Acheron and Cocytus, the squalid Charon with his ferry - boat on the Styx, the vast throng of departed spirits pleading to be taken across the river, huge Cerberus barking from his triple throat, the Elysian fields on one side, Tartarus on the other, and Lethe, the river of forgetfulness—until Aeneas has the desired interview with his father, who opens to him the book of the future and unfolds the philosophical conception of the universal spirit that breathes through Nature. Instead, however, of leading the hero back by the same route to the entrance at Avernus, the poet makes Anchises dismiss his son by the "Ivory Gate." [2] The poet, borrowing the idea of this gate from Homer's two portals of dreamland, made use of it as a convenient way of restoring Aeneas to daylight without taking him through all the scenes which he had already traversed. Virgil does not tell

---

[1] Tibullus also gives a picture of the lower world (I. iii. 57-82).

[2] *Id.* VI. 895. Virgil states that through this gate false visions were transmitted to the upper world. Why he should have chosen this exit for his hero has never been satisfactorily explained.

us, however, if indeed he had formed any conception
himself, whereabouts this second opening to upper
air was situated.   He probably felt that among the
strangely mysterious Campi Phlegraei, with their
densely wooded lonely hills and valleys, their
mephitic pools and their steaming crevices, there
must lie hidden some other "Charon's ditch"
that might serve as appropriately for exit, as
Avernus did for entrance, to the regions below.[1]
At all events, as Virgil described his hero's descent
into the underworld as a reality and not a mere
dream, he had to restore Aeneas to upper air not
too far away from the ships which were drawn up
on the beach at Cumae.   That the Trojan leader
was supposed to emerge from his subterranean
journey at no great distance from where he had
begun it, is indicated by the abruptness and brevity
of the narrative:—"he took his way to the ships
and rejoined his comrades; then bore straight
along the shore to the haven of Caieta."

In an earlier chapter (p. 70) reference was
made to the service that may have been rendered
to the reform movement of Augustus by the
publication of Virgil's *Georgics*.   In a different
way and appealing to other human instincts, the
Æneid was probably still more effective for the
same purpose.   From beginning to end that poem
is one grand pæan of patriotism.   Legend and

---

[1] Ovid in his account of the journey of Aeneas and the Sibyl into
the infernal regions, does not make use of the Ivory Gate, but brings
the two travellers back through the darkness (*Metam*. XIV. 120).

history, poetry and romance, antiquarian research and philosophical speculation, idylls of peace and tumults of war, the rude dangers of the sea and the quiet beauties of the land, the gods in heaven and the spirits in Orcus are all enlisted in the poet's service with the one grand object of the glorification of Rome. In working out this theme, Virgil displays in even a higher degree that regard for the national religion which was so apparent in the *Georgics*. He brings us into the very presence of the immortals and makes us witnesses of their interest in human affairs. But above all, in spite of inconsistences and self-contradictions which seem so conspicuous to a modern reader, Virgil's detailed picture of the underworld, the unquestioning belief which he reveals in the immortality of the soul and in the reality of future rewards and punishments, could not fail to exert at the time a powerful effect on the minds of the great body of his fellow-countrymen. There is truly a deep pathos in this sustained effort of the poet to stem the advancing tide of indifference and scepticism, and by his renewed and earnest presentation of the national religion, to rally the community to its acceptance. That faith had sufficed for the men who, frugal and industrious in peace as they were valiant and triumphant in war, had made Rome the mistress of the world. Consecrated by tradition, and intimately linked with a thousand memories in the glorious history of the Republic, it appealed to Virgil's loyal affection for the past.

Yet while he clung to it, he was not insensible to the teachings of philosophy and would fain reconcile these with the faith of his fathers. Never was his immortal line more applicable than to his own case :—

"Sunt lacrimae rerum, et mentem mortalia tangunt."[1]

In these chapters I have tried to show that during the last decades of the Roman Republic and the first century of the Empire there lived many men in whom the love of Nature was strongly developed, and who found in her presence, watching and wondering, some of their purest pleasure and joy. This devotion, although less comprehensive and intense than its representative has grown to be in the modern world, was warm and fruitful. It gave rest and refreshment to politicians wearied with their labours for the State, it afforded food for thought to philosophers of every school, and it inspired some of the greatest poets of antiquity who doubtless kindled a reflex of their own enthusiasm among readers all over the vast dominions of Rome. While much of the inner life of men in the

[1] The solemn exposition of the Stoic doctrine of the "Anima Mundi," which Anchises delivers to his son Aeneas at their impressive interview in the lower regions, would hardly have been inserted in this striking manner if it did not express the opinion of the poet himself. There is a notable difference between the presentation of the subject in this passage (*Æn.* VI. 724), and the earlier statement in *Geor.* IV. 221, where Virgil refrains from committing himself to the adoption of the doctrine.

antique world can with difficulty and only imperfectly be realised by us, since it was so largely
made up of features that undergo constant change
with the progress of time, such as religion, politics,
manners, customs, habits and associations, Nature,
on the other hand, though also ever changeful,
retains the same bright freshness and renews her
youth and beauty with each return of spring.   Her
life and charm make their appeal to us as they
did to men two thousand years ago.   The simple
chords which were then awakened in the stately
cadence of Latin prose and in the rich music
of Latin poetry still vibrate in our ears to-day.
Where they find a sympathetic response in our
hearts they bring us into closest touch with the
inner soul and spirit of the best of the Romans.
For they express the instinctive joy of man in
the world around him—that

> Primal sympathy
> Which having been must ever be,

and which, as a universal bond, gathers into one
common brotherhood the peoples of every century
and of every tongue.

INDEX

Printed at
The Edinburgh Press,
9 and 11 Young Street.